TOWING and the LAW

A Collection of 101 Informative Articles

Michael P. McGovern

TT Publications Inc.
Winter Springs, Florida

TOWING and the LAW

© 2011 Michael P. McGovern

The McGovern Law Firm
P.O. Box 5536
Knoxville, Tennessee 37928
(865) 686-4891
michael@themcgovernlawfirm.com

This publication was created to provide you with accurate and authoritative information concerning the subject matters covered; however, this publication was not necessarily prepared by persons licensed to practice law in a particular jurisdiction. The publisher is not engaged in rendering legal or other professional advice and this publication is not a substitute for the advice of an attorney. If you require legal or other expert advice, you should seek the services of a competent attorney or other professional.

Publisher: TT Publications Inc.,
203 West SR 434, Winter Springs, FL 32708

All rights reserved. No part of this book may be reproduced or transmitted in any form by any means, electronic or mechanical, including photocopying, recording, or by any other information storage and retrieval system, without permission from the Publisher.

Cover Design: Christina Wright,
TT Publications Inc., Winter Springs, FL
Back Cover Photography: Chad Smith,
2319 Digital Media, Knoxville, TN, www.2319digital.com

ISBN: 978-0-615-44393-5

Printed in the United States of America

Dedicated to my parents, Ben and Joan McGovern,
founders of Cedar Bluff Towing, Knoxville, Tennessee

TABLE OF CONTENTS

Chapter 1 Law Enforcement Rotation Lists and Contracts

Access and Bidding

§ 1:1	I Hear You Knocking but You Can't Come In	2
§ 1:2	Court Orders Low Bid Contracts for Towing on New Jersey Toll Road	4
§ 1:3	The Trouble with Governmental Towing Service Bids	6
§ 1:4	On the Dotted Line	9
§ 1:5	The Bidding Game	11
§ 1:6	So Close, But So Far Away	14
§ 1:7	What Gives You the Right …?	16
§ 1:8	What Gives You the Right…? The Sequel	18
§ 1:9	The Future of Freeway Towing	20
§ 1:10	The "Point To" Test	22
§ 1:11	Special Rules for Municipal Contracting	24
§ 1:12	Minimum Equipment Requirements in Bid Specs	26
§ 1:13	Not the Only Game in Town	28

Administration

§ 1:14	High-Bid Franchise Contracts	31
§ 1:15	Conflicts of Interest	34
§ 1:16	The Commonality Conundrum	37
§ 1:17	So What Have You Done for Me Lately?	39
§ 1:18	Playing by the Rules	41
§ 1:19	The Burden of Proof	43
§ 1:20	Prove It	45
§ 1:21	The "Perfect" Rotation Towing System	47
§ 1:22	No Discrimination in Enforcement of Rotation Policy, Says Court	49
§ 1:23	Rhode Island Supreme Court Rejects Franchise Tow Contract	51
§ 1:24	Owner Requests	53

Suspension and Cancellation

§ 1:25 Tow Operator Wins in U.S. Supreme Court 56
§ 1:26 Working Without a Safety Net 58
§ 1:27 Cancellation Clauses 60
§ 1:28 The Right to Gripe...62
§ 1:29 Michigan Jury Slaps Rude Town Manager 64
§ 1:30 Pennsylvania Towing Operator Wins Retaliation Lawsuit ..66
§ 1:31 Counting Your Chickens..68

Rates and Pricing

§ 1:32 Taking the Bad with the Good..71
§ 1:33 The Antitrust Minefield 73
§ 1:34 Recovered Stolen Vehicles: Forced to Tow for Free.............75
§ 1:35 Rotation Towing List Price Ceilings 77

Chapter 2   Private Property (Trespass) Towing

§ 2:1 When to Let It Go 80
§ 2:2 Patrol Towing..82
§ 2:3 Rate Caps Put Tow Companies in Squeeze 84
§ 2:4 Drawing a Line in the Sand..86

Chapter 3   Safety and Safety Regulations

§ 3:1   Federal DOT Regulations: A Primer.....................................89
§ 3:2   What You Don't Know Might Hurt You 91
§ 3:3   Size and Weight Exemptions...93
§ 3:4   Risky Business..96
§ 3:5   Hours of Service Rules for Tow Truck Drivers.....................98
§ 3:6   Move Over, Buddy...100
§ 3:7   Tow Cars, Not People 102
§ 3:8   Duty of Care..104
§ 3:9   A Breakdown in Protection 106
§ 3:10 Proper Truck Maintenance Can Be the Best Defense 108
§ 3:11 Like a Moth to Flame 110
§ 3:12 Delay Causes Roadside Tragedies.......................................112
§ 3:13 CDL Review 114
§ 3:14 Tough New CDL Rules 116
§ 3:15 Hidden Dangers 118
§ 3:16 Stranded Drivers Beware...120

Chapter 4   Vehicle Impounding and Possessory Liens

§ 4:1 You Gotta Know When to Hold 'Em 123
§ 4:2 Police Department Holds..125

§ 4:3	Vehicle Forfeiture: Who Really Loses................................127
§ 4:4	When Nikki Wants her Nikes..129
§ 4:5	A "Good Faith Effort" 131
§ 4:6	Care, Custody and Control..133
§ 4:7	Gate Crashers 135
§ 4:8	Lien Sale Theft Case Trumped by Federal Deregulation...137
§ 4:9	Damage Release Forms 139
§ 4:10	The Bankruptcy Quandary..141

**Chapter 5   Federal Trucking Deregulation Law:
               Regulation of Safety and Non-Consent Tow Rates**

§ 5:1	Deregulation and the Tow Truck Industry 144
§ 5:2	Supreme Court Deals Setback to Towing Deregulation....146
§ 5:3	Deregulation's Death Rattle?...148
§ 5:4	The Short and Unhappy Life of Towing Price Deregulation..150
§ 5:5	Price Controls: Naughty or Nice? 152

Chapter 6   Local Licensing Laws

§ 6:1	Tow Truck Licensing Laws...155
§ 6:2	A Tale of Two Cities 157
§ 6:3	Big Win in the Big Apple 159

Chapter 7   Administration, Dispatching and Staffing

§ 7:1	Disability Act Regulations Make Hiring Complex.............162
§ 7:2	How Much Should You Know Before You Tow?...................164
§ 7:3	Criminal Past Not Always Roadblock to Towing Future ...167
§ 7:4	All Dressed Up and No Place to Go 169
§ 7:5	Driver's Arrest-Related Injuries Covered by Workers Compensation 172
§ 7:6	Vicarious Criminal Liability..174

Chapter 8   Billing and Collection

§ 8:1	A Dividing Issue 178
§ 8:2	*I'm Mad As Hell, and I'm Not Gonna Take This Anymore!* 180
§ 8:3	Who Is Going To Pay?..182
§ 8:4	A Good Start 184
§ 8:5	Sue 'Em All, Let the Judge Sort 'Em Out............................186
§ 8:6	Deadbeat Driver Dodges License Suspension 188
§ 8:7	A No-Win Proposition?..190
§ 8:8	Salvage Vehicle Abandonment by Insurance Companies 192

Chapter 9   Miscellaneous

§ 9:1   You Can Fool Some of the People Some of the Time..........196
§ 9:2   Cutthroat Competition..198
§ 9:3   Scanning for Dollars 200
§ 9:4   The Truth about AAA 203
§ 9:5   I'll Show You Mine if You'll Show Me Yours 205
§ 9:6   In the Zone 207
§ 9:7   The Taxman Cometh 209
§ 9:8   The Unfairest of Them All 211
§ 9:9   Vehicle Damage Claims..214
§ 9:10 Registration Program for Interstate Towing......................216
§ 9:11 Guns and Tow Trucks...218
§ 9:12 Finding a Competent Attorney..221
§ 9:13 Government-Operated Vehicle Storage Facilities 223
§ 9:14 It Makes No Cents: Payment in Pennies 225

INTRODUCTION

In late 1993, ***Tow Times*** Editor Tim Jackson telephoned me and asked if I would write one or two articles for the magazine focusing on legal issues in the towing industry. I said, "Sure." That was over 17 years and almost 200 articles ago.

My first "Legaleze" column appeared in the February 1994 issue. Since then I have recapped dozens of significant court rulings and provided general overviews on a myriad of legal issues facing tow operators. In many of the articles, I drew upon my personal experiences as attorney for hundreds of towing companies across the U.S. and as a former tow truck driver.

Over the years, my office has received many inquiries from tow company owners seeking back copies of Legaleze columns. A typical request starts out something like, "I've got this legal problem and I remember reading one of your articles in ***Tow Times*** a while back about a similar situation." Usually, we can pinpoint the particular article and are happy to accommodate by sending a copy. I have also been flattered to learn that some readers cut out and save every Legaleze article, keeping them in a binder for future reference.

It finally dawned on me that there was no single publication providing general legal information for the towing industry. With this book, I have attempted to provide the automotive towing businessman with that long-needed legal handbook.

I started by separating the wheat from the chaff. Topics with no continuing viability, and those of limited jurisdictional scope, were eliminated. Where applicable, discussions were updated with new case law or legislation. Formal case citations and statutory references were added, which should be of tremendous value to attorneys representing towing companies. In the end, a decade and a half of Legaleze articles was pared down to 101 of the most significant legal topics.

I hope you will find *TOWING and the LAW* useful in your day-to-day operation. I envision it as a quick reference for the most common legal questions that arise. I should, however, caution that *TOWING and the LAW* is only a starting point. If you are faced with any matter involving the application or interpretation of law, you should always seek the advice of a competent attorney.

Michael McGovern
Knoxville, Tennessee
March 17, 2011

Chapter 1 Law Enforcement Rotation Lists and Contracts

Access and Bidding

§ 1:1   I Hear you Knocking but You Can't Come In 2

§ 1:2   Court Orders Low Bid Contracts for Towing on New Jersey Toll Road 4

§ 1:3   The Trouble with Governmental Towing Service Bids 6

§ 1:4   On the Dotted Line 9

§ 1:5   The Bidding Game 11

§ 1:6   So Close, But So Far Away 14

§ 1:7   What Gives You the Right …? 16

§ 1:8   What Gives You the Right…? The Sequel 18

§ 1:9   The Future of Freeway Towing 20

§ 1:10 The "Point To" Test 22

§ 1:11 Special Rules for Municipal Contracting 24

§ 1:12 Minimum Equipment Requirements in Bid Specs 26

§ 1:13 Not the Only Game in Town 28

2 TOWING and the LAW

§ 1:1 I Hear You Knocking but You Can't Come In

Tow calls originating from a police agency rotation tow list generate substantial revenues from towing, recovery labor, storage, secondary tows, vehicle salvage, and, in many cases, mechanical or auto body repairs. Additionally, the work is fairly steady and predictable: accidents happen regularly, vehicles are continually being stolen or abandoned requiring recovery and towing, and police agencies are also major sources of referrals or breakdowns.

Given the revenue generated by law enforcement towing, police agency referrals are often considered to be of particular importance to new towing companies. I am frequently asked by the owners of towing firms: "The sheriff/chief of police/highway patrol won't let me on the rotation list. Don't I have a right to be on the list?"

The questions are easy; the answers are not. Whether a towing company has a right to receive tow calls from a police agency depends on a number of factors, including state and local laws, the police department towing rules and regulations, the towing company's equipment and facilities, and local practices and procedures.

If a towing company wishes to be admitted to a local towing rotation list, it must first find out what criteria or qualifications exist with regard to the rotation list. Are there written rules and regulations that spell out in detail what the police agency requires of its approved towing firms in terms of equipment, storage facilities, insurance, response time, etc.? If the towing company meets all of these criteria then it is usually a simple matter of demonstrating that capability and applying for admission to the list pursuant to the procedure set forth in the rules.

One point to keep in mind about towing list qualifications: they must be reasonable based upon the particular needs of the police agency. It would certainly seem reasonable for any local authority to require all authorized towing firms to have two tow trucks, a secure storage facility, and response time of 40 minutes or less. On the other hand, it would probably not be reasonable for a police agency to require seven tow trucks all painted green and white (which happen to be the number of units and colors of a competing towing firm), have a storage facility of a specific size and dimension (which happens to be identical to the facilities of a certain local firm), and a business location within three blocks of the city hall (which happens to correspond to the location of the same company). Obviously, in the latter example the police agency specifications have been intentionally "doctored" to favor one particular company to the exclusion of all others. That would be an unnecessary and unreasonable classification and could not lawfully serve as the basis to exclude otherwise objectively qualified towing firms from the rotation list.

What if the towing firm meets all the criteria, written or unwritten, yet despite proper request is still not admitted to the rotation list? Can it legally force its way onto the list? It depends.

Courts have looked to the amount of discretion reserved by the local police agency in admitting towing firms to the rotation list to determine whether or not a towing firm has a right to be admitted to a rotation list. If the written rules and regulations, or ordinance, sets forth the qualifications in unambiguous terms, spells out an application process and directs the chief or sheriff to admit —without reservation or discretion — all towing firms that meet the qualifications, a legal right to be admitted to the rotation list might be found. By meeting the specifications for the list, a towing company would have a legal right to be on the list because placement on the list is "automatic," not discretionary. If, however, some discretion or decision is reserved to the police chief or sheriff regarding new towing companies and that discretion is exercised reasonably and not for unlawful purposes, a company declined admission to the list would not be able to claim a legal right to be on the list. (See § 1:7).

It has been my experience that most law enforcement agencies are more than willing to approve towing companies for admission to rotation lists. The key factors are that the new company meets all the reasonable specifications demanded by the jurisdiction and complies with the formal or informal application process.

4 TOWING and the LAW

§ 1:2 Court Orders Low Bid Contracts for Towing on New Jersey Toll Road

The Garden State Parkway runs approximately 120 miles along the New Jersey coastline from near New York City to lovely Cape May. It is a limited-access toll highway and is one of the heaviest traveled thoroughfares in the nation.

To facilitate the removal of wrecked and disabled vehicles from its lanes of travel — there are about 50,000 incidents each year— when it opened in 1954 the Parkway was divided into 15 towing "zones." A towing contractor was assigned to each zone for a five-year period with the exclusive right to tow all wrecked or disabled vehicles within that zone. And by "exclusive," I mean exclusive. No other companies were allowed to tow vehicles off the Parkway, even if a vehicle owner specifically requested a non-Parkway towing firm. A motorist had the choice of being towed by the zone operator to the nearest Parkway exit (where presumably, the motorist can obtain repair service or another tow) or to the zone operator's place of business.

Motorists are charged directly for all towing services rendered; however the rates for such services are regulated by the Parkway.

For most of the Parkway's existence, the towing zones were automatically renewed to the existing operator every five years so long as there were no complaints or service problems. No new towing operators would be considered unless there were glaring problems with the zone operator. Nor was there a public bidding or competitive selection process for the tow zones. The Parkway took the position that the interest of public safety and convenience, furthered by quality towing service, outweighed any benefits that might be derived from a bid system. In that monopolistic environment, the tow zones were 10- to 15-mile-long towing fiefdoms.

In 1990, the Parkway instituted an informal rating system. The system, dubbed the "Mooney System" after Pat Mooney, the Parkway employee who developed it, ranked perspective zone towing companies according to certain subjective criteria, e.g. quality of the firm's equipment, reference from other customers, experience, safety record and proximity to the Parkway. The Mooney System did not, however, take into consideration towing rates and did not incorporate any type of competitive bidding process. The highest-ranked tow firm in each zone, based upon the subjective criteria, was awarded the five-year appointment from 1990-1996, the Mooney rating resulted in only two new zone contractors being appointed.

N.E.R.I. Corporation is in the business of towing, storage and automobile repair. The company's owner, Joseph Neri, had attempted to obtain a towing zone since 1984. Every application had been rejected. Finally, he sued the Parkway and the existing contractor. He contended that the Parkway could not arbitrarily appoint towing companies to the zones, even under the Mooney System, and that New Jersey law required that the Parkway advertise the zones for public bid. On December 31, 1996, the New Jersey Supreme Court agreed with Mr. Neri.

In *N.E.R.I. Corporation v. New Jersey Highway Authority*,[1] the state high court held that the Garden State Parkway tow zones must be competitively bid. The court found that the state statute requiring the Parkway to publicly advertise for bids on contracts valued over $7,500, and to award such contracts to the "lowest responsible bidder," applied to the Parkway tow zones.

The court rejected the argument of the Parkway that the bid law was applicable only in situations in which the Parkway itself was spending over $7,500. It did not matter that the motorists and not the Parkway paid the towing fees.

The supreme court also refused to accept the defendant's argument that towing services are exempt from the state competitive bidding law because automotive towing is a "professional service," which is exempt from the bidding law. While recognizing that towing requires "special skills," it held that the "professional service" exemption was intended by the legislature to apply only to professions such as architecture, engineering, law and other occupations which require a prolonged formal course of specialized training.

With the stroke of Judge Garibaldi's pen, the four-decade stranglehold on Parkway towing by 15 New Jersey towing firms came to a crashing end.[2]

---

[1] 686 A.2d 328 (N.J. 1996)
[2] Current Parkway towing procurement regulation: N.J. Admin. Code 19:9-2.13

§ 1:3 The Trouble with Governmental Towing Service Bids

Over the past 25 years I have reviewed hundreds of bid proposals for emergency towing services. Some of the common problems that I see:

Inadequate bid specifications

Many towing bid proposals are woefully lacking in the bid specifications. To put it bluntly, the drafter of the bid proposal simply doesn't understand what is needed in terms of equipment and service—and perhaps doesn't take the time to learn. Writing proper specifications for a towing contract is not a simple task.

Many bid specs adequately address the obvious requirements, e.g., response time, size of storage lot and number of trucks required, but get bogged down on the more complicated provisions: equipment specifications, insurance requirements, communications, recordkeeping, driver qualifications, etc. In many bid proposals, the later specifications are often extremely outdated or, worse, simply omitted from the bid proposal.

Undisclosed bid evaluation method

Unlike a non-towing bid proposal which usually seeks a single type of product or service in multiple quantities, towing service bids often require the potential contractor to bid on multiple "items" of service in multiple quantities. Additionally, towing bids usually call for the bidder to bid items based on different pricing methods: some at a flat rate, some on an hourly basis (e.g. labor and heavy-duty towing) and others on a daily basis (e.g. storage). Despite those unique difficulties, towing bid proposals frequently fail to disclose how the winning bid is to be determined. The bidder is faced with a classic case of mixing apples and oranges. Without advance notice of the evaluation methodology, the bid process cannot result in a rational, legal bid.

Consider the following two bids:

ABC Towing
1. Light duty towing   60.00
2. Heavy-duty towing   125.00
3. Storage (outside)   10.00
4. Storage (inside)   18.00
5. Road service   40.00

XYZ Towing
1. Light duty towing   85.00
2. Heavy-duty towing   125.00
3. Storage (outside)   15.00
4. Storage (inside)   1.00
5. Road service   5.00

Who is the lowest bidder? That depends entirely on how the bids are evaluated. If the low-bid is determined by the lowest overall cost under the contract (i.e. a weighted bid), ABC Towing prevails because there are usually more light-duty calls than heavy-duty calls, more outside storage than inside storage, and hardly ever any road service required. ABC was clearly the lowest bidder on the "most common" contract items light-duty towing and outside storage.

On the other hand, if the bids are analyzed on a simple average basis, XYZ Towing wins the bid with an average bid of $46.20 compared to ABC's $50.60. Under the simple average method, XYZ's apparent mathematical gamesmanship — bidding high on the high volume items and low on the low volume items — pays off.

In public bidding, the law requires that the bidders, so far as possible, be put on terms of perfect equality, so that they bid on substantially the same proposition and on the same terms. If the bid proposal does not specify the manner in which the bids for various towing services are to be analyzed and the most responsible bid determined, I would suggest that such a bid is prima faciae invalid. Without that advance disclosure in the bid specifications, potential contractors are simply shooting in the dark.

Nondisclosure to the vehicle owner: the "zero bid" problem

I can go into my files and pull out any number of towing bid contracts wherein the successful bidder bid anywhere from $0 to $10 for light-duty emergency towing. A logical person would look at those bids and ask. "What sense does that make?" or "What's going on here?" But these contracts are commonly approved and signed by government entities all across the country. Does that mean that towing services bid for in the contract are actually performed at that rate? Not necessarily.

A zero towing bid, or any below-cost towing bid, is one of the most manifest fallacies in government procurement. It is made possible by this unadulterated fact: *The person who is expected to pay the contracted towing fee isn't even aware there is a contract.*

All too often a zero or below-cost bid is simply a deceptive means by which a towing contractor acquires the exclusive right to emergency tow work and then surreptitiously charges rate for services rendered pursuant to the contract. The contractor can get away with it because he knows (1) the person paying the bill —the vehicle owner or his insurer — has no knowledge of the existence of the towing contract and (2) even if they are aware of the contract, they frequently don't complain because they fully expect to pay a reasonable rate for towing. The other party to the contract — the city or county — doesn't care if its tow vendor is overcharging because it's not paying the tow bills, so it just looks the other way.

8 TOWING and the LAW

The solution to the below-cost bid problem is quite simple: mandatory disclosure of the terms of the contract to the paying customer. Any low-bid contract should require the winning contractor to disclose the contract rates on every invoice for services rendered pursuant to the contract. The consequence of a failure to disclose, or failure to charge the bid price, should be termination of the contract.

§ 1:4   On the Dotted Line

Suppose a city police department used a rotation towing list for over 20 years. There were eight local towing companies on the list. Whenever the police department needed towing service as the result of an accident, breakdown, arrest, abandoned vehicle, etc., it simply referred to its tow list and called the next available towing company.

Then, the city council voted to eliminate the rotation tow list in favor of a single city-wide towing vendor. The city manager recommended a low-bid contract. Following the bidding procedures set forth in the state statutes, the city published an Invitation to Bid (ITB), soliciting bids for towing and storage services to be provided at the request of the city police department. The bids set forth various specifications to be met by the successful bidder. In addition to the usual requirements concerning response times, driver qualifications and recordkeeping obligations, the ITB mandated that the contractor have a minimum of three light-duty tow trucks; a lighted, fenced storage facility; $1 million in liability insurance and high-tech communication equipment in each truck.

All of the eight rotation towing companies submitted bids, including a company I will call Lakeshore Towing. Lakeshore was a top-notch operation and met most of the bid specifications, but it was not in 100 percent compliance. To fully comply with the contract terms it would be necessary for Lakeshore to purchase another truck, acquire some new communication equipment, increase its insurance and improve storage lot fencing. Nevertheless, the owner of Lakeshore submitted a bid knowing that if he was the successful bidder he could quickly meet all the contract requirements.

After reviewing the bids received, the city council determined that Lakeshore Towing was the lowest responsible bidder and authorized the city manager to award the city-wide contract to that firm within 30 days — conditioned on Lakeshore coming into full compliance with the specifications. Based on that action by the city council, over the next month Lakeshore Towing invested thousands of dollars in necessary trucks, communications equipment and storage facility improvements and bought more insurance to come into compliance.

While Lakeshore was gearing up for the contract, the seven other former rotation towing companies — those who lost the bid and were soon to be excluded from any police towing work — were frantically appealing to the city politicians to return to the rotation towing system. They prevailed. After Lakeshore had upgraded its operation in preparation for the contract, but before the contract had actually been executed by Lakeshore and the city manager, the city council met and voted to reject all the bids and restore the rotation towing system.

Of course, Lakeshore's owner cried, "Foul!" Having invested substantial sums of money in reliance upon the city council's previous vote authorizing the city manager to award him an exclusive city-wide contract, he was back to receiving only one-eighth of the total calls as one of the eight rotation list participants. "I want the city to reimburse me for all the expenses I incurred to comply with the contract specs," he demanded.

Unfortunately, Lakeshore will not recoup its start-up investment from the city. The city was not contractually bound until the contract was actually executed. In the 1996 case of *Jenkins v. City of Little Rock*,[1] the Arkansas Court of Appeals held that when the governing body of a municipality votes to authorize a city manager to enter into a contract with the apparent winning bidder for a towing contract, that resolution, by itself, does not bind the city to the prevailing bidder. In other words, the deal is not final until the ink is dry on the contract. In my hypothetical above, in the absence of the signed contract, the owner of Lakeshore Towing made the expenditures at his own risk.

If confronted with a similar dilemma, the prudent tow operator should protect himself by insisting upon the execution of the written contract conditioned upon the towing contractor coming into compliance within thirty days of signing. Provided that the winning contractor timely complies, the city would be contractually bound for the term of the contract.

---

[1] 915 S.W.2d 298 (Ark. Ct. App. 1996)

§ 1:5 The Bidding Game

Your towing company meets or exceeds all the bid specifications for the city's lucrative law enforcement towing contract. You have fully and accurately completed the bid proposal. Your bid prices objectively appear to be the lowest of all the bids submitted, but your firm is not awarded the contract. The city grants the contract to a competitor that submitted a higher bid. Or the city rejects all the bids and then, when the contract is re-bid, another company bids lower and is awarded the bid.

Do you, as the unsuccessful bidder, have grounds for a lawsuit against the city in either situation? Against the winning bidder? If there is a basis for a lawsuit, what can you recover?

What are the rules?

Most states have rules, regulations, constitutional provisions or legislative enactments bearing on the subject of competitive bidding for public contracts. Municipalities and counties often have their own ordinances or rules pertaining to competitive bidding. Those state and local laws are designed to prevent favoritism, fraud or corruption in the award of contracts and to obtain the best products or service at the lowest possible price. Generally, they require public notice or advertisement of the bid, fair and unambiguous bid specifications, public opening and an award to the lowest responsible bidder. The content of the bid rules and regulations, if they are applicable to public towing contracts, dictates the answers to the questions posed above.

Find out if the rules apply to you

First, one must determine if the laws and rules governing competitive bidding even come into play when a municipality seeks towing services. Local governments often contend that they do not have to comply with bidding rules when contracting for towing services because the tow bills are paid by the motorists or their insurance companies, not the government. But several appellate court rulings have rejected that argument. (See § 1:2). In some jurisdictions, however, the bid laws only apply to the procurement of goods and products, not services, so the bidding rules do not apply to towing service contracts.

How bids are accepted and rejected

If there are no formal bidding rules that apply, a municipality may procure towing service in any responsible manner. A rotation towing list is one common method of obtaining towing service, but some cities prefer to establish a working relationship with a single towing vendor working under a formal agreement.

In those jurisdictions where no formal bidding laws apply, in the absence of fraud, collusion, illegality or action that is clearly arbitrary, a city's choice of towing contractor is subject only to the requirement that it be "in the best interest of the taxpayers." That is true even if, although not required by law to do so, a city voluntarily initiates a formal competitive bidding process. Thus, following what appears to be a competitive bidding process, the contract might actually be awarded to other than the lowest bidder. Under those circumstances, as long as the contract award was not the result of collusion or some other illegal activity, the lowest bidder could not prevail on a claim that the city did not fully comply with the competitive bid laws.

Starting the bid process all over again

What if — after a mandated competitive bid process — a city rejects all the bids submitted and starts the bid process all over again? This happens frequently in bids for towing services, usually because the bid specs are confusing or ambiguous and, after the bid opening, one of the losing bidders complains that he or she did not understand the terms of the specs and, as a result, made a mistake in their bid proposal. (All too often a rebid will occur when the contract is not won by the towing firm whom the city surreptitiously would prefer as its towing contractor.) Most state bid laws, and towing bid specifications themselves, provide for rejection of all bids. Again, the city usually must have a rational basis, such as ambiguity in the specs, potential for litigation or "not in the best interest of the taxpayers," to reject all bids. However, as a practical manner, some justifiable reason for rejection of all bids can almost always be put forth by the city.

The lowest bidder can take action if contract is not awarded

Finally, consider the case of a legally mandated competitive bid process in which the city simply ignores the unquestionably lowest bid, even though the bidder is responsible and meets all the bid specs, and awards the contract to a higher bidder. The low bidder may have a cause of action against the city if the law of the jurisdiction provided the city with no discretion in the award of the bid. If the city was required, without reservation, to award the contract to the "lowest responsible bidder," it would be legally wrong for the city to award the contract to any bidder other than the lowest responsible bidder.

If, on the other hand, the law or bid specs expressly reserved to the city the right to award the contract to the bidder whose bid was "in the best interest of the taxpayers" or provided the city with similar discretion in the award of the contract, the city need only act in good faith in the award of the contract. (See § 1:12). A losing bidder, even the apparent bid winner, is unlikely to prevail in a lawsuit against the city if the city retained any discretion in the award of the contract and had some reasonable basis for its eventual contracting decision.

As noted above, the laws and rules pertaining to competitive bidding, especially as they apply to public towing, vary from state to state, indeed from city to city. Readers with questions or concerns about public towing bids are encouraged to seek the advice of a competent attorney.

§ 1:6   So Close, But So Far Away
Residency requirements

I often get calls from towing operators who are somehow being treated differently than their competitors. "I'm being discriminated against," they complain.

A residency requirement is one method of governmental discrimination that frequently affects towing businesses. Participation on a city or county towing list is often denied to towing companies which, except for the fact that their principal business location and/or storage facilities are located outside the city or county, would otherwise have a legal right to be on the list.

But let's get something straight: Governments regularly engage in discrimination. The mere fact that discrimination is evident does not necessarily mean that the Equal Protection Clause, which protects citizens from unlawful discriminations, has been violated. There are both legal and illegal discriminations.

For example, most states do not permit unsupervised persons under the age of 16 years to operate motor vehicles on public roads. Do those laws discriminate against persons on the basis of their age? Of course they do. Is it unconstitutional? No. A local ordinance forbids women from entering a men's restroom in a restaurant during business hours. Does that discriminate against persons on the basis of their gender? You bet it does. Is it a violation of the Equal Protection laws? No.

The point, of course, is that not all governmental discrimination is unlawful. Generally, the law permits governments to discriminate in economic matters if there is some rational basis for the discrimination.

With regard to regulations that discriminate among business entities, the United States Supreme Court has said that governments "are accorded wide latitude in the regulation of their local economies under their police powers, and rational distinctions may be made with substantially less than mathematical exactitude."[1] In other words, as long as they can show some justifiable basis for a business regulation that results in a discrimination, governments do not have to be perfectly fair to all businesses and do not have to treat all businesses exactly alike. When a local economic regulation is challenged solely as violating the Equal Protection Clause, the courts consistently defer to legislative determinations as to the desirability of particular statutory discriminations.

Does a residency requirement in those situations protect the economic interests of the towing firms located within the city or county and discriminate against a towing company whose lot is located, say, only one-half (1/2) mile from the city or county border? Of course it does. Is it a lawful discrimination? Well, let's see:

What is the government's interest? A municipality clearly has a legitimate interest in ensuring that tow trucks respond to police tow calls in a timely fashion. A local government also has a legitimate concern about the convenience of vehicle owners and police officers who are required to pick-up or examine vehicles at storage facilities. But does a residency requirement rationally address those concerns? Doesn't a response time requirement, e.g. 20 minutes, satisfy a city's interest in response time without the necessity of a residency requirement? A mandatory response time would seem to be the only rule that is necessary. If a tow truck can respond in a reasonable amount of time, it should make no difference where the tow company's storage yard is located. A city's concern about response time can be addressed without unnecessarily discriminating against nonresidents.

The issue of convenience to the vehicle owners or the police department is a bit trickier. Doesn't convenience depend on where the person traveling to the storage facility is coming from? Sometimes an out-of-town storage lot may actually be more convenient to a vehicle owner than one located within the city or county. But what if a city ordinance or police department regulation prohibits police officers from traveling outside their jurisdiction in furtherance of an investigation?

Finally, what about a local governing body's interest in supporting the business of local citizens? Is that interest, standing alone, a legitimate basis for discriminating against nonresident towing companies?

There are no hard and fast rules in these cases. As noted above, whether or not a residency requirement violates the Equal Protection Clause in the federal constitution turns on whether there is any legitimate governmental interest that compels the restriction and, also, whether or not the restriction actually furthers that interest.

State statutes may also come into play. For example, a New York statute provides that any restriction or regulation imposed by a municipality upon nonresident businesses desiring to "carry on any lawful business or calling" within the municipality, must be "necessary for the proper regulation of such trade, business or calling."[2] Thus, in order to limit rotation list participation to residents only, a New York municipality must demonstrate that such a restriction is somehow necessary to the regulation of nonconsensual towing.

(See also § 2:4 regarding residency requirements in private property impounding regulations).

---

[1] *New Orleans v. Dukes*, 427 U.S. 297 (1976)
[2] N.Y. McKinney's General Municipal Law, § 80

§ 1:7 What Gives You the Right . . . ?

Billy Bondo is in the auto body repair business, operating Fender Bender Body Shop. He does not own a tow truck. Instead, whenever Bondo needs a tow for one of his customer's vehicles, he calls up his long-time friend, Harvey Hook of Hook's Wrecker Service. Harvey has been providing Fender Bender with towing service for over 20 years, delivering prompt, quality service for a reasonable fee.

One day, Curtis New of New Towing walks into the front office of Fender Bender and asks to speak to the owner. Billy Bondo comes to the counter.

"Hey, I hear you've been sendin' all your towing business to Hook's Wrecker," says Mr. New. "Well listen, I'm new in town and I need some accounts so I want you to start using me and Hook's Wrecker on a rotating basis. From now on, you call Hook's for one tow then me for the next tow and so on."

Can you imagine the puzzled look on Billy Bondo's face? You might expect him to ask Mr. New, "What gives you the right to get any tow calls from me?!" In fact, you might characterize Curtis New's demand as rather ridiculous.

Yet on a regular basis, tow operators throughout the nation walk into the offices of their local law enforcement agencies with similar demands: "I've got good equipment, a secure storage lot and lots of insurance, so put me on your rotation tow list."

Does the law enforcement agency have to use the towing company? Or legally speaking, does the towing company have a right to the police agency's towing referrals?

All citizens do, of course, have certain legal rights under the law. There are, for example, laws that provide a right to vote, the right to an attorney in a criminal prosecution and, in most states, the right to health care and a smoke-free workplace. But is there any law or regulation that a tow operator can point to that gives him or her a *legal entitlement* to the towing work dispatched by a given police agency?

In some jurisdictions, the answer is "yes." Several states and many local governments have enacted statutes, ordinances or towing list rules specifically providing that all tow applicants that meet certain minimum equipment, facility and safety criteria will be added to a list to receive tow calls from their police agency. For example, an Oklahoma statute provides that when law enforcement agencies in cities of less than fifty thousand population are in need of wrecker service, "*all* [qualified] wrecker operators located near or in the city limits ... *shall* be called on an equal basis as nearly as possible."[1] There, a tow operator can literally point to the law that gives him the right to receive tow calls.

Law Enforcement Rotation Lists and Contracts

But in the absence of such a law or regulation, the answer is probably "no." If there is no specific law that compels a law enforcement agency to add a towing company to that agency's tow list, placement on the list is completely up to the reasonable discretion of the law enforcement agency. A sheriff or police chief is free to select whichever tow company or companies he chooses as long as the selection is not based solely on a prohibited classification such as race, color or gender. That is true even if the aspiring tow company meets all the requirements set forth in any applicable call list rules and regulations — and even if the wannabe towing operation is *more qualified* than others being used by the police agency.

Unless there is a law or rule mandating that every complying company "shall be" or "must be" placed on the list, admission to the tow list is a discretionary privilege, not a legal right. A policy or regulation stating that a towing company "may be" admitted to the list or "will be considered" for the call list upon application is not sufficient to establish a legal entitlement to participate. (See § 1:1).

Some will say there is a difference between Fender Bender Body Shop and a law enforcement tow list because the latter is run by a governmental entity: "I'm a taxpayer. That should give me a right to tow for the police department if I meet all the requirements." However, a tow operator's mere status as a taxpayer does not give rise to a legal entitlement to be on a rotation towing list. If that were the case, every taxpayer would have a right to a government job.

Before seeking work from a law enforcement agency, a tow operator would be well advised to first determine whether the law provides him with a legal entitlement to towing referrals. In other words, is there a law or regulation that guarantees him a place on the call list if he meets the minimum equipment and performance requirements? It is the difference between a *privilege* and a *right* — which makes the difference between *asking* and *demanding*.

---

[1] Okla. Stat. tit. 47, § 952

§ 1:8 What Gives You the Right . . . ? The Sequel
Questions and Answers

In the previous section, I addressed the question of whether towing companies have a legal right to receive tow call referrals from law enforcement agencies. I concluded by stating that unless there is a specific law or regulation giving towing companies a legal right to receive tow calls from a governmental agency, a tow company likely has no legal basis upon which it might demand admission to participate on a rotation list or similar tow call list. Here are some follow-up questions and answers:

"Doesn't the 1994 federal deregulation' law give all tow operators a right to be on police call lists?"

The federal statute deregulating intrastate trucking eliminated traditional economic regulations imposed by governments upon motor carriers, for example, market entry restrictions (certificates of need and necessity) and price controls (tariffs) on consensual transactions. (See § 5:1). So, is a police department that limits participation on its tow list essentially "regulating" the towing industry and thereby violating that federal law?

A number of federal courts have held that local governments are not "regulating" the towing industry when they select vendors to perform nonconsensual tow work at their request. In 1999, I represented a tow operator in Texas who filed a lawsuit contending that a city's award of its towing contract to just one tow operator violated the federal deregulation law. Ultimately, the federal court of appeals rejected his claim. (See § 1:35). The appellate court said there was a difference between a city obtaining towing services for its own needs and, on the other hand, regulating transactions between a towing company and a third party customer. In the former situation, the court held that the city was acting "as a typical private party would act in seeking a towing service, and [the deregulation law] should not apply." That is true, said the court, even though the vehicle owner or insurance company, and not the city, pays the tow bill.

Since a police department which limits the number of towing services providing nonconsensual towing for its department is not "regulating" the towing industry, it is thus free to select whichever tow company, or companies, it chooses for its nonconsensual tow work without running afoul of the federal deregulation act.

"What about the federal antitrust laws? Don't they prohibit closed towing lists?"

Maybe. First, the federal antitrust laws, which forbid anticompetitive activities and monopolies, come into play only if it can be established that the towing service required by the law enforcement agency is "an integral part of interstate transportation."[1] Secondly, it must be shown that the municipality has so-called "market power" over the business of towing within its jurisdiction. Third, the municipality must be found to have entered into an agreement or conspiracy with the "favored" towing companies to exclude others. Even then, a municipality may be immune from an antitrust lawsuit if its action in limiting participation on the tow list is based upon some state law or policy to displace competition in the field of law enforcement towing.[2]

> *"There is a law in my state that requires competition in local government procurement. Doesn't that law give me a right to receive my fair share of police department tow calls?"*

State or local procurement ("bid") laws may require police agencies to submit their nonconsensual towing work to an open and public competitive bidding process with an award to the lowest responsible bidder. Whether or not a city, county or state agency must comply with the competitive bid laws when contracting for towing services depends upon the precise language of the bid laws. Some state bid laws only apply to government procurement of *"goods," "products," "purchases," "improvements,"* or *"construction"* — not *"services"* — so the bidding rules don't apply to towing service contracts. Procurement laws relating to "services" frequently do not require public bidding. For example, Indiana law provides that the purchasing agency of a municipality may use any manner it "considers appropriate" in obtaining needed "services." In those jurisdictions where no formal bidding laws apply to the procurement of towing services, a city's choice of towing contractor is only subject to the requirement that it be "in the best interest of the taxpayers."

Even if the applicable bid law does require public bidding for towing services, the law merely gives a qualified towing company the right to submit a bid for the tow work. A statutory right to bid is important because it gives a tow operator at least a chance at the often-lucrative towing contract, but the right to submit a bid does not guarantee a contract or any share of the tow work from the governmental entity letting the bid.

---

[1] *U.S. v. Yellow Cab,* 332 U.S. 218 (1947)
[2] *Parker v. Brown,* 317 U.S. 341 (1943)

§ 1:9 The Future of Freeway Towing
Federal judge approves Houston's revised SafeClear program

Many years ago when a client told me about the "chip" towing system in Houston, Texas, I thought he was joking:

Tow truck drivers monitor police radio scanners. When a wreck or breakdown call goes out, the drivers race to the scene. Dozens of tow trucks gather at the site. All the drivers then throw a copper coin, or "chip," into a hat and pull out one or two, depending on how many vehicles are involved in the incident. The tow truck drivers whose chips are pulled "win" the right to tow the vehicles. All the other drivers leave the scene.

But it was no joke. Chasing with chips was the towing method used in Houston for over 50 years. However, on January 1, 2005, the chip-towing firms were booted off Houston's limited access highways. On that day, citing safety concerns and the need for more efficient highway incident management, the City of Houston implemented its SafeClear program.[1] The Houston freeways were divided into 26 segments or zones. Contracts were issued to local towing companies to patrol the freeways for wrecked or disabled vehicles. When a SafeClear tow truck arrives, a vehicle owner has two choices. One, he can accept a free tow to a safe location just off the freeway from where he can make further road service or towing arrangements. The City pays the SafeClear tow truck a $50 fee for each "free" tow. The other option is to hire the SafeClear truck to tow the vehicle from the point of disablement to any location within 20 miles for a fixed fee of $138.

Significantly, the law prohibits unauthorized tow trucks from appearing at the scene of a freeway wreck or breakdown. No more tossin' chips. Furthermore, in the interest of quick clearance and avoidance of secondary accidents, the law did not allow vehicle owners to request the services of a non-SafeClear tow truck, i.e., an "owner's request" (OR).

About two months after the SafeClear law went into effect, the tow companies that did not win contracts organized under the name Houston Professional Towing Association and filed a lawsuit in federal court challenging the new tow program. They alleged that it violated the 1994 federal trucking deregulation law. One of their principal complaints was the "no OR" rule. And they had plenty to complain about: A Rice University study revealed that 25 percent of all towing in Houston comes off the freeway system and that freeway towing generated revenues of more than $28 million over a seven-month period in 2005.

On August 31, 2005, federal district Judge Kenneth Hoyt ruled that, although the SafeClear program was a valid safety regulation, the deregulation law did forbid the City from completely denying non-contracted tow companies the right to service their customers on the freeways.[2] He issued an injunction; however, he gave the City an opportunity to amend the ordinance to remedy the illegal "no OR" rule.

The City, realizing that unrestricted ORs meant a return to chasing and the downfall of the SafeClear program, scrambled to fix its freeway towing ordinance. The challenge: How to permit legitimate ORs while at the same time ensuring quick removal of wrecked and stalled vehicles from the freeways. After three months of studies and hearings, the city council crafted a revised ordinance. The new SafeClear law allows the owner of a vehicle wrecked or stalled on a freeway to call a state-licensed tow operator of their choice, provided that the selected tow company can respond to the scene before the investigating police officer determines, based on the location of the vehicle, traffic conditions, and other factors relating to traffic incident management, that the vehicle must be moved for safety's sake. The "no chasing" rule remains intact. The revised SafeClear program went into effect on December 1, 2005.

The towing firms without SafeClear contracts were not satisfied. According to them, as a practical matter, the new program still shut them out of freeway towing. Because only SafeClear trucks are allowed to patrol the freeways, the non-contractors contended that it was virtually impossible for them to safely get to a tow site in time to satisfy a police officer. The group asked the court to hold the City in contempt of the injunction for effectively continuing to ban ORs.

On March 22, 2006, Judge Hoyt heard arguments in the case. In *Houston Professional Towing Association v. The City of Houston, Texas*, he ruled that the City was not in violation of his August 2005 order.[3] In a brief two-page written decision, he said that the provision of the law "that frustrated the right of a private citizen to choose his towing company has been removed. Hence, a stalled vehicle on a freeway may be towed by a towing company of the owner's choosing as long as the owner contacts the towing company and the tow operator arrives within a reasonable period of time." He concluded that the current SafeClear ordinance "does not, by its language or spirit, violate the [injunction]."

---

[1] Houston Code of Ordinances, Art. III, Chapter 8, Div. 2
[2] No. Civ. A H-05-0323, 2005 WL 2121552 (S.D. Tex. Aug. 31, 2005)
[3] No. Civ. A H-05-0323, Order (S.D. Tex., March 22, 2006)

§ 1:10 The "Point To" Test
Legal right to rotation calls stems from laws and contracts

I field lots of phone calls from tow company owners. A recurring topic is law enforcement rotation-type towing lists. Usually, the caller's firm has been denied placement on a list, been removed from a list, or was just not getting their "fair share" of dispatched calls. They want to sue the sheriff, the city or the state police for "violating their legal rights."

What "legal rights?" Many towing company owners seem to think that just because they have a tow truck, a vehicle storage lot, adequate insurance, and all the other trappings generally needed to perform law enforcement towing, they have some "legal right" to an equal share of tow calls from a law enforcement agency. But legal "rights" are established in constitutions, by Congress and state legislatures, and in contractual agreements. A tow operator must look to those sources to see whether they have any legal footing as to a rotation list.

For many years I have relied upon what I call my "Point To" Test. Can a tow operator point to a state law or a contract that guarantees him work from a law enforcement agency?

The court in *Morley's Auto Body v. Sheriff Hunter* used my "Point To" Test.[1] In that 1995 case, a Florida towing company contended that its legal rights were violated when it was removed from a county rotation list without just cause. Even though the sheriff had adopted detailed written regulations governing his rotation list, the federal appeals court focused on the absence of any state law: "Because the [tow company has] not, and apparently cannot, point to any Florida statute, state administrative regulation, or any other source of Florida law that provides the asserted entitlement in remaining on the wrecker rotation list, we hold that they have failed to allege a [legally enforceable] interest."

On the other hand, an Oklahoma statute provides that law enforcement agencies in smaller cities shall dispatch "all [qualified] wrecker operators located near or in the city limits ... on an equal basis as nearly as possible."[2] So, in contrast to the owner of Morley's Auto Body, some tow company owners in the Sooner State can actually point to a law giving them a legal right to receive tow calls on a fair-share basis.

Even in the absence of a state law, a tow operator might enjoy a *contractual right* to rotation calls. But in order to be enforceable, a rotation towing agreement must be specific and executed in accordance with state contract law. A simple list of equipment and insurance requirements prepared by the law enforcement agency does not suffice.

Piecknick Towing was a tow provider for the Pennsylvania State Police (PSP). The informal PSP rotation guidelines designated certain zones for each tow company. When the PSP began dispatching a towing service from a neighboring zone into Piecknick's zone, he filed suit. He argued that the PSP rules gave him an exclusive right to all calls in his zone. But the federal court of appeals in *Piecknick v. Commonwealth* disagreed, saying, "[W]e do not believe the [PSP rotation] guidelines create an enforceable contract between the towing services on the list and the State Police .... [The PSP rotation policy] is too vague and indefinite ..."[3]

However, compare the Piecknick ruling with the 2008 court decision in *Ronald Kadluboski v. City of Wilkes-Barre, Pennsylvania*. Kadluboski, who does business under the name City Towing, held a five-year towing contract with the city, executed in conformity with general contract law. About midway through the contract term, after a closed-door meeting of a number of city officials without any notice to Kadluboski, it was determined that City Towing had breached the contract by unspecified performance failures. The city unilaterally terminated the contract.

Kadluboski sued. On September 15, 2008, noting that the "first question" to be considered was whether Kadluboski had "a [legal] interest in the continuation of his towing contract," the federal trial judge held that the tow operator indeed had a legally protected interest.[4] Unlike Piecknick, Kadluboski had something he could point to — an enforceable contract — that specifically gave him a legal right to the city towing work. The court determined that, because Kadluboski had a legal right, and because the contract represented "a large portion" of his business with "potentially devastating consequences" upon termination, he should have been provided an opportunity to respond to any claims of contract deficiencies *before* the contract was pulled out from under him. By not giving him that chance, the city violated his rights.

So, if there is no state law or contract granting a legal entitlement, what is the nature of the interest a tow operator has in a place on a rotation list? It is merely a privilege that can be given or taken away, usually at the reasonably-exercised discretion of the government entity or law enforcement agency. Clearly, that is a risky way to do business. A towing firm might invest thousands, if not hundreds of thousands of dollars, in equipment and facilities to perform law enforcement towing with no guarantee that the business generated from the police agency will continue.

The solution? A state law or contract you can point to.

---

[1] 70 F.3d 1209 (11th Cir. 1995)
[2] Okla. Stat. tit. 47, § 952
[3] 36 F.3d 1250 (3rd Cir. 1994)
[4] No. 3:06-cv-2062, 2008 WL 4279879 (M.D. Pa., Sept. 15, 2008)

§ 1:11 Special Rules for Municipal Contracting
Enforceability requires dotting I's and crossing T's

Municipalities generally have particular ordinances, or rules, that specify how city contracts are to be awarded and finalized. For example, an ordinance for the City of Pasadena, California, provides that: "All contracts shall be in writing, and shall be executed in the name of the City of Pasadena by an officer or officers authorized to sign same. All contracts shall be approved as to form by the City Attorney before the execution thereof."

In October 1999, the City of Pasadena sent a written proposal for a five-year franchise towing contract to potential towing contractors. Derderian Bros. Corp. d/b/a Johnnie's Tow Service, and several other towing firms, signed a letter accepting the terms of the proposed franchise agreement. The city manager and the finance director signed off on the written agreement. On November 8, 1999, the city council approved three towing firms for contracts, including Johnnie's Tow Service.

Johnnie's and the other two companies began operating under the written franchise agreement. Then, less than two years into the five-year contract, the city determined that it wanted to change the terms of the contract. It sent new bid invitations to eight towing firms. Five companies, including Johnnie's Tow Service, submitted bids. In April 2002, the city council awarded new franchise contracts to just two companies. Johnnie's Tow Service was not one of them.

Johnnie's sued, claiming that the city breached the five-year franchise agreement approved by the city council in November 1999. The case wound up in the California Court of Appeals. In a 2004 opinion, that appellate court first checked the contracting requirements in the city's law: "The plain language of the city charter requires: a writing; execution by an authorized agent; approval by the city attorney as to form of the contract prior to execution; and approval by the city council." In *Derderian Bros. Corp. v. City of Pasadena*, the court noted that, although the 1999 contract was in writing, had been signed by an authorized agent of the city, and had even been approved by city council, "[T]he city attorney never approved any franchise agreement as to form." Because the city law specifically requires that the city attorney approve any contract before it may be executed, the court concluded that "the alleged November 8, 1999, agreement was not entered into in compliance with the charter, [therefore] no contract existed between [Johnnie's Tow Service and the city]."[1] Johnnie's was SOL.

In April 1987, the City of Little Rock, Arkansas, published a request for bids for towing and vehicle storage services. Among the bids received was one submitted by Asher Wrecker Service. After reviewing all bids, the city's Board of Directors adopted a resolution authorizing the city manager to execute a contract with Asher Wrecker Service. The resolution was approved by the Board on June 2, 1987. Asher Wrecker began towing for the city even though the city manager had not yet signed the contract.

After only a few days, a dispute arose after Asher Wrecker claimed that some additional terms were being imposed by the city. Asher Wrecker withdrew its bid. A competing towing company was then awarded the contract. Years later, Asher Wrecker filed a lawsuit against the City of Little Rock for breach of contract. Asher Wrecker claimed that its signed bid constituted a contract offer. It argued that when the Board adopted the resolution awarding the towing work to Asher Wrecker, a binding written contract was created. According to Asher Wrecker, by thereafter adding new terms, the city breached the contract approved by the Board on June 2, 1987.

In a 1996 ruling, the Arkansas Court of Appeals disagreed. In *Jeff Jenkins d/b/a Asher Wrecker Service v. City of Little Rock*, the court held that a resolution by the governing body of a municipality authorizing the execution of a contract does not, by itself, bind the city to the intended contractor. "A plain reading of the ... resolution indicates that the city had not contractually bound itself in writing. Rather, it only authorized the City Manager to award a contract to Asher Wrecker Service. There is no evidence, nor is it contended, that the City Manager signed a written contract with Asher Wrecker Service as authorized by the resolution," said the court.[2]

Both Johnnie's Tow Service and Asher Wrecker lost because the contracts they were attempting to enforce were not executed in full conformity with the applicable laws governing municipal contracting. Lesson to be learned: When it comes to municipal towing contracts, no deal is done until all pre-contract requirements have been met and the ink on the signatures is dry.

---

[1] No. B171975, 2004 WL 2106603 (Cal. Ct. App., Sept. 22, 2004)
[2] 915 S.W.2d 298 (Ark. Ct. App. 1996)

§ 1:12 Minimum Equipment Requirements in Bid Specs
No fudging allowed, says New Jersey appellate court

"Rules are made to be broken." Apparently that old saying does not apply to towing contract bid specifications. According to a 2009 New Jersey court decision, bidding rules can be bent slightly, but they cannot be broken.

Any proper towing contract bid, or Request for Proposal (RFP), contains an itemization of equipment and services to be furnished by the winning bidder. Typically, the RFP will require a specified number, size and type of tow trucks, for example, two Class A (light-duty) tow trucks, a rollback, and one Class C (heavy-duty) unit. The bid specifications will also set forth the criterion for the vehicle impound facility, minimum insurance coverage, response time, recordkeeping standards, driver qualifications, etc. — all which must be met by a responsible bidder.

Despite the seemingly mandatory language of most RFPs, in some states contracting agencies have the discretion to ignore or waive some specifications when it suits their purposes. Indeed, an RFP will often contain a clause permitting the contracting agency to "waive any informalities, irregularities, or technical defects" in the bid. In short, under some circumstances, governments can award a contract to a bidder that does not fully comply with all the specifications set forth in the RFP.

Whether or not a particular bid specification can be waived by a contracting agency depends on whether the specification is essential to the contract. As stated by an Ohio court, "So long as a bid complies with the specifications in all material respects, and contains no irregularities which give one bidder a competitive advantage over others, the bid will be deemed responsive, notwithstanding the omission of an item called for by the specifications." For example, the inadvertent absence of a signature on a bid submission might be deemed a mere irregularity.

So what constitutes a "material," non-waivable specification in an RFP for towing services? That was the question facing a New Jersey court in the case of *Cioffi's Towing Service Inc. v. Borough of Collingswood*.[1]

In 2008, the borough sought bids on a three-year contract to provide towing services. Among those minimum standards set forth in the RFP was a requirement that the contractor maintain the following equipment: One heavy-duty wrecker, one medium-duty wrecker, one light-duty wrecker and one flatbed truck.

The lowest bidder was Helmrich Transportation Systems, a fourth-generation towing firm based in Pennsauken. However,

Helmrich's list of equipment revealed it did not have a tow truck conforming to the medium-duty specifications. The borough decided to ignore the medium-duty truck requirement because, according to the chief of police, there was very little demand for medium-duty service anyway. It awarded the contract to Helmrich.

The only other qualified bidder, Cioffi's Towing, which did have all the required equipment including a medium-duty unit, sued the borough, claiming that it should have been awarded the contract. Since there was no dispute that Helmrich's did not comply with the medium-duty truck requirement, the court accurately noted that the only question in the case was whether that "specific noncompliance constitutes a substantial and hence non-waivable irregularity."

While acknowledging that some aspects of bids can be waived in "a sensible or practical way," in its October 2009 opinion, the appellate court said that the materiality of the requirement of a medium-duty wrecker in the Collingswood bid was "patently obvious." It held as follows:

"A towing operator's possession of the equipment deemed necessary to fulfill the municipality's towing requirements is essential to the undertaking. In inviting bids, the municipality expressly stated that the bidder would be required to have three wreckers, and made that known in mandatory terms, directing that the operator's bid 'shall' meet the minimum requirement of three wreckers of the various sizes specified. This mandatory requirement could not be waived upon the municipality's later disavowal of its own specification."

In a strong rebuke to the borough, the court's written opinion went on to say: "The municipality's waiver of the three-wrecker requirement provided Helmrich with an advantage in the bidding process that strikes at the very heart of the [bid law] which was intended to encourage competition ... There can be no doubt that the three-wrecker requirement could well have discouraged others, who did not possess that necessary equipment, from bidding, or could have influenced the amount of the bids submitted by those that did. By permitting Helmrich to skirt the bidding specifications, the municipality created a bidding procedure that was capable of becoming a vehicle for corruption or favoritism ..."

The court concluded that Helmrich's lack of a medium-duty tow truck constituted a material discrepancy that the municipality could not waive. It ordered that the contract be awarded to Cioffi's Towing.

In light of the court's ruling, perhaps the more appropriate adage when it comes to minimum equipment requirements in towing contract RFPs is "Rules are rules."

---

[1] L-3706-08, 2009 WL 3460308 (N.J. Super., Aug. 26, 2009)

§ 1:13 Not the Only Game in Town
Court says preferential police towing deal not monopoly

The City of Malvern, in south central Arkansas, is the county seat for Hot Spring County and home to two towing companies, Phil Bailey Towing and Beason Services. The tiny town of Rockport (population 792) shares a border with Malvern but it has something that Malvern does not – an interstate highway (I-30) running through it.

Pursuant to a written directive issued by the chief of the Rockport Police Department (RPD) whenever towing service is needed by the RPD due to a traffic accident, arrest, breakdown, etc., the only towing company located in Rockport, Tanner's Towing, is to be called. If Tanner's is not available, the RPD turns to the sheriff's department rotation list, which includes the two companies from nearby Malvern.

The towing companies in Malvern previously served on a Rockport rotation towing list with Tanner's, but annexations by the City of Malvern devoured their business locations, leaving Tanner's as the only towing company in Rockport. Those Malvern companies claim that the annexation did not change their response times; they can still respond to RPD calls as quickly as Tanner's. In fact, Beason Services is only 400 yards from Tanner's tow yard – just a bit farther than a Tiger Woods tee shot. But now, if the RPD needs a tow truck, those former Rockport businesses can only wait and hope that Tanner's is unavailable.

Fed-up with sitting on the sidelines watching Tanner's get first dibs on the lucrative interstate highway work, Bailey and Beason sued Rockport, claiming that it had given a monopoly to Tanner's in violation of the federal antitrust laws. The Sherman Antitrust Act forbids any contracts, combinations or conspiracies in restraint of trade.

On November 16, 2010, Judge Robert Dawson, of the federal court in western Arkansas, said that "no illegal monopoly exists" in Rockport. In the order handed down in the case of *Phil Bailey Towing and Recovery, et al. v. City of Rockport*,[1] he pointed out that vehicle owners/drivers at RPD tow-a-way sites are free to request any towing company they wish, that the Malvern-based plaintiffs still receive tows from the secondary county rotation list, and that those out-of-town companies continue to perform other non-RPD towing within the Rockport city limits. In other words, Tanner's Towing does not have exclusive rights for all towing in Rockport; it only has a preferential position with regard to the police towing. According to Judge Dawson, that does not constitute a violation of the federal antitrust laws.

The ruling does not come as a surprise. Over 30 years ago, a Rhode Island towing firm sued the City of Cranston after it was removed from that city's towing list. In *Federal Auto Body Works Inc. v. Cianci*,[2] the former rotation tow company alleged that the closed rotation tow list constituted a monopoly in violation of the antitrust laws. In his February 1980 ruling, a superior court judge held that a rotation list favoring some tow companies over others for police tows did not violate the antitrust laws: "Every tow operator in the city is able to engage in the towing business."

In *Brumfield Towing Service Inc. v. City of Baton Rouge*,[3] the plaintiff towing firm claimed that contracts with local competitors for the exclusive right to police-generated towing violated the antitrust laws. In a 1996 ruling, the Louisiana federal judge said, "[T]he city, as a consumer of towing services, has, for itself and the general public, selected the tow truck operators with whom it chooses to deal. That election is simply the operation of the free market and in no way represents a 'restraint of trade' ...."

In 1998, a group of towing companies in North Carolina challenged the appointment of a single tow operator, Horn's Garage and Wrecker, to perform all the towing for the local sheriff's department. Like the plaintiffs in the other cases, they contended that the arrangement was a restraint of free trade in violation of the antitrust laws. But the judge in *Winston-Salem Wrecker Ass'n. v. Barker* said that there was no proof of any agreement or conspiracy between the preferred towing firm and the sheriff. Furthermore, according to the court, even if there was such an agreement, because other opportunities existed for towing businesses in the county, the sheriff did not control the towing market.[4]

The message from the courts seems to be clear: Absent an overt conspiracy in a jurisdiction where a police agency's referrals constitute an appreciable portion of the local towing market, exclusive arrangements for a police agency's towing work will not be found to violate the antitrust laws.

---

[1] No. 10-6005, 2010 WL 4750880 (W.D. Ark., Nov. 16, 2010)
[2] No. CA 78-1742, 1980 WL 336033 (R.I. Super., Feb. 14, 1980)
[3] 911 F. Supp. 212 (M.D. La. 1996)
[4] Case No. 98-CVS-4369 (N.C. Super. Ct., 21st Dist., J. Todd, Oct. 28, 1998)

Administration

§ 1:14 High-Bid Franchise Contracts 31

§ 1:15 Conflicts of Interest 34

§ 1:16 The Commonality Conundrum 37

§ 1:17 So What Have You Done for Me Lately? 39

§ 1:18 Playing by the Rules 41

§ 1:19 The Burden of Proof 43

§ 1:20 Prove It 45

§ 1:21 The "Perfect" Rotation Towing System 47

§ 1:22 No Discrimination in Enforcement
of Rotation Policy, Says Court 49

§ 1:23 Rhode Island Supreme Court Rejects Franchise
Tow Contract 51

§ 1:24 Owner Requests 53

§ 1:14 High-Bid Franchise Contracts

The concept of a high-bid franchise contract is really quite simple: A city issues an Invitation to Bid (ITB) for the emergency towing within its jurisdiction. In addition to the usual specifications, such as equipment requirements, storage facilities, 24-hour service, insurance, etc., the bid sets forth the number of tow calls expected to be performed by the successful bidder. Additionally, the rate for towing is pre-set in the ITB. Thus, by multiplying the expected number of tows by the predetermined price, the prospective bidder can ascertain the expected revenue to be generated under the contract. The bidders are then asked to bid the amount of money that they will pay for the contract rights, with the highest bidder winning the contract. In other words, the right to receive the police towing calls is sold to the highest bidder. Put another way, the bidder who agrees to kickback the most of his revenues to the city as a franchise fee and, thereby, retain the least revenue for himself, wins the contract.

Who wouldn't like this deal?

Consider the following hypothetical municipal high-bid contract proposal: 1,000 expected emergency tow calls per year at a set rate by the contract of $100 per tow. That's $100,000 per year in expected towing revenues under the contract. ABC Towing submits a bid of $40,000 and, as the "highest" bidder, wins the contract. Note that ABC's expected gross revenue for the term of the contract has now dropped to $60,000 ($100,000 less the $40,000 franchise fee kickback) and his average revenue per call is not $100 per tow but only $60 per tow. Assuming that ABC Towing can make a profit with a total average gross profit of only $60 per emergency call, one may think that the high-bid system is the preferred system for municipal acquisitions of towing services. After all, isn't everybody happy? The towing company should be satisfied with the net revenues and the city is raking off $40,000 toward the city coffers. Who wouldn't like that deal?

The vehicle owners, that's who! They're paying $40 too much every time a vehicle is towed by the city police department. The vehicle owners are paying $40 over and above the actual cost of providing the towing, and that excess amount is going directly to the city's general treasury. That's a tax — a tax imposed only on people who suffer the misfortune of having their vehicles towed. It is that economic impact upon the vehicle owner that makes the high-bid franchise contract unconstitutional and illegal in most, if not all states.

Because the towing fee paid under a high-bid franchise towing contract includes a franchise fee that amounts to a "towing tax" and because only those people who have their vehicles towed pay that tax, franchise towing contracts result in an illegal, discriminatory tax imposed upon vehicle owners who have their vehicles towed at the request of the city. Although a city might be justified in charging a small administrative or user fee to cover the costs incurred in administering a towing contract, that charge must be commensurate with the actual cost of providing the service. In most cases, the franchise fee collected under a franchise contract far exceeds any reasonable administrative cost. After all, that's the whole point in the city franchising the contract — putting money in the city treasury.

In 1983, the New Jersey Supreme Court reviewed a high-bid towing contract. In that case, the average "per tow" franchise fee collected by the tow contractor as part of the total towing fee (and then passed through to the city by payment of the franchise fee) was much higher than the amount reasonably related to the city's costs relating to the towing contract. The bidding procedure's primary purpose was simply to nourish the municipal treasury without relationship to the municipality's actual costs in administering the towing system.

In *Gross v. Ocean Township*,[1] the court said: "Although license and permit fees may be imposed to meet regulatory expenses, we are not dealing here with such an exaction. Whatever regulatory responsibilities are retained by the [city], their costs have not been shown, and it is not pretended that they are even colorably related to the amount of the successful bid."

The court then noted that, generally, municipalities have no revenue-raising power except as granted by the legislature, and that no New Jersey statute authorized municipalities to raise revenue through a high-bid franchise bidding scheme. Unanimously, the seven supreme court justices agreed that, although the system was profitable to the municipality, it was legally improper because the municipality had no authority from the state legislature to raise revenues in such a manner. In effect, the city was indirectly taxing vehicle owners for arranging for emergency towing on their behalf. That tax was not authorized by law and was discriminatory in nature because it was imposed only on people who had their vehicles towed under the terms of the contract.

Other than the legal problems, high-bid contracts have a practical downside. Since the towing fees charged under the franchise contracts are artificially inflated to include the hidden kickback to the municipality, the contracted towing firm takes the brunt of any criticism from vehicle owners about excessive towing fees. In the example above, the towing fees charged to vehicle owners are 50 percent more than the true cost of towing and storage. Unbeknownst to the vehicle owner, that 50 percent excess is being paid to the city. But who do you think would likely get the blame for those inflated charges?!

High-bid franchise-type towing contracts have one unique feature not found in other emergency towing systems — revenue generation for the benefit of the general municipal treasury. But in almost all cases, such revenue generation is illegal because it constitutes an indirect discriminatory tax not authorized by law. (See § 1:23).

---

[1] 457 A.2d 836 (N.J. 1983)

§ 1:15 Conflicts of Interest

The chief of police is part owner of a towing company that participates on the city police department's rotation list... A state highway patrol captain's nephew has a towing company on the state's rotation tow list... The owner of a towing company serves as a part-time reserve officer for the city police department... A city councilman's daughter is the wife of the owner of a towing company that has submitted a bid for the city's towing business.

What do these situations have in common? They all involve nepotism and conflicts of interest.

Government officials — whether elected, appointed, or hired — are expected to act in the best interest of the citizenry without regard to their own personal interests or prejudices. Because the potential for exploiting their position of power is great, government officials are held to high standards of conduct. An abuse of government power can subject the official to criminal charges, for example, bribery and graft. Other official conduct, although short of criminal corruption, can give the appearance of governmental impropriety. Nepotism and favoritism are common examples of such suspect activity.

Let's face it, most high-ranking government officials or employees gained their offices or jobs largely because of their political clout. Once they take their office or position, they don't forget how and who got them there. Political patronage is as American as apple pie.

But the federal and state constitutions place some limitations on patronage. For example, the U.S. Supreme Court has held that a tow operator cannot be removed from a city rotation towing list because he supported the mayor's campaign opponent. (See § 1:25). That is a violation of the tow operator's First Amendment right of speech and association. Additional restrictions on patronage are found in state and local bidding laws as well as the statutory codes of ethics for governmental officials and employees, which are designed to further curtail patronage, nepotism and conflicts of interest in government.

As you might expect, public scrutiny of a government official is keenest when he or she is obtaining goods and services on behalf of the government entity. Referring to the first paragraph of this article, aren't the ears of every competing towing company going to perk up each time the scanner broadcasts an "owner's request" for the chief of police's towing company or the captain's nephew? And who wouldn't smell a rat if the city councilman's son-in-law was awarded the towing contract even though his bid wasn't the lowest or most responsive?

Conflicts of interest in government are becoming increasingly unavoidable because more and more candidates for public office have diverse financial holdings and business interests. A conflict of interest differs somewhat from pure political patronage in the sense that the government official in the former situation has a personal financial stake in the governmental action. A blanket prohibition against any and all financial conflicts of interest would be stifling to our representative system of government. Many good candidates for government offices or jobs would be disqualified due to their private interests and investments. Recognizing the dilemma, the legislatures of most states have enacted governmental ethical codes in an effort to encourage participation in government while, at the same time, avoiding real or perceived improprieties.

A typical government ethics code requires an elected government official to publicly disclose any financial interest, direct or indirect, that he or a family member has in a proposed acquisition of goods or services by the government he represents. Failure to disclose is a crime in some states. Even though the particular legislative rules may permit the "conflicted" official to participate in the discussion, in most cases that official will be excluded from the vote on the intended purchase. For instance, in my example above, the council member's son-in-law would be eligible to bid on the contract but the councilman should be excused from voting and, in most instances, from the deliberation of the issue because one of his family members has a financial interest in the outcome of the bid.

What if one government official has the sole authority to make decisions regarding towing service? Do the same ethical rules apply to the police chief or sheriff who has a personal or family interest in a towing company on a rotating call list? It would appear so. Governmental ethical rules are quite broad in their scope, often pertaining to any "public servant." Some ethical codes outright forbid public officials with employment or procurement authority from hiring or contracting with businesses in which they or their family members have any financial interest. The public policy underlying those laws is the avoidance of even the appearance of impropriety by government officials.

Some state statutes specifically address the obvious risk of conflicts of interest associated with law enforcement officers and towing companies. An Oklahoma law provides that "[n]o officer of the Department of Public Service or any law enforcement officer of any political subdivision of the state shall have any interest, financial or otherwise, in a wrecker or towing service nor shall a wrecker or towing service employ such officer."[1] That law has been interpreted to prohibit a towing company owner from serving as a reserve police officer. In New York City, the law pertaining to city marshals emphasizes that "[n]o marshal or member of his or her immediate family shall maintain any financial interest, direct or indirect, in a ... towing company."**2** The fact that those laws exist highlights the potential for nepotism and conflicts of interest in the business of governmental towing.

---

1 Okla. Stat. tit. 47, § 956
2 N.Y. McKinney's NY City Civ. Ct. Act, §1601-a

§ 1:16 The Commonality Conundrum

I recall speaking with a tow operator from a small town in Arizona many years ago about his local towing rotation list. He told me that there were 21 companies on the list. I was surprised, given the small size of the town. He explained: The list started out with the three companies in town. Then one company owner got the bright idea to create a "dummy" company, using the same towing equipment and same storage yard but a different name on some magnetic door signs, then adding the "new" company to the rotation list. Instead of receiving one in every three calls (1/3 of all the calls dispatched), he then got two in every four calls (1/2 of all the calls).

Of course, the other companies couldn't stand for that too long, so they created their own dummy companies to add to the rotation list. Once everybody got two companies on the list, the real distribution of calls was back to one-third to each company (2 out of every 6 calls), so somebody created yet another dummy company to gain an advantage and the cycle started all over again. Finally, each of the three original companies had seven "sham" companies on the tow list for a total of 21 names on the rotation towing list.

Many government entities attempt to curb the above-described syndrome by enacting "common ownership" restrictions in their tow list rules or contracts. For example, "No tow operator shall be directly or indirectly involved in the towing business of any other tow operator." Clearly, a police agency has a legitimate interest in eliminating sham companies. They create inefficiencies and complicate dispatching. Sometimes, however, those provisions serve to exclude legitimate companies from participation. Common ownership of towing businesses, in and of itself, does not necessarily mean that the businesses are "shells" or "shams" created merely to gain an economic advantage on the tow list.

Common ownership can result from the purchase, consolidation, or merger of one towing company with another existing towing company. Such a purchase or merger does not result in a new business entity.

With regard to a police department towing list, the acquisition of one towing company on the rotation list by another company on the rotation list changes absolutely nothing. It does not create any additional administrative burden on the police department — the number of tow companies remains the same — and there is no change in the distribution of tow calls. In that situation, the police department has no legitimate governmental interest in eliminating one of the companies from the rotation tow list merely on the basis of commonality of ownership.

On the other hand, the formation of a new company by an existing rotation company owner does add to the administrative burden of the police agency and redistributes the volume of tow calls. Those are the evils that governments mean to address with "common ownership" restrictions, but they often do so with too broad of a brush and sometimes preclude both the sham companies as well as legitimate commonly-owned firms.

To avoid the inequities and possible illegalities of "common ownership" prohibitions in contracts and tow list regulations, government entities would be well-advised to avoid complete bans against common ownership of towing companies. Instead, governmental agencies should focus in more detail on those factors that separate legitimate commonly-owned companies from the illegitimate, or "sham," companies. For example, how was the common interest derived? Was there a legitimate sale and purchase for value? What is the extent of the common interest? Do the companies use the same towing equipment? Do they share the same storage yard? Are their operations covered under the same insurance policy? Do they have separate business licenses and file separate tax returns?

Those factors serve to identify sham companies created merely for the purpose of gaining an unfair advantage on the rotation towing list. Governments and their police agencies should carefully review each situation involving common ownership interests and make a determination, under all the circumstances, whether or not companies owned wholly or in part by the same individual, partnership, or corporation should be permitted.

§ 1:17 So What Have You Done For Me Lately?

You think all those free tows that you give law enforcement agencies might pay off for you someday? So did poor John Doleszny of Tri-State Towing in Brattleboro, Vermont.

On the morning of May 26, 2000, Doleszny was hauling a vehicle on Canal Street without having activated his flashing beacon lights. A city police officer traveling the opposite direction observed Doleszny's tow truck operating without the flashing lights, which the officer believed was in violation of the law. The officer turned around and followed the tow truck for several blocks, at one point clocking its speed in excess of 45 miles-per-hour in a 25 mile-per-hour zone. He signaled Doleszny to pull over.

The officer approached the tow truck and asked Doleszny for his driver's license. He informed Doleszny that he was stopped for towing without using his emergency flashing lights and for speeding, but said he was only going to write him a ticket for the speeding violation.

Concerned about getting points charged against his driving record, Doleszny pleaded with the officer to cite him for failing to use his flashing lights rather than for speeding. So far so good. But when Doleszny supposedly offered to tow the police officer's personal vehicle for free should he ever need towing in the future, he found himself in court defending against a charge of bribing a police officer.[1]

At trial, the police officer testified that when Doleszny realized he would be getting a speeding ticket he asked if there was "any way we can work this out" and the officer asked him what he meant by that. According to the officer, Doleszny then said that "he could tow my car for free" and explained that he had towed the police department's cars for free in the past.

Doleszny took the stand in his defense and said that, yes, he had asked the officer for a "break" based on the free towing that he had provided in the past for the police department. He said that he was only attempting to persuade the officer to write him a ticket for failing to illuminate the emergency lights rather than speeding and he denied offering the officer anything in return for dispensing with the speeding ticket. In fact, Doleszny testified, he could not afford to tow the officer's vehicle for free.

The jury found Doleszny guilty of bribery and the court sentenced him to thirty days of probation. Doleszny appealed.

The main legal issue in the appellate court was whether or not it was appropriate for the judge to allow the jurors to ask their own questions during the course of the trial. After each testifying witness answered questions from both attorneys, the jurors were permitted to submit additional questions to the judge, who then consulted with the attorneys and decided whether or not to pose the question to the witness. After the witness answered the jurors' questions, the lawyers were allowed to ask follow-up questions. In *State of Vermont v. John Doleszny*,[2] the Vermont Supreme Court decided that juror questions, if handled properly by the trial judge, are okay. The high court consequently upheld Doleszny's bribery conviction.

What I found particularly interesting about the ruling, and the case in general, were the questions asked by the jurors. One of the jury questions submitted to the arresting officer was quite perceptive: Had Doleszny specifically "used words about towing a police car or towing your personal car or neither?" The officer responded that the tow truck driver had "told me that he could tow my car for free."

After Doleszny's testimony, the jury had several additional questions for him. Interestingly, they wanted to know the make and model of Doleszny's tow truck and of the vehicle being towed. The defense attorney objected, arguing that the answer was irrelevant, but the judge allowed it, saying it was a legitimate question and "doesn't hurt anybody."

The curious jury also asked Doleszny: "Why have you towed police cars for free in the past?" Good question. He replied that it was done "as a courtesy." The prosecutor jumped up and asked him why he had towed police department vehicles for free when he had testified earlier that he could not afford to tow the officer's personal car for free. Another good question. Doleszny said that it was just a "general business practice" among the local towing companies.

Here's the question I wish the jury had asked: "Mr. Doleszny, do you still tow police cars for free?" But I'm afraid his answer might have resulted in yet another charge against Doleszny—contempt of court for cursing.

---

[1] Vt. Stat. Ann., tit. 13 § 1101(a)(1)(bribery)
[2] 844 A.2d 773 (Vt. 2004)

§ 1:18 Playing by the Rules
Enforcing rotation list rules and regulations

In Nextel Cup racing, if a NASCAR official catches a driver or team breaking a league rule the sanctions can be swift and severe. Rough driving, equipment cheating or cursing on television can draw a fine, loss of precious Cup points and, in some cases, suspension. If an NBA player breaks the rules of conduct, for example, by climbing six rows of arena seating to punch a spectator in the face, he can count on being suspended for the remainder of the season and forfeiting his earnings.

Most rotation towing lists are governed by written rules and regulations which set forth certain guidelines such as equipment specifications, response times, minimum levels of insurance, storage yard requirements and dispatching procedures. The typical rotation list rules also contain prohibitions against "call jumping" or "wreck chasing," obtaining multiple spots on the list by using bogus company names, skipping calls without good cause, etc. Suspension or permanent removal is normally called for in the event of a violation.

But what if the rules are routinely violated by one of the participating towing companies and nothing is done about it by the administrating law enforcement agency? In the "game" of governmental towing rotation lists, the rules are often broken without the offending "player" suffering any fine or sanction. The "referee" plainly sees the foul but never throws his penalty flag or blows his whistle. Such "non-calls" can be quite frustrating for the complying companies. What can be done?

In sports, referees are not expected to be perfect in all their calls. Likewise, our legal system does not require law enforcement officials to be perfect in their enforcement of laws and regulations. Otherwise, it would be a valid defense to a speeding citation that every driver who was speeding at the same time and place did not also receive a ticket. Nevertheless, police officers may not intentionally discriminate in the enforcement of a particular law. For example, if an officer *only* issued speeding tickets to minority drivers or *only* to vehicles registered in Ohio that would be persuasive evidence of discriminatory enforcement, which is a violation of the constitutional right to be treated equally under the law.

As applied to a towing rotation list, that means that non-enforcement or unequal enforcement of rotation list regulations will give rise to a legal cause of action only when there is a clear pattern of purposeful or invidious discrimination in the treatment of companies by the regulating authorities. Mere laxity in enforcement is not enough. Evidence that the rules are being enforced against one company and not another, standing alone, is not enough to establish a claim for discriminatory enforcement. Some tangible proof of an intent on the part of an enforcing officer to treat rotation companies differently is essential to any equal protection case. In a successful case, however, a plaintiff can recover money damages in the amount equal to the additional revenue he would have received as a member of the rotation list had any non-complying firms not been on the list.

Alternatively, a rule-abiding tow company owner frustrated by non-enforcement of the rules against other rotation towing companies might petition for a writ of mandamus. A writ of mandamus is an order from a court commanding a government official to carry out his or her non-discretionary official functions. If the rotation list regulations have certain mandatory requirements, e.g., all towing companies "shall" or "must" meet certain standards or criteria, and the police agency has no discretion to waive the requirement for any participating company, a court may, by means of a writ of mandamus, direct the head of the agency to carry out his or her official duties and enforce the rules. Depending on the terms of the regulations, such court-ordered enforcement could result in the suspension or removal of any non-complying firms.

There is another, more compelling, reason why law enforcement agencies should strictly enforce their rotation list rules and regulations. The rules are intended to aid police agencies in efficient procurement of needed towing services. They also foster towing safety. Customers and passersby can be killed or injured by faulty tow trucks, defective towing equipment and unskilled drivers; vehicles are often stolen from unsecured storage yards; and tempers usually flare whenever there is unfairness in the administration of a law enforcement tow list. Avoidance of such injury, loss and controversy seems reason enough for strict enforcement of rotation list rules and regulations.

§ 1:19 The Burden of Proof
Getting a grip on political retaliation

In the spring of 1997, when Roger Whitmore of Automotive Services, in Zion, Ilinois, was approached for a financial contribution to the re-election campaign for the sheriff, he refused. Whitmore was backing the sheriff's challenger. The incumbent sheriff eventually won re-election in 1998. Shortly after the election, the county tow zones were adjusted. Whitmore's zone was reduced by half, which translated to a 75% drop in annual revenues. Whitmore sued the sheriff, the county and a number of competing towing companies. He claimed that the dramatic cut in his zone was the result of a politically-motivated conspiracy.

Without a doubt, it is unlawful for an elected official to take revenge against a tow operator for his lack of support in an election campaign. That rule of law was established thanks to the perseverance of the late Jack Gratzianna of O'Hare Truck Service in Chicago.

In 1993, after almost 30 years of participation on a municipal police department tow list, Gratzianna's towing company was removed after he supported the losing candidate in the city's mayoral race with financial contributions, yard signs and votes. I represented Jack and his company in a lawsuit alleging that Jack's right to free speech and association was violated when the mayor retaliated against Jack for his campaign activities. That litigation ultimately wound up in the U.S. Supreme Court. In the landmark decision of *O'Hare Truck Service v. City of Northlake*, the Court held that the First Amendment protects independent government contractors like towing firms from political retaliation. (See § 1:25).

But a claim of political retaliation must still be supported by competent evidence or proof. In the O'Hare Truck Service case, the mayor never denied that Gratzianna was suspended because of his actions in the election campaign. In another retaliation case, I represented a Tennessee tow operator who was kicked off a rotation tow list the day after an election in which he supported the losing candidate for sheriff. The re-elected sheriff was torpedoed at trial by a secretly-recorded audio tape in which he was heard to tell my client that he was taken off the tow list because he was "too involved in politics."

In most instances, however, the evidence of retaliation is not so convincing. Mere speculation or assumption about the motivation behind the punitive actions of a government official following an election will not win the day in court. The danger of filing a lawsuit without adequate proof is demonstrated by Whitmore's case.

Other than the bare fact that his towing area had been reduced after the election, Whitmore had no hard evidence that the sheriff's reconfiguration of Whitmore's tow zone was directly related to his adversarial campaign activities. There was no "smoking gun" tape recording, no concrete testimony confirming payment of bribes, and no evidence that other contributors to the sheriff's opponent had been victims of retaliation. In fact, another tow company that donated money to the opponent actually gained territory in the sheriff's post-election realignment. Furthermore, the sheriff insisted that the towing zones were realigned only to "maintain organizational efficiency."

In March 2004, the federal judge dismissed the case of *Roger Whitmore's Automotive Services v. Lake County* calling the lawsuit a "knee-jerk" reaction to the sheriff's zone realignment.[1] In her strongly-worded opinion, the judge said that after five years of bitter litigation Whitmore had "nothing to show other than a collection of loosely connected facts" and "a tale of intrigue ... worthy of a novel." If the change was politically motivated, asked the court, why did the sheriff not readjust the zones in 1997 immediately after Whitmore refused to contribute? The judge also pointed out that Whitmore's claim of retaliation was contradicted by the fact that, even though the size of his towing area was cut, Whitmore continued to receive calls dispatched from the sheriff's department. If the sheriff wanted to punish Whitmore "he could have taken away the entire towing area," said the court.

The judge said Whitmore was a "disgruntled businessman who attempted to utilize the judicial process to harass the County" and threw out the case. To make matters worse, labeling Whitmore's case "frivolous," the judge ordered him to pay $114,486 in attorney's fees and costs incurred by the county and the sheriff.

Whitmore's case serves as a warning to all potential towing litigants to have solid evidence before suing government officials for politically-motivated wrongdoings. Suspecting political retaliation, bribery and corruption is easy, but proving it can be very difficult.

---

[1] No. 99-c-2504, 2004 WL 723842 (N.D. Ill., March 31, 2004)

§ 1:20 Prove It
Documenting rotation list violations

It is an unfortunate truth of the towing industry that many rotation towing systems are the object of improper manipulation by law enforcement officials. To put it bluntly, nepotism, favoritism and old fashioned patronage, in complete disregard of the official rotation list, often results in a favored towing company receiving far more than their proportion of calls.

Eventually, a tow operator on the "short side" of the favoritism stick, increasingly frustrated with not getting his "fair share," complains to the chief law enforcement officer about the situation:

Tower: "I'm not getting my fair share of rotation calls!"

Officer: "What makes you say that?"

Tower: "I listen to the scanner and I can tell I'm not getting all my calls."

Officer: "I can assure you that I will not tolerate any favoritism by my officers or dispatchers. If you can give me a specific instance where you think you were skipped or denied a call, I will definitely look into it."

Tower: "Well, there was that time about a month ago when there was an owner's request for Smitty's Towing. No way that coulda' been an owner's request because the car in the wreck was from out of town."

Officer: "What was the date of that accident?"

Tower: "I don't remember exactly."

Officer: "Where was the accident?"

Tower: "Somewhere out on Highway 30, I think."

Officer: "Who was the officer?"

Tower: "I don't know."

Officer: "How do you know the vehicle owner was from out of town?"

Tower: "Somebody told me, but I don't remember who."

Officer: "Did you have the tag number of the car?"

Tower: "Um ... maybe somewhere."

Officer: "Well, I'd like to help you but ..."

Not a very effective complaint.

Before lodging any complaint about the improper manipulation of towing calls by a law enforcement official, the prudent tow operator will accurately document all the facts supporting the allegations. If there is a specific incident which raises a question, e.g., a suspicious personal request for another company on the rotation call list, all of the available details should be recorded in writing: date, time and location of the accident, name of the other company, and name or number of the officer requesting the tow. Usually, much of this information is obtainable over the scanner.

Most police agencies maintain a written dispatch log of tow calls. Those logs generally detail the date, time and location of the calls, reason for the call and name of the dispatched towing company. More often than not those logs also contain additional information about the call, such as officer's name, vehicle owner's name and address, and destination of the tow. Those dispatch records are helpful in confirming or dispelling suspicions about call list manipulation. If a law enforcement official is sincere about maintaining the integrity of his or her tow system, they should be willing to provide any tow operator with copies of the logs. If there is resistance to a request for the logs, they can be obtained by a subpoena or a proper request made pursuant to the state Freedom of Information laws.[1]

Verifying bogus "personal requests" can be most challenging. If police officers are calling in false personal requests for favored towing companies, the tow call logs will be in order. In other words, the logs will accurately reflect an "owner's request," even a phony one. If there is suspicion of falsified owner's requests for accident tow calls, a tow operator can obtain copies of the accident reports (public records), usually for a small fee, then contact the vehicle owners identified on the accident report to verify whether or not they did indeed request the specific towing company as the tow log or accident report indicates. In order to establish a pattern of falsified personal requests made for a particular tow operator, it may be necessary to review hundreds of accident reports and interview dozens of vehicle owners.

If you feel you are the victim of improper manipulation of a tow call list, gather your facts before you confront the proper authorities. You will establish immediate credibility and perhaps remedy the problem without the need for any further action. If the problem persists, and a lawsuit becomes inevitable, you will already have your most compelling evidence at hand.

---

[1] www.nfoic.org (state FOI laws)

§ 1:21 The "Perfect" Rotation Towing System

Rotation towing lists are a simple and practical means of procuring emergency response towing for law enforcement agencies, but they are also the source of many legal and practical problems. Over the years, I have handled many lawsuits over the use, or misuse, of a governmental rotation towing program. A client once asked me, "How would you describe the 'perfect' rotation program?" I told him that I had not yet seen the perfect rotation system, but his call gave me cause to ponder ...

In my opinion, a "perfect" rotation towing system would include the following:

First, there would be a state statute providing state and local law enforcement agencies with clear authority to use a rotation tow list. That would avoid the havoc that reigns in Missouri. About seven years ago, Mark Robbins of I-44 Towing in St. Clair was tossed off the Missouri State Highway Patrol (MSHP) rotation list. He contended that he was unjustly removed, but the MSHP ignored his pleas for reinstatement. He eventually sued the MSHP, arguing that the state legislature never gave the MSHP the legal authority to operate a rotation tow list in the first place.

In June 2006, a Cole County judge agreed.[1] He entered an injunction ordering the MSHP to stop "creating, maintaining or enforcing a rotation list of towing or wrecker operators" and left everybody scratching their heads wondering what to do. So in the perfect towing world there would be a state law giving state and local police departments the authority to use a rotation towing system.

Next, there would be a clear and concise set of written rules and regulations. A well-written rotation policy eliminates many questions and problems regarding the administration of the rotation list. What are the qualifications for admission to the list? Equipment, storage facility, insurance? What is the application process? How will the calls be allocated? What constitutes a valid owner's request? What is expected of a rotation list participant regarding response time, processing of vehicles, recordkeeping, etc.? Ideally, the towing industry would have input into the drafting of the rules and the regulating agency would be receptive to proposed revisions as the need might arise.

In a perfect world, favoritism and nepotism would be prohibited and the prohibition strictly enforced. Upon submission of evidence that favoritism has been shown for one towing company over another, e.g. manipulating the list by calling in false "personal requests" or allowing one company to respond to the scene of accidents while excluding others, the offending police officers would be subject to severe sanctions for violating the rules, including suspension. The towing company knowingly receiving the favored treatment would be subject to suspension from the list.

Wreck chasing, or call jumping, would be expressly prohibited. Wreck chasing is just plain cheating. In a perfect towing world, the ban against wreck chasing would be stringently enforced and violators would be suspended from the tow list.

One of the most important aspects of an idyllic towing program would be accurate recordkeeping on the part of the police agency and free access to that information by the towing list participants. Suspicion underlies many towing list disputes: Are the other companies getting more calls than me? Was that personal request call I heard on the scanner legitimate? Did I get skipped yesterday? There would be accurate logs and tow-in reports kept on every rotation call, including the date and time, location, vehicle owner's name, address and phone number, reason for the tow, and the name of the company dispatched. These records would be open and readily available upon reasonable notice to any towing company with a question about the administration of the rotation list.

Rates might be regulated (since the regulation of non-consent towing rates is permitted by federal law), but only after public utility-type hearings. (See § 1:35). Rates would not be based on commercial, non-emergency rates, or what I call the "dart board" method. They would be determined only after input from the towing industry and a complete analysis of costs of operation, return on investment, and other factors relating specifically to emergency response towing.

Finally, the perfect rotation program would provide for some type of arbitration or mediation process when things go wrong. For many tow operators, the revenue derived from a rotation list is extremely important to the financial viability of the business. A rotation list participant faced with suspension or expulsion should be entitled to at least an opportunity to respond to a complaint before being removed from the list and, if necessary, given an opportunity to appeal to a non-law enforcement entity.

---

[1] *Mark Robbins d/b/a I-44 Towing v. Missouri Highway Patrol*, No. 05AC-cc01104 (Mo. 19th Circuit Ct., June 20, 2006)

§ 1:22 No Discrimination in Enforcement of Rotation Policy, Says Court
Safety concerns motivate police action

Daniel Habhab is of Lebanese descent. He and his family own and operate Habhab's Towing, Auto & Truck Repair in Ames, Iowa. In an effort to generate business, Daniel began patrolling Interstate 35 around Ames and Ankeny, soliciting towing and repair work from motorists.

Habhab's cruising was of concern to the local law enforcement agencies. The police officers claimed that some of Habhab's activities were unsafe. For example, Habhab's vehicles sometimes cut across the highway median to get to potential customers.

Of course, Habhab was also violating the state and county rotation towing policies. Pursuant to those policies, a trooper or deputy asks the driver of a wrecked or disabled vehicle if they have a preference for a tow truck company. If the motorist does not have a preference (as is usually the case), the officer calls in a request for the next-scheduled towing company on the rotation list. Like all such lists, those rotation lists were created to distribute the work evenly among the companies on the list. However, as a result of his interstate patrolling, Habhab was receiving an exorbitant number of "preference" calls for accidents and breakdowns.

In April 2002, the sheriff wrote a letter to Habhab warning him about his practices. He said that "responding to accident scenes without being called creates an unsafe environment for all involved." He asked that Habhab "not respond to accident scenes without first being called or requested." Undaunted, Habhab continued patrolling the highways, searching for wrecked and disabled vehicles.

A month later, there was an incident between a state trooper and Habhab. A trooper came upon a vehicle stopped in the median and Habhab was already at the scene offering his services. The trooper approached Habhab and asked, "You get called to come out here or you just drive by?" When Habhab admitted he had not been called, the trooper told him to "take off." The trooper told Habhab, "We'll call when we need a tow truck." Habhab left the scene.

When the next scheduled rotation tow truck arrived at the scene, the trooper chatted with the driver. He mentioned that Habhab previously filed a complaint against certain troopers for not giving him his fair share of calls. The trooper also said, "We're racists, too — 'cause he's from the Middle East, he's Arab, so ... you got a throw that card into it too, you know."

In December 2004, Habhab filed a federal court lawsuit against cause of his ethnicity and national origin in violation of his constitutional right to equal protection under the law. Habhab's allegations included, among other things, claims that the troopers encouraged potential customers to hire other tow truck companies, ordered Habhab to leave a towing site despite having been hired by the vehicle owner, and threatened Habhab with criminal charges if he continued to follow his business practices.

The federal judge dismissed Habhab's case in September 2007. Habhab appealed.

In an opinion issued on August 7, 2008, the U.S. Court of Appeals for the Eighth Circuit upheld the trial judge and rejected Habhab's discrimination claim. In the case of *Daniel Habhab v. William Hon*,[1] the court said that, as a threshold matter, Habhab had to show that the state troopers treated him differently than the owners of other towing companies because of his ethnic background.

However, Habhab could not prove that tow truck businesses owned by Caucasians or persons of other race or ethnicity were treated more favorably by the troopers. Any tow truck driver patrolling the interstate like Habhab, regardless of race or ethnicity, was treated the same by the state troopers. The court said, "Habhab's general and conclusory allegations reflect nothing but tension between the state troopers and Habhab because of Habhab's business practices."

With regard to the trooper's reference that Habhab was from the "Middle East, he's Arab," the court said that comment did not amount to unconstitutional racial discrimination. The statement "was not pervasive or severe enough to amount to racial harassment," according to the appellate court.

Habhab also contended that the troopers' inquiries to stranded motorists, such as "Are you sure you want to use these people?" or "Do you want me to call a service you want to use?" were racially motivated. But the court said those questions alone did not demonstrate the troopers were racially biased against Habhab. "These inquiries reflect the troopers' intention to communicate to the motorists they had other options, because other towing services were available and the motorists did not have to use Habhab simply because Habhab was the first at the scene," stated the court.

The *Habhab* decision is the latest in a long line of cases demonstrating that claiming unlawful discrimination based on race, nationality, gender, age, etc. is one thing; proving it is another.

---

[1] 536 F.3d 963 (8th Cir. 2008)

§ 1:23 Rhode Island Supreme Court Rejects Franchise Tow Contract

Long court battle ends in victory for Providence tow operators

Franchise towing contracts are one of my pet peeves. Under a franchise contract system, sometimes called a "high bid" contract, a city issues an invitation to bid for its emergency towing services. The rates to be charged to the vehicle owners (or their auto insurance companies) for towing and storage services are *pre-determined* in the bid request. Potential contractors are asked to bid the amount of money that they will pay as a franchise fee for the right to service the contract, with the award going to the highest bidder. Put another way, the winning towing firm is the one that agrees to kickback the most of its projected contract revenues to the city and retain the least revenue for itself.

For example, a franchise bid proposal might provide that the eventual contractor can anticipate 1,000 emergency tow calls per year at a contract rate of $100 per tow, or $100,000 per year in expected towing contract revenues. ABC Towing wins the contract by agreeing to pay the city a $40,000 annual franchise fee. After payment of that fee, ABC's expected gross contract revenue drops to $60,000 ($100,000 less the $40,000 fee). ABC's average revenue per call is not the $100 collected, but only $60 per tow. The city gets the other $40 per tow via the franchise payment.

Driven by revenue-starved municipalities, the use of franchise towing contract bids has increased in recent years. However, I have long contended that most franchise towing contracts are unlawful because municipalities do not have legal authority – granted by the state legislature – to generate revenues through the device of selling towing work to the highest bidder. (See § 1:14).

I had an opportunity to test that theory in early 2003 when I was contacted by "Captain" Jim Robbins, president of the Rhode Island Public Towing Association (RIPTA), which represents the PUC-regulated towing firms in that state. His group wanted to put a halt to a franchise towing contract being proposed by the City of Providence.

The city's contract scheme came on the heels of the "Operation Plunder Dome" scandal in which former mayor Vincent Cianci and others were sent to federal prison for taking bribes from tow operators in return for a share of the 10,000 tows dispatched annually by the city. The new mayor, David Cicilline, announced a plan to eliminate the citywide rotation towing system and replace it with four zones serviced by two towing providers per zone. The 14 rotation towing companies would have to vie for those eight contracts.

Significantly, bidders were required to specify how much of a "referral fee" they would pay to the city. The referral fee had to be at least 20 percent of their PUC-regulated towing fees and at least 10 percent of their regulated storage fees. The city anticipated $300,000 in such fees from the winning towing contractors to help defray a projected budget shortfall in 2004. Obviously, preference would be given to the bidders that agreed to rebate the largest percentage of their contract revenues to the city.

I, along with Pawtucket attorney Michael Horan, sued the city on behalf of RIPTA and the rotation towing companies, including Grasso Service Center. We contended that the city did not have any authority to auction its emergency towing services to the highest bidder. Also, because the PUC laws forbid a certificated tow operator from refunding or rebating any portion of its regulated rates, we alleged that the city's proposed contract was preempted by those PUC regulations.

The city, of course, responded that it had authority from the state legislature to implement its proposed revenue-generating contract. It further defended the "referral fee," arguing that the PUC laws prohibiting towing fee rebates only outlawed kickbacks made directly to the vehicle owner-customer.

A court battle raged for almost six years that included two appeals to the Rhode Island Supreme Court. Finally, on January 15, 2009, in *Grasso Service Center, et al., v. Alan Sepe*,[1] the supreme court ruled in favor of the RIPTA. After a thorough analysis of the facts and law, the state's high court concluded, "[W]e are of the opinion that [there is no] specific delegation of legislative authority to the city to enter into contracts with certificated towers based on competitive bids for a percentage of the tower's [regulated fees]."

With regard to the statutory prohibition against service fee rebating, the court also agreed with RIPTA. "There is no language that indicates that the [state legislature] intended to exempt municipalities from the statutory prohibition against splitting a portion of the rate. Accordingly, we are of the opinion that a tow operator may not pay or agree to pay a remittance to a municipality, and we are equally satisfied that Providence may not require such a payment in exchange for a position on a tow list," the court said.

The ruling is a sweeping victory for the Rhode Island towing industry and should serve as ammunition for tow operators everywhere who are battling against franchise towing contracts.

---

[1] 962 A.2d 1283 (R.I. 2009)

§ 1:24 Owner Requests
Right to choose towing firm should be honored

I was in college, driving a tow truck on nights and weekends for my family's towing company. One hot summer day, in the middle of a pop-up thunderstorm, I happened upon a rear-end auto accident on a divided highway. I stopped behind the wreck and activated my truck's emergency lights to protect the crash scene from oncoming traffic. I did not even get out of my truck. The driver of one of the vehicles came up to my truck window and asked if I would tow his car to his house. I said, "Sure," and told him to tell the police officer when he arrived that I had been hired to tow his vehicle. When the patrol car showed up, I started hooking to my newest customer's wrecked car. However, the officer, who I later discovered was related to the owner of a competing tow company, angrily told me to leave the scene. He said he had already called for the "next scheduled" company on the rotation list.

"But," I protested, "the car owner specifically asked me to tow this car! This is an owner's request. The rotation list doesn't apply."

When I continued to hook up the vehicle, the patrol officer charged back at me. To make a long story short, things quickly turned ugly. I wound up handcuffed, sitting in the back of the squad car, steaming mad, and facing a plethora of criminal charges. I wish I knew then what I know now.

With some limited exceptions, the driver of a vehicle involved in a wreck or breakdown has the right to hire the towing company of their choosing. If a wrecked vehicle is blocking traffic or otherwise causing an eminent danger, public safety might override a vehicle owner's desire to hire a towing company that would be a long time in arriving. Also, the driver of a vehicle being impounded for criminal investigation or forfeiture typically has no right to choose the firm providing the transportation to the impound lot. Otherwise, though, an owner's request (an "OR") for a specific towing firm should be honored by the police agency responding to the incident.[1] Indeed, a vehicle owner's right to indicate a preference for towing service is acknowledged in most law enforcement towing rules and regulations.

So what if a renegade police officer intentionally refuses to honor a valid OR? Besides getting mad like I did, a tow operator also has a cause of action for interference with a business advantage. Since a vehicle owner has the right to contract for your services, a tow operator has a reciprocal right to fulfill the contract. Any intentional interference with that contractual relationship is actionable.

On August 15, 1990, the late Jim Hoagland, of north Indiana's Hoagy Wrecker Service, was turned away from a commercial account's vehicle by a police officer. Claiming that the local merchant had specifically requested his services, Hoagland sued in federal court, claiming that the police officer had violated his civil rights and interfered with his services contract. The judge in *Hoagy Wrecker Service v. City of Fort Wayne*[2] dismissed the federal civil rights claim but added that if the officer was not acting within the scope of his authority, i.e., he was acting out of personal animosity or malice in denying the OR, then Hoagland "had a remedy in the form of a state action for tortious interference with contract."

In November 2007, the Ohio Court of Appeals held that the chief of operations for the E-911 dispatch center in Athens County might be liable to a towing company for lost revenues if it could be proven that the E-911 chief was improperly diverting calls to one of the other tow companies on the city rotation list. In the case of *David Dolan d/b/a JD's Towing v. City of Glouster*,[3] the appellate court made clear that a public official is not protected by governmental immunity in a lawsuit brought by a towing firm for tortious interference with a business relationship, even if the business relationship is with the governmental entity that employs the official, if that official acts with malicious intent and outside the scope of his or her designated duties.

Although being denied an OR is infuriating and can, in many instances, give rise to an enforceable legal claim, the cost of pursuing a court action for one lost light-duty tow call usually makes a lawsuit unfeasible. Being cheated out of an OR for a heavy-duty rollover might be a different matter. In any event, perhaps the best approach to OR abuse is prompt communication with a supervising officer, including a thorough explanation of a vehicle owner's right to the towing firm of his choice and of the potential for unneeded litigation.

---

[1] *See Stucky v. City of San Antonio*, 260 F.3d 424 (5th Cir. 2001)
[2] 776 F. Supp. 1350 (N.D. Ind. 1991)
[3] 879 N.E.2d 838 (Ohio Ct. App. 2007)

Law Enforcement Rotation Lists and Contracts **55**

Suspension and Cancellation

§ 1:25 Tow Operator Wins in U.S. Supreme Court 56

§ 1:26 Working Without a Safety Net 58

§ 1:27 Cancellation Clauses 60

§ 1:28 The Right to Gripe 62

§ 1:29 Michigan Jury Slaps Rude Town Manager 64

§ 1:30 Pennsylvania Towing Operator Wins
   Retaliation Lawsuit 66

§ 1:31 Counting Your Chickens 68

§ 1:25 Tow Operator Wins in U.S. Supreme Court
High court rules against political patronage

In a landmark decision for the towing industry and for all independent contractors who do business with government entities, on June 28, 1996, the U.S. Supreme Court proclaimed that the First Amendment of the U.S. Constitution forbids political patronage as a factor in the selection and retention of towing service operators.

In the case of *O'Hare Truck Service v. City of Northlake, Illinois*,[1] Justice Anthony Kennedy, writing for a 7-2 majority of the court, rejected the argument of the City of Northlake that because the Chicago-area towing firm and its owner, Jack Gratzianna, are independent contractors they should not have been allowed to bring suit when the company's place on the city's towing rotation list was terminated in retaliation for Gratzianna's support of the incumbent mayor's campaign opponent.

The background of the *O'Hare* case is really quite simple and will probably sound familiar to many towing company owners: For approximately 30 years, O'Hare Truck Service (OTS) participated on a list of local towing companies which received emergency calls on an alternating or rotating basis. During the mayoral campaign in 1993, the incumbent mayor, Reid Paxson, approached the company's president, Jack Gratzianna, about a campaign contribution. Gratzianna advised the mayor that he couldn't support him unless certain changes were made in the way the rotation list operated. Mr. Paxson refused to make the requested changes, so Gratzianna refused to contribute to Paxson's campaign. In fact, Gratzianna then actively supported Paxson's opponent in the mayoral election, placing the opposite candidate's campaign posters in his place of business and bumper stickers on his tow trucks. Mr. Paxson won reelection as mayor of Northlake and promptly booted Gratzianna and OTS from the city's towing rotation list.

The trial court dismissed the case before it even got to trial, holding that, unlike government employees who have a constitutional right to participate in election campaigns without fear of reprisal, independent contractors to a governmental agency have no similar protection under the First Amendment and their employment status is subject to denial or revocation based on purely political decisions. Basically, the lower court was of the opinion that the benefits derived from a governmental entity by an independent contractor were somehow less important than those delivered by an employee.

In its seven-page majority opinion, the Supreme Court overruled the lower courts. Emphasizing that the Constitution does not "draw the line" between independent contractors and employees, Justice Kennedy said:

> There is no doubt that if Gratzianna had been a public employee whose job was to perform tow truck operations the city would not have discharged him for refusing to contribute to (the mayor's) campaign or for supporting his opponent... We cannot accept the proposition that those who perform the government's work outside the formal employment relationship are subject to what we conclude is the direct and specific abridgment of First Amendment Rights.

Although the *O'Hare* case was based on political retaliation against a towing company, the decision will likely have ramifications far beyond towing. Any independent government contractor, including trash haulers, insurance agents, cleaning services, etc., are now assured of protection from retaliation based on political preferences.

Nevertheless, this case may have more significance to the towing industry than any other type of business. Almost anybody who owns a tow truck knows that political retaliation and favoritism often accompany the selection process for towing for a city, county or state police agency. This Supreme Court ruling should lead to more purchasing decisions by government agencies based on the quality of towing services, not political support and favors.

The *O'Hare* case represents the first time that a case involving an automotive towing company has reached the United States Supreme Court. Fortunately, it also represents the first major victory for the towing industry in our nation's highest court.

---

[1] 518 U.S. 712 (1996)

TOWING and the LAW

§ 1:26 Working Without a Safety Net

I just got kicked off the rotation list . . . !

I receive a lot of telephone calls that start out that way. No doubt, being suspended or removed from a rotation towing list can be both emotionally and financially devastating. The tow operators who call me usually want immediate reinstatement to the tow list and reimbursement from the police agency for all revenues from rotation list calls that have been lost.

Sometimes it is readily apparent that the tow operator's legal rights have been violated. For example, if he has evidence that he was removed from a rotation list because of his activities in an election campaign, because he spoke out on a public matter on which the chief of police or sheriff disagreed, or as a consequence of unlawful discrimination, e.g., because of the tow operator's color, race, gender or religion, he would have a valid civil rights claim.[1] The federal and state constitutions forbid government officials from taking punitive action against individuals in those and other specific circumstances.

But if the tow operator is removed for some other reason — perhaps a heated disagreement with the police chief, an allegation of overcharging or maybe a change in the tow list specifications — whether or not he has a valid legal claim for reinstatement or money damages depends on the precise nature of the business relationship with the law enforcement agency. In those situations, the phone conversation might continue like this:

Caller: I want to sue the city for a million dollars for taking me off the list!

Me: Well, do you have a written contract with the police department?

Caller: No, my name is just on a list posted in the dispatch office.

Me: Is there a state or local law that requires the police department to use all qualified tow operators on a rotation tow list?

Caller: Not that I know of.

With those answers, the outlook is not good for the aggrieved tow operator. In the absence of some constitutional infringement or a state law which guarantees a spot on the rotation list, whether a tow operator has any legal remedy for being suspended from a tow list usually hinges on whether he holds a contract that provides him with some enforceable right to the work received from the rotation tow list. No contract, no legal right. No legal right, no remedy.

The law of contract has a long and revered history. The freedom to enter into contracts is a constitutionally-guaranteed right with roots dating to medieval England. Contracts are very powerful tools because they provide certainty in business transactions and establish understandings upon which the contracting parties may rely in the conduct of their business. Businesses which engage in long-term transactions without written contracts, for example, most towing companies serving on rotation lists, are much like tightrope walkers working without safety nets. One misstep and it might be all over.

Many towing operators who are removed from a tow list for reasons that do not rise to the level of a clear constitutional violation have a difficult time accepting the fact that they may have no legal recourse for reinstatement or money damages:

Caller: But I bought over $100,000 in trucks and equipment, and leased a big storage yard, just so I can provide good service to the police department! How can they just kick me off over a lousy disagreement? How am I going to pay for these rigs?

Me: If you bought all that equipment just to serve on the police department rotation tow list and you didn't get a written agreement for a specified term beforehand, I'm afraid you invested in that equipment at your own risk.

A bank doesn't make loans without first obtaining a written agreement (a promissory note) spelling out exactly how it is going to get its money back from the borrower. A commercial developer doesn't rent office buildings without a written agreement (a lease) guaranteeing its future income stream of rental payments. If the borrower or tenant fails to make the expected payments, the bank and landlord have legal rights that are enforceable in a court of law. Yet towing companies throughout the nation routinely invest tens of thousands of dollars in equipment and facilities to serve their law enforcement customers with absolutely no written assurance of a return on that investment and no legal recourse if the revenues from the tow list are suddenly terminated. As many unhappy towing company owners have discovered, that can be a very risky way to do business.

Caller: I hear what you're saying, but there's no way that my local police department would ever give contracts to the rotation tow operators.

Me: Then you've got a decision to make.

I realize that many police agencies do not, or will not, provide their rotation tow operators with enforceable written contracts. I also know that towing for police agencies can be quite lucrative for the participating towing companies. However, much like tightrope walkers, those companies who choose to serve on tow lists without contracts better be willing to accept the risk that someday they might fall — without a safety net.

---

[1] U.S. Const., amend. I and amend. XIV

§ 1:27 Cancellation Clauses
Contract revenues can be cut short

Service contracts are vital to most towing businesses. Contracts with law enforcement agencies, motor clubs, auto and truck dealerships and other customers ensure the steady stream of towing and storage revenues needed to pay overhead expenses and earn a profit. Long-term contracts are particularly important because they provide the guaranteed revenue for major capital expenditures. For example, a three- or four-year contract with a police agency can provide the funding for new tow trucks, office buildings and vehicle storage facilities.

However, despite the significance of service contracts to towing companies, many police and auto club contracts include a provision similar to the following: *This contract may be cancelled by either party without cause upon giving 30 days notice to the other party.*

As a practical matter, a towing company holding a four-year law enforcement contract that includes a 30-day "without cause" cancellation clause does not have a four-year contract; it has a 30-day contract.

Towing firms routinely invest tens of thousands of dollars of operating capital in new towing equipment, long-term leases and improvements, communications equipment, insurance, employees and employee benefits, etc., on the basis of a newly-acquired auto club or police contract. Many of those companies have seen their investments squandered when a 30-day "without cause" cancellation clause is impetuously invoked by the club or police agency.

Not fair, you say? Unfortunately, "without cause" termination clauses in commercial contracts are routinely upheld by the courts. Unlike consumers, whom the law protects from unreasonable provisions in certain contracts, business entities are generally presumed to be on an even playing field with other businesses or government agencies when they are negotiating or bidding on commercial contracts. There is a presumption of validity of all terms and conditions in commercial contracts, including termination clauses. In other words, towing businesses are generally free to enter into contracts based on any terms they agree to — even unwise or ill-advised ones like "without cause" cancellation clauses.

Most contract termination clauses are mutual, meaning that either party can cancel under the conditions specified. However, termination clauses in many police towing contracts are unilateral. Only the police agency can cancel without cause. Those one-sided termination clauses have been upheld by the courts as long as they provide for reasonable notice to the terminated towing company.

What if a contract with a 30-day "without cause" clause is cancelled immediately without the requisite 30 days notice. May the terminated party sue for breach of contract? Sure, but several courts have held that the money damages recoverable are limited to only the net profits that the terminated contractor would have received during the 30-day period following the cancellation. The courts have reasoned that since the contract was cancelable at any time simply by giving 30 days notice, 30 days of net revenue is the most the terminated party could ever expect to recover for a wrongful breach of the contract.

Much time and effort is spent in the negotiation of the terms to be included in law enforcement contracts. Towing company owners and government officials haggle over equipment specifications, towing and storage rates, designation of zones and other matters. The cancellation clause, way in the back of the proposed agreement, is often completely overlooked. For the reasons set forth above, it should not be. Such a clause renders one of a towing company's most valuable business assets wholly and completely at risk — as vulnerable as a new tow truck without insurance. The contract which provides a police agency with the right to terminate "without cause" leaves a non-breaching towing company exposed to the discretion (and often political whims) of government and law enforcement officials.)

Ideally, early termination of a towing service agreement by an auto club or law enforcement agency should be only "for cause," for example, faulty or unsafe towing equipment or practices, repeated failure to respond to calls for service, cancellation of insurance, etc. Even then, termination should come only after the towing firm is provided with a fair opportunity to cure whatever deficiency prompted the termination notice. However, if a "without cause" termination provision is unavoidable, it should provide for a substantial notice period and perhaps predetermined compensation.

TOWING and the LAW

§ 1:28 The Right To Gripe

Towing service owner Larry Lucas, who had been on the towing list for the Monroe County (Michigan) Sheriff's Department for almost 30 years, went to a Board of Commissioners meeting to complain about favoritism and corruption.

Among other things, he complained that one of his competitors, a "high end" contributor to the sheriff's political campaign, had been dispatched to calls in Lucas' area. Lucas then explained to the Board that he tried to get maps from the Sheriff's Department that showed the areas, but to no avail. Lucas finally received a copy of the map and, much to his distress, discovered that his towing zone had been decreased by one-third. His former territory had been given to another one of the sheriff's campaign contributors. Additionally, at the Board meeting, Lucas reported an incident wherein one of the sheriff's political cronies delivered a message to him from the sheriff that if Lucas did not "back off" on his public complaining he would be removed from the tow call list.

Sure enough, after a report of Lucas' heated speech to the Board appeared in the local newspaper, the sheriff removed Lucas from the tow list. In a letter to Lucas, the sheriff said that Lucas was being penalized for "the accusatory remarks about the Sheriff and his wrecker policy [he] made before a Board of Commissioners meeting."

At about the same time that Lucas was voicing his complaints in Michigan, Sarah Gable was operating Case Towing in southern Ohio, near Cincinnati. Her firm was on the rotation call list for the Ohio Highway Patrol (OHP) but she was not getting her fair share of calls. She felt she was being discriminated against because she was female, so she lodged a sex discrimination complaint with the OHP. In a direct and immediate response, her firm was immediately kicked off the tow list by an OHP official.

Both Lucas and Gable filed lawsuits claiming that the law enforcement agencies violated their constitutional rights under the Petition Clause of the First Amendment to the United States Constitution.[1] That provision prohibits any governmental entity or agent from "abridging... the right of the people... to petition the government for a redress of grievances." In simple terms, U.S. citizens have a constitutional right to "bitch" and gripe about their government — federal, state, or local — without fear of reprisal. It is one of the most fundamental rights incorporated into the Bill of Rights by our nation's Founding Fathers.

Lucas' case was dismissed by the trial court judge. Gable won a $55,000 jury verdict. Both cases ended up in the federal court of appeals.

In the opinion issued in the case of *Lucas v. Monroe County*,[2] the Sixth Circuit started by saying that "Freedom to criticize public officials and expose their wrongdoing is at the core of First Amendment values..." With respect to the subject of favoritism and unfairness in the disbursement of government benefits, the court noted that "tow calls are a classic issue of community concern." Concluding that Lucas had "presented overwhelming evidence" that his removal from the tow call list was motivated by his constitutionally-protected public criticism of the Sheriff's Department, the appellate court reversed the lower court's dismissal of Lucas' case. Lucas eventually received a significant monetary settlement and, after the election of a new sheriff, was reinstated to his tow zone.

In *Gable v. Lewis*,[3] the same federal court of appeals reiterated that it has been clearly established "that the submission of complaints and criticisms to ... public agencies like a police department constitutes petitioning activity protected by [the First Amendment]." The court went on to uphold the jury award in Gable's favor.

It is important to note that Gable never proved that the OHP was discriminating against her on the basis of her gender. She did, however, prove to the satisfaction of the jury and the appellate court that the motivating factor in the decision of the OHP to remove her company from the tow list was the mere filing of the sex discrimination complaint. The point being that, regardless of whether or not the discrimination complaint would have eventually proven to be meritorious, Gable had every right to air her complaint.

The bottom line is that even though a law enforcement official may not like what a tow operator has to say in a public forum about a tow call system, he best respect the right of the tow operator to do so.

---

[1] U.S. Const., amend. I
[2] 203 F.3d 964 (6th Cir. 2000)
[3] 201 F.3d 769 (6th Cir. 2000)

§ 1:29 Michigan Jury Slaps Rude Town Manager
Tow company receives verdict of almost $700,000

What began as a request for help turned into a nightmare for Dave and Teri Wojahn of Dave and Teri's Towing in Vienna Township, Michigan.

It all started in July 2001 when Dave and Teri's impounded a wrecked vehicle for the township. As the only towing firm located in the small township, Dave and Teri's enjoyed an exclusive arrangement to provide towing services for the town. Shortly after the tow and impound, the vehicle owner appeared at the storage lot demanding access to his vehicle. He was in a highly agitated state, extremely loud and belligerent. The Wojahns' daughter, Stephanie Nelson, the company's office manager, was in the tow office at the time.

In accordance with standard procedure, Stephanie requested registration and insurance information from the car owner before admitting him into the tow yard. At that point, the vehicle owner went into a rage. He cursed violently and directed a gender-based vulgarity at Stephanie. The entire episode was captured on the towing company's video surveillance equipment.

Within a few days, Dave Wojahn took the videotape to the Genesee County Sheriff's Department seeking to press charges against the insulting vehicle owner under a local law prohibiting the use of profanity in front of women and children. But both the sheriff and the county attorney refused to prosecute.

Wojahn, along with his daughter, Stephanie, then took the video to the town supervisor, Tony McKerchie. His response was quite unexpected. He blamed Stephanie for the confrontation. After watching the video, he pointed at her and said to Wojahn, "There's your problem. You need to get rid of her and hire a man."

Not long after that incident, McKerchie told Wojahn to add a $50 "processing fee" to all township tow calls. When Wojahn objected, McKerchie told him, "You do what I tell you or I'll put Dave and Teri's out of f—king business!"

Wojahn refused to kowtow to Supervisor McKerchie's unreasonable demands and, obviously, would not fire his daughter. So, true to his word, McKerchie embarked on a campaign to put Dave and Teri's out of business. First, he pushed through a change in the township's towing policy to allow out-of-town towing firms to receive calls. After that new policy was implemented, Dave and Teri's Towing, which had been the township's exclusive towing service provider for many years, stopped receiving any tow calls for tows within the township.

Then, Supervisor McKerchie contacted law enforcement

officials in neighboring jurisdictions and obtained commitments from them not to use Dave and Teri's.

Unfortunately, McKerchie's deliberate and malicious acts were successful. Business waned. The Wojahns were forced to sell their tow trucks to pay the company debts. Dave and Teri's Towing eventually folded in 2005.

"It was like dying a slow death," said Teri Wojahn. "It was not pleasant at all." But before closing its doors, the towing firm, joined by Stephanie Nelson, filed a federal lawsuit against Vienna Township and its supervisor, McKerchie, contending that their civil rights had been violated. In particular, they claimed that the town and its supervisor had violated the First Amendment by retaliating against them for airing their complaint. They further alleged that McKerchie's insistence on an all-male towing staff was unlawfully discriminatory in violation of their constitutional rights to equal protection of law.

The trial began in early May 2007. Although McKerchie denied making the blatant discriminatory comment, and denied that he connived to ruin the Wojahns' business, the jury was unconvinced.

Perhaps the most compelling testimony during the five-day trial came from the Genesee County sheriff who was forthright in confirming that Supervisor McKerchie had, in fact, persuaded him not to use Dave and Teri's Towing for sheriff department tow calls. After a short deliberation, the jury returned a verdict for both the towing firm and Stephanie Nelson.[1] The jurors were obviously outraged by McKerchie's conduct because in addition to awarding Dave and Teri's Towing over $350,000 in lost profits, past and future, it hammered him for $250,000 in punitive damages. The federal jury also decided that McKerchie had violated Stephanie's civil rights and awarded her $78,000, including $50,000 in punitive damages.

"I'm elated," Teri Wojahn said after the verdict was announced. "Justice has been preserved."

Indeed.

---

[1] *Teri Lynn Ent., Inc. v. Vienna Township*, No. 03-cv-70196, Judgment (E.D. Mich., May 7, 2007)

§ 1:30 Pennsylvania Towing Operator Wins Retaliation Lawsuit
Jury awards $3.25 million

In March 2008, a federal court jury in Harrisburg, Pennsylvania, awarded tow operator Jimmy Schlier and his tow company, Schlier's Towing, a verdict in the amount of $3.25 million. The jury determined that the Pennsylvania State Police violated Schlier's civil rights when it removed his tow company from PSP rotation tow list in 2002, and then refused to reinstate the firm in 2003. In a newspaper account following the verdict, Schlier thanked the jury. Perhaps he should have also thanked the late Jack Gratzianna, of O'Hare Truck Service in Chicago.

The First Amendment of the U.S. Constitution prohibits government officials from restricting an individual's speech or political affiliation. For example, an elected official cannot fire an employee because the employee supports the official's opponent in a political campaign. The First Amendment also gives citizens the right to petition the government for redress of grievances. In other words, we have a right to gripe and complain about perceived wrongs in government.

In 1993, O'Hare Truck Service was removed from a local rotation towing list after an election campaign in which Gratzianna actively and openly supported the challenger to the incumbent mayor. Gratzianna sued, claiming that he was retaliated against in violation of his right to free speech and association under the First Amendment. But the trial court said that those constitutional protections only applied to government employees, not independent contractors, and threw his case out. Not one to go quietly, Gratzianna appealed. I represented him on the appeal. The case eventually wound its way to the U.S. Supreme Court. In 1996, in a decision of major significance, the high court ruled in *O'Hare Truck Service v. City of Northlake, Illinois*, that the right to be free from government retaliation should apply equally to both government employees and independent contractors. (See § 1:25).

"We cannot accept the proposition that those who perform the government's work outside the formal employment relationship are subject to what we conclude is the direct and specific abridgment of First Amendment rights," said the Court.

Fast forward to 2002. Schlier had been an authorized PSP towing company in eastern Pennsylvania since the 1970s, but he had growing concerns about the administration of the PSP rotation list. In early 2002, Schlier began lodging complaints to the PSP internal affairs office, contending that his company was being treated unfairly.

For several years, Schlier had also been towing vehicles to the PSP impound facility and making auto repairs on PSP vehicles. His invoices for those services, totaling about $20,000, were ignored. Schlier began insisting that the PSP pay those bills.

Law Enforcement Rotation Lists and Contracts   67

Additionally, as a rotation towing firm, Schlier's was often called upon by the PSP to impound vehicles that were the subject of criminal investigations and ordered to put those vehicles on "hold." Over the span of about 10 years, more than 40 vehicles were put on hold by the PSP, including the two buses involved in the tragic Penn State bus wreck in November 1999. For over two years, those buses remained on "hold" in Schlier's storage yard. In July 2002, Schlier began demanding that the PSP also pay him the storage fees relating to those investigatory holds.

The PSP's response to Schlier's complaints and demands? In August 2002, they kicked Schlier's company off the PSP rotation towing list for six months. I immediately wrote a letter to the PSP's attorney objecting to the removal of Schlier's company from the PSP call list. In my letter, I referenced the *O'Hare Truck Service* Supreme Court ruling and, prophetically, wrote, "[A]s any potential juror would readily see, [the captain's] actions are purely vindictive." The PSP stubbornly refused to reinstate Schlier to the rotation towing list.

In November 2002, on behalf of Schlier and his towing firm, I sued the PSP in the Pennsylvania Board of Claims (BOC) for payment of all of the outstanding invoices due to Schlier, including over $500,000 in storage fees on the "hold" vehicles. After six months, in March 2003, Schlier applied for reinstatement to the PSP rotation list. But the PSP refused to reinstate him, largely because he had filed the claim with the BOC.

Schlier then filed a civil rights lawsuit in federal court, contending that the PSP officers had violated his fundamental rights to free speech and his "right to complain." At trial, Schlier was able to prove the retaliatory motive of the PSP officers and, through the testimony of financial analysts, showed the monetary impact that the removal from rotation had on his company. Schlier took the witness stand and said that the episode caused him tremendous mental and emotional distress. He testified that he was not himself, that he took sleeping pills, quit going to industry trade shows, and that he was generally in fear of his future.

On March 20, 2008, the obviously outraged jury hammered the PSP officials with a verdict of $1 million in favor of Schlier's towing business and $2.25 million in favor of Schlier individually.[1] In 1996, Jack Gratzianna cracked opened the door for tow operators nationwide to take action against abusive practices of government officials that infringe on First Amendment freedoms. In March 2008, Jimmy Schlier busted through that door.

---

[1] No. 3-04-cv-1863, Judgment (M.D. Pa., March 20, 2008)

§ 1:31 Counting Your Chickens
Assessing damages in cases involving business loss

"Hey, Towing Company Owner, a judge has just determined that your company was unlawfully removed from a police rotation list! Whattaya gonna do next?"

No, you are not going to Disney World. First, you must prove your damages.

There are two fundamental aspects of civil lawsuits seeking monetary compensation: liability and damages. Liability is a finding that a defendant unlawfully caused you to suffer a financial loss. The damages phase of the case is the calculation of those monetary losses. For example, in a car accident case, if the defendant driver is found to have been negligent (liable), the plaintiff driver must then prove his or her losses (damages). Typically, those will be medical bills, lost wages and compensation for pain and suffering.

Likewise, a towing company plaintiff seeking reimbursement for a loss of business must also demonstrate both liability and damages. Proving the former is often far easier than proving the latter.

In a case involving the unjust removal of a towing firm from a police rotation list or breach of a towing contract, the core component of damages is lost profits. How much money did the business actually lose as a result of the defendant's wrongful action? It is important to note that the focus of the damages inquiry is on lost *profits*, not lost *revenues*. That means a prevailing towing litigant must be prepared to present evidence of the gross revenue lost less any expenses that were avoided. A loss of 100 tow calls at an average of $150 per tow does not equate to $15,000 in damages. The variable expenses for fuel, labor, maintenance, insurance, etc. must be deducted to establish the lost net profit.

In most lawsuits involving rotation lists or towing contracts, it is easy to compute the exact number of lost calls by analyzing the police towing logs. In other cases, the number of lost calls can be fairly estimated by reference to call volume for the corresponding time periods in prior years. The average gross revenue per call can be calculated from prior receipts.

Lost profits will not be awarded based on sheer conjecture or speculation, but reasonable estimates are admissible. Good documentation is essential to proving lost profits. Unfortunately, there have been many hollow victories in cases in which towing companies were clearly wronged but received only nominal damages due to poor recordkeeping.

The expected profits from the sales of unclaimed impounded vehicles, or parts from those vehicles, might also be an element of damages. In the California case of *All Points Towing v. City of Glendale*,[1] the city breached its contract for towing services. At trial, the towing firm was awarded $27,776 for lost profits on towing services and more than four times that amount, or $116,000, for lost profits on the sale of parts from abandoned vehicles. The court of appeals upheld the award, holding that such losses were clearly foreseeable in the event of a breach.

In the mid-1990s, a Florida jury determined that the civil rights of my towing firm/body shop client were violated when the sheriff removed it from his rotation call list without due process. The jury awarded damages of over $200,000, the majority of which was compensation for lost profits on the auto bodywork that would have been performed on the impounded vehicles.[2]

Depending on the legal theories raised and the applicable state or federal laws, a winning towing plaintiff might also recover his attorney's fees from the defendant. That is critical because absent such "fee shifting" provisions it would be financially unfeasible to file some meritorious, but monetarily small, claims.

A note about punitive damages: Punitive damages are intended to punish a defendant for conduct that is willful, reckless or malicious. Such damages are rarely awarded in business-type litigation and some states bar the assessment of punitive damages against governments or government officials acting in their official capacities. Nevertheless, punitive damages have been deemed appropriate in towing cases involving particularly outrageous conduct by government officials acting outside the scope of their authority. A case in point is *Terri Lynn Ent., Inc. v. Vienna Township*, in which a Michigan jury awarded $250,000 in punitive damages after a spiteful, gender-biased town supervisor retaliated against the towing plaintiff for lodging legitimate complaints, forcing it out of business. (See § 1:29).

Finally, there is one category of cases in which an award of lost profits is rarely allowed. Those are lawsuits brought by towing companies claiming that they were denied a bid contract despite being the lowest or most responsive bidder. A successful towing litigant in those cases can obtain prompt injunctive relief compelling the issuance of the contract, or rebid of the contract, but cannot recover profits lost during any period of time it was wrongfully deprived of the contract. The reasoning is that the bid laws were enacted primarily for the protection of the public, not individual bidders. Although lost profits are usually not recoverable, a plaintiff who successfully challenges a towing bid award will ordinarily be awarded the expenses incurred in preparing its bid, and any rebid, and its attorney's fees.

---

[1] 735 P.2d 145 (Ariz. Ct. App. 1987).
[2] *Morley's Auto Body v. Sheriff Hunter*, No. 2:92-cv-00271, Judgment, (M.D. Fla., March 10, 1994)

70 TOWING and the LAW

Rates and Pricing

§ 1:32   Taking the Bad with the Good 71

§ 1:33   The Antitrust Minefield 73

§ 1:34   Recovered Stolen Vehicles: Forced to Tow for Free 75

§ 1:35   Rotation Towing List Price Ceilings 77

§ 1:32 Taking the Bad with the Good

If you tow for a government or police agency, invariably you are going to be dispatched to tow junk or abandoned vehicles to your storage yard. Nobody will come to claim the worthless hulls and you will be forced to sell the vehicle for scrap. Usually just getting to the point where you can sell the vehicle requires a great deal of time and expense — registration searches, certified notices, newspaper ads, etc. — not to mention the unpaid towing and storage fees.

I am often asked: "Can the police department *make* me tow those junkers?" The short answer to the question is that, with regard to your business decisions, the police department can't *make* you do anything that you don't want to do. If you don't want to haul those junk vehicles, then simply remove your company from the call list or invoke the cancellation clause of your contract. However, I understand that is not always a viable solution.

The long answer is that it depends on the nature of the agreement or understanding between your company and the police agency or government entity. If the existing contract or rotation rules specifically call for the towing of abandoned vehicles as part of the services to be provided, and you were aware of those terms prior to signing the contract or joining the rotation list, you would be hard pressed to now complain about towing the derelict vehicles.

The more pertinent question is what to do when faced with a proposed *new* contract that includes a provision requiring you to tow the "no pay" junk vehicles? Can you complain and, if so, on what grounds?

In my opinion, contracts for the towing of abandoned or junk vehicles should be separated from the contracts or rotation lists for accidents, arrests and breakdowns. There should be two separate contracts or rotation agreements: one for calls paid for by the owners or insurers and another for abandoned and junk vehicles in which the towing and storage fees (at least to a maximum amount) are paid to the towing firm directly by the government entity initiating the call. A contract which combines both the "paid" and the "no pay" calls creates an improper subsidy.

Consider, a hypothetical city towing contract under which the successful bidder would tow all accident and breakdown vehicles as part of the services to be provided under the contract. In addition, the winning towing company would be required to pick up all stray dogs in the city throughout the term of the contract. Ridiculous? Yes, but it is no different than requiring the towing firm to pick up all "stray" vehicles. What the city is asking the towing firm to do is provide a service for free that they would otherwise have to pay to get done.

Such conditions in towing contracts are unfair at best and illegal at worst since this amounts to contract subsidization which is prohibited under many state and local bidding laws.

Discussions with the city, county or state officials prior to the letting of a contract bids or finalization of rotation list regulations might go a long way toward eliminating this unjust but all-to-common practice in government towing.

§ 1:33 The Antitrust Minefield

The caller explained that the city council in his small town was considering enacting a new ordinance to regulate the local towing businesses. The proposed ordinance set forth certain safety specifications, such as equipment and insurance requirements, but in addition — and this was the reason for his telephone call to me — the city intended to set a maximum price for towing services rendered pursuant to the city police rotation list. The proposed fees were, in the opinion of the caller and other towers in his area, unreasonably low. They devised a plan to protest the new law.

"All of us have gotten together and decided to strike," he said. "We've agreed amongst ourselves that if the police department calls any of us for a wrecker, we'll just tell them we are unavailable. We're gonna let all those wrecks and abandoned vehicles sit out there in the middle of the streets. You think that might get us anywhere?"

"Yes," I replied. "I think it might get all of you locked up in the federal penitentiary for violating the antitrust laws."

The federal antitrust laws are designed to promote and protect economic competition.[1] Most states also have antitrust laws that mirror the federal laws. Both the federal and state laws are founded on the policy that in a freely competitive market each competing business generally will try to attract customers by cutting prices and increasing the quality of its products or services. The customer, or consumer, benefits from such free enterprise and inefficient businesses will eventually lose out in the competitive battle. That's the theory.

To promote free enterprise and competition, the federal and state antitrust laws prohibit certain types of "anticompetitive" conduct. For example, it is unlawful to enter into an agreement with one or more competitors to refuse to deal with certain customers. Such an agreement is commonly referred to as a "boycott" and is what the telephone caller had described to me.

It is also unlawful for a towing company to agree to limit the geographical areas in which it will operate in return for a reciprocal agreement from a competitor. Suppose, for instance, that a municipality solicited bids for emergency towing services and that, for the purpose of bidding, the city was divided into zones: A and B. Separate bids were to be submitted for each zone. It would be unlawful for one towing company to agree with a competitor that he would only submit a bid for zone A if the competitor would only bid in Zone B.

Obviously, agreements among competitors to establish uniform prices for towing services ("price fixing") is prohibited under the antitrust laws. This is a particularly troublesome area for towing operators because government agencies sometimes actually encourage towing competitors to establish uniform prices. I am aware of numerous occasions in which a police chief, highway patrol captain or sheriff, concerned about divergent pricing for police-ordered towing services, has directed local towing forms to "get together" on their towing fees or to "come up with an equal tow rate." The tow operator following that directive would be committing a "per se" violation of antitrust laws.

There are both criminal and civil penalties for violating antitrust laws. The penalties can be severe and the towing industry is by no means immune from prosecution. In 1988, fifteen towing firms in Maine were charged in a conspiracy to fix prices in a proposed towing bid.[2] That same year a group of towing company owners in central Florida held a meeting to discuss a pending bid proposal where they were secretly tape recorded by a police officer masquerading as a representative of one of the towing firms. In 1993, seventeen towing business owners in Arizona faced $7.6 million in civil penalties for allegedly agreeing not to compete among themselves for a state towing contract and were also accused of agreeing to boycott the competitor who won the bid by refusing to provide him with back-up service.[3] Numerous other towing companies found themselves as defendants in antitrust civil suits, which have proven that triple damages may be awarded to a prevailing plaintiff.

The U.S. Department of Justice and state antitrust enforcement agencies take the antitrust laws very seriously. So should you.

---

[1] 15 U.S.C. § 1 (Sherman Act)

[2] *State v. Randy's Inc.*, No. 88-467, 1988 WL 247975 Consent Decree, (Me. Super. Ct., Androscoggin Co., Nov. 30, 1988)

[3] *State v. Northern Arizona Towing Assn.*, et al., No. CV-93-18730, Consent Decree (Ariz. Super. Ct., Maricopa County, November 1995)

§ 1:34 Recovered Stolen Vehicles: Forced To Tow For Free

It starts out as a normal tow: The owner of a parking facility or apartment complex calls a local towing service, complaining about a vehicle that has been abandoned on his property. The towing company removes the offending vehicle and impounds it at its secured storage facility. In accordance with the state law concerning abandoned vehicles, the towing firm sends certified letters to the vehicle owner and lien holder advising of the location of the vehicle, the reason for the tow, and the amount of towing and storage fees that must be paid to retrieve the vehicle.

But then, six weeks later, this happens: A city police officer appears at the towing company office. It turns out that the impounded vehicle had been reported stolen before it was abandoned. The police officer, hand resting on his sidearm, orders the tow operator to release the vehicle to the owner — without charge. Or he tells the tower to take the stolen vehicle to the city impound facility — without charge.

He has no warrant or court order. When the tow operator resists, demanding payment of his accrued charges before releasing the vehicle to the owner or the police department, things get ugly. Finally, under threat of arrest or removal from the city rotation towing list, the tow operator relents, releasing the vehicle and forfeiting all of his charges.

We are all sympathetic to the plight of the victim of a vehicle theft. But why should the towing company that recovered the vehicle be compelled to provide free towing and storage services when it recovers a stolen vehicle?

Most stolen vehicles are covered by comprehensive insurance that is available to pay the towing and storage fees related to the vehicle recovery. There is no reason why a multi-billion dollar insurance company from Hartford, Bloomington or Northbrook should receive the benefit of free towing and storage services at the expense of a small towing business.

If, for reasons of public policy, a governmental agency feels that victims of crime, or their insurers, should not have to incur the costs of recovering the stolen vehicle, then that well-intending government might establish a fund for victims of stolen vehicles from which reasonable towing and storage fees might be paid. Those fees might eventually be recovered as restitution if the crook is ever brought to justice. Indeed, in *People v. Clay*[1] the Colorado Court of Appeals held that a towing company recovering a stolen vehicle is a "victim" under the state criminal restitution law and upheld an order directing a convicted car thief to pay $1,480 in towing and storage fees, even those that accrued during the police department evidentiary "hold."

In any event, there is no justifiable reason for the innocent towing company to be penalized by forfeiture of its hard-earned fees. Of all the persons or entities involved in a vehicle theft and recovery — the owner, the lien holder, the insurance company, the thief, the law enforcement agency, etc. — the towing company is the most "innocent." The towing company did not place the vehicle at risk to be stolen, did not steal the vehicle, and did not earn thousands of auto loan interest or insurance premiums on the vehicle. All it did was spend its time, equipment and labor in recovering the vehicle, expecting to be paid a reasonable fee for its services. Of course, recovering stolen vehicles can be one of the most difficult tow jobs because the vehicles are usually stripped of their wheels and tires.

But, more importantly, in most cases it is improper for a police agency, under a show of force, to coerce a towing company owner into releasing an impounded vehicle without proper authorization and without charge.

Under the laws of most states, a tow operator enjoys a possessory lien on all vehicles that are lawfully towed to its storage facility. That means that a towing company has a legal right to maintain possession of the vehicle until all reasonable charges are paid. If those fees are not paid, the towing company can sell the vehicle at a lien foreclosure sale.

Without a court order and payment of accrued charges, or a pre-existing contractual arrangement, a police officer has no right to insist upon the free release of a recovered stolen vehicle. To threaten arrest or economic sanctions against a tow operator for refusing to release a vehicle on which he has a possessory lien smacks of extortion. It is a civil rights violation because the tow operator is being deprived of his property interest (his possessory lien) without just cause and without due process.[2] In the eyes of the law, it is no different than a police officer demanding that a tow operator surrender his wallet or else suffer removal from the tow list.

If, out of compassion for a hapless, uninsured victim of an auto theft, a towing company voluntarily chooses to waive its fees, that's one thing. But being forced to do so — under threat of arrest or expulsion from a towing list — that's another thing altogether.

---

[1] 74 P.3d 473 (Colo. Ct. App. 2003)

[2] U.S. Const., amend. XIV

§ 1:35 Rotation Towing List Price Ceilings
Unlawful rate regulation or lawful voluntary agreement?

About once a week I get a phone call from a towing company owner complaining that some law enforcement agency is "illegally regulating" his towing fees. Typically, the caller's company participates on a city or county rotation towing list. The towing list is governed by an ordinance or rule that includes a towing rate cap. In some instances, a maximum tow charge is being proposed for the first time. The tow operator, dissatisfied with the rate, contends that the local government is engaging in unlawful price regulation. Most likely, it is not.

"Regulation" is a government entity imposing itself, without any direct interest, on the interactions between two private parties. Certainly, a ceiling on the fees allowed to be charged by rotation list towing companies is an example of a government entity imposing itself. But by setting a maximum towing fee for rotation list calls, is a government controlling an interaction between two private parties? On the surface, rate ceilings certainly seem to be a regulation of the financial transaction between the rotation towing company and the vehicle owner. But the courts see it differently.

In February 1999, in the case of *Cardinal Towing v. City of Bedford*,[1] I stood before the federal court of appeals in downtown New Orleans and argued that an exclusive, single-vendor contract for tows from sites involving police investigation was an unlawful regulation of the nonconsensual towing market. In doing so, I emphasized that the vehicle owners (or their insurance companies) paid the towing bills, not the police agency. Although it noted the "odd structure of the towing industry," the appellate court disagreed. It said:

> *Nonconsensual tows do not involve any opportunity for market interaction on the part of the owner of the vehicle. The real decision is made by the party who ordered the tow, who chooses both to remove the vehicle and the party to perform the service.... This structure, while somewhat distorted by the fact a third party gets left with the bill, is in its relevant essentials an ordinary market for services. But in this oddly bifurcated market, the party requesting the tow is undeniably also acting as a consumer, and when the City requests a tow it should be treated as a consumer.*

In other words, the towing firm's "customer" in a rotation towing system is the law enforcement agency, not the vehicle owner – despite the fact that the vehicle owner pays the bill. Under the reasoning of the court in *Cardinal Towing*, a government entity is reasoning of the court in *Cardinal Towing*, a government entity is not regulating financial transactions between the rotation tow companies and the vehicle owners when it implements a fee schedule; it is merely setting forth terms by which it will deal with those towing companies that voluntarily choose to participate on its tow list. Those terms include a maximum towing fee and an agreement by the towing firm, often implied, to collect the fee directly from the vehicle owner or their insurer. In the absence of the latter requirement, the police agency would have to pay the towing charges, then seek reimbursement from the vehicle owner.

Two years after the Cardinal Towing decision, in *Fort Bend County Wrecker Ass'n v. Wright*,[2] a Texas appellate judge put it this way:

> The Sheriff's Department is not setting prices. They are creating an invitation to contract. Those wrecker companies who do not wish to tow for the ... Sheriff's Department can charge any tow fee they choose. The Sheriff's Department has merely set a fee limit as a standard to determine with whom it will contract.

By setting maximum prices for rotation tow calls, a law enforcement agency is not *forcing* its rates on any towing firm. If a rate cap is unacceptable, a tow company can simply elect not to participate on the rotation list. (If no company is willing to perform at the stated rates, the agency might be compelled to adjust its pricing schedule.)

Section 14501(c) of title 49 of the U.S. Code prohibits state and local governments from regulating the price charged for transportation of property by motor carriers, including towing companies. Some think that statute proscribes rotation list price controls. However, section 14501(c) does not forbid rate caps in rotation list ordinances or rules because, as explained above, such maximum fees are not price regulations in the first place. They are simply conditions that law enforcement agencies require of those towing companies that choose to be on a particular rotation tow list. Section 14501(c) only prohibits government entities from regulating the price charged in consensual transactions between a towing firm and a private third-party, for example, commercial accounts, motor clubs, calls from Yellow Pages® ads, etc.

---

[1] 180 F.3d 686 (5th Cir. 1999)
[2] 39 S.W.3d 421 (Tex. Ct. App. 2001)

Chapter 2   Private Property (Trespass) Towing

§ 2:1   When to Let It Go 80

§ 2:2   Patrol Towing 82

§ 2:3   Rate Caps Put Tow Companies in Squeeze.........................84

§ 2:4   Drawing a Line in the Sand 86

TOWING and the LAW

§ 2:1   When to Let It Go
Use of deadly force rarely justified

I received a newspaper clipping reporting on a towing incident in which a woman tried to prevent her improperly-parked BMW from being removed from a shopping center parking lot in Great Neck, N.Y. When the woman saw that her vehicle was about to be towed, she began arguing with the tow truck driver. Her pleas evidently fell on deaf ears because the tow truck driver drove away "with the woman standing on a running board, hanging on to the side door of the tow truck," according to a Nassau County police report. The tow driver allegedly kept going for about two miles before he was stopped by police officers. He was charged with reckless endangerment and violation of several town ordinances.

Tow truck drivers are sometimes faced with situations in which people place their lives in jeopardy to prevent the towing of their vehicle or to avoid payment of a towing fee. The scenario described above is one. Occasionally, a vehicle owner will jump onto a vehicle about to be towed without his consent, i.e., a repossession or private property impound. There have also been incidents in which a vehicle owner has snuck into a tow yard, located and started his impounded car, then sped recklessly through the storage yard, driving out — or crashing through — the entrance gate.

Does the law permit the owner of a towing company to pull out a pistol and squeeze off a few shots at the fleeing gate-runner? Can a tow truck driver legally drive away with a private impound vehicle in tow after the vehicle owner has jumped onto the vehicle or onto his tow truck? Of course not. All that is at stake in any of those situations is a tow bill. The vehicle owners are attempting, albeit foolishly, to avoid paying an impound fee. But the law does not permit a tow operator to endanger the life of a person, even a vehicle owner acting stupidly, for no purpose other than to protect his tow bill.

When a tow operator is confronted with one of those potentially-violent situations the proper response is to back away and seek appropriate legal remedies. For example, in the case of a gate-runner, the tow operator should simply call the police and swear out a criminal warrant against the perpetrator. In most states the tow operator has a possessory lien, i.e., a legal right to maintain possession of the vehicle until the bill is paid, so the owner may be guilty of criminal theft of his own vehicle.

Identifying the defendant is easy enough: the vehicle make, model and license tag number should be on the tow-in form. The investigating law enforcement agency can obtain the owner's name and address from the appropriate state department of motor vehicles.

Private Property (Trespass) Towing   **81**

The tow operator may also sue the vehicle owner in civil court for the amount of the tow bill, any damages to other cars or the yard gate, court costs and, in some states, his attorneys fees. The claim might be covered under the vehicle owner's auto insurance policy.

Likewise, if someone jumps on a vehicle about to be towed or stands unyielding between your tow truck and the vehicle, the law does not permit you to forcefully remove them, threaten them with physical harm or otherwise put them in a life-threatening situation. Your proper recourse is to seek the assistance of a law enforcement officer or, alternatively, disconnect from the vehicle, leave the scene and then seek your civil remedies. Nothing good can come to you from escalating the confrontation. You can later file a civil suit against the vehicle owner or attempt to collect a "show up" or "drop" fee from the person who requested the removal of the trespassing vehicle.

Although the law does not permit you to use, or threaten to use, physical force to collect a tow bill, you are justified in using force, and in some situations even deadly force, if your own life or personal well-being is endangered. For example, if you are physically assaulted by a crazed vehicle owner and placed in a reasonable fear of serious bodily harm or death, the law permits you to use whatever force is necessary under the circumstances to protect yourself and others. The law would likely excuse your actions if you shot a 250-lb. madman who lunged at you with a knife while you were hooking up to his car. But the same would not be true if the assailant was a drunk 95-lb. college coed who charged at you armed only with a nasty snarl and ruby-red fingernails.

As usual, the law boils down to common sense and a balancing of the value of competing interests. It is legally unacceptable to engage in a physical confrontation, with the attendant risk of serious bodily injury, over a tow-away or a tow bill. In the heat of the moment, when he might feel the urge to use force, a tow operator should exercise restraint. The law ranks the value of life and personal safety above the price of a tow.

§ 2:2 Patrol Towing
New law raises new questions

Patrol towing, or contract towing, is a simple concept. A business or multi-unit residential complex gives a blanket authorization to a towing company to remove and impound vehicles that are parked in violation of "No Parking" signs or community parking rules. For example, a homeowners' association might contract with a towing firm to tow away all vehicles that do not display current parking permits and those that are parked in fire lanes. A tow truck will then monitor, or patrol, the parking lot, usually 24/7. When the driver sees a parking violation, he immediately removes the offending vehicle.

Done in a professional and safe manner, patrol towing is a valuable service that can be an essential element of parking control. It is a tremendous benefit to property owners or managers. They do not have to be on the property at 3 o'clock in the morning to direct the towing of unauthorized or improperly parked vehicles.

Critics of patrol towing — primarily vehicle owners who flagrantly disobey parking signs and rules — claim that the practice leads to towing abuse and physical altercations. The most frequent complaints are based on the speed at which the vehicle removal can occur ("I was only parked there for 5 minutes!"), lurking tow trucks, excessive price and the gruff behavior of towing company representatives.

Unfortunately, there have also been documented reports of violent confrontations and outright thievery by some tow operators, for example, towing properly parked vehicles after falsifying the towing report or doctoring pre-tow photographs to indicate a parking violation.

Largely in response to the misconduct of a few outlaw towing firms, several state legislatures enacted laws requiring that a property owner or agent be physically present at the scene of a nonconsensual tow-away, regardless of the time of the tow, and sign off on a written impound authorization. Evidently, some legislators feel that tow truck operators cannot be trusted with making towing decisions.

In 2002, I represented the owner of a "patrol towing" company in a federal lawsuit seeking an injunction to stop the City of San Diego from enforcing the California on-site authorization law. John Tillison claimed that the state law was illegal because the economics of intrastate trucking, including automotive towing, had been deregulated by Congress. A 1994 federal law said that states may only regulate tow truck companies in matters relating to safety and the price charged for nonconsensual towing. (See § 5:1). Tillison argued that the on-site authorization law was an unlawful regulation of his business practices that had nothing to do with price or safety.

The City countered that the on-site authorization law was not trumped by the federal deregulation law because it fell within the so-called "safety exception." Having a property owner or agent at the scene of a nonconsensual tow tended to avert confrontations if the vehicle owner appeared, reasoned the City. It offered statistical evidence showing the number of phone calls for police assistance at the scene of nonconsensual tows.

When Tillison took the witness stand at trial, I asked him whether an on-scene authorization eliminated disputes with vehicle owners or otherwise furthered any safety interests. Speaking from 25 years of experience, he testified, "If the vehicle owner comes out, it doesn't matter if there's ten people there authorizing the vehicle to be towed. If he wants to be confrontational, he's going to be confrontational." It was a marvelously perceptive answer that cut the heart out of the City's defense.

The trial judge ruled in Tillison's favor, finding that the California law did not further any safety interests.[1] He even suggested that the presence of a third person at the scene of the tow-away may actually *create* a dangerous situation. The court struck down the state law, holding that it was an economic regulation that violated the 1994 federal law. Following the court's ruling in *Tillison v. San Diego*, the use of patrol towing grew throughout California and the nation.

But as the practice of patrol towing expanded, the public outcry in protest also escalated. Ultimately, the critics took their pleas to Washington, D.C. They convinced Congress to change the federal law that Tillison had relied upon in his victory. Buried deep inside the 900-page highway re-authorization bill enacted by Congress in 2005 was a small but important change to that 1994 law. Congress carved out an additional exception to towing deregulation by granting state governments the power to enact laws requiring a property owner, lessee or agent, to be present at the time a nonconsent tow is made from private property.[2]

So, is patrol towing a thing of the past? Don't pull a white sheet over it yet. Congress only gave state governments the *authority* to enact laws requiring on-scene tow-away authorization. Which states choose to actually exercise their new found power remains to be seen. Those considering adopting such a law, or retaining an existing one, would be wise to heed John Tillison's words.

---

[1] *Tillison v. City of San Diego*, No. 01-cv-2373, Decision (S. D. Calif., Feb. 28, 2003), rev'd 406 F.3d 1126 (9th Cir. 2005)
[2] 49 U.S.C.A. § 14501(c)(5)

§ 2:3 Rate Caps Put Tow Companies in Squeeze
Fuel cost increases highlight problem with rate regulations

If you tow vehicles in nonconsensual situations, more likely than not, the rates you charge for towing and storage are regulated by some governmental entity — a state legislature, county commission, board of aldermen, etc. For example, if your company is on a rotation list for a municipal police department, maximum rates are probably set forth in the ordinance or regulation that establishes the rotation list. The maximum allowable rate for private property impounds (PPIs) may also be fixed by state or local law.

Even in the best of economic times, it can be difficult for tow operators to get needed rate increases for nonconsensual tows. Typically, once a rate is established by the governing body, the rate is published in the code book, stuck on a shelf and forgotten. Because few local laws regulating tow rates contain a provision for periodic rate review or a cost of living adjustment, many years can pass without an increase.

Tow companies engaged in nonconsensual towing, eventually forced to beg for a raise, often discover that there is not even a formal procedure by which they can compel the governmental agency to conduct a rate review. Informal pleas to city councils or other regulatory bodies for justified rate increases are frequently met with looks of feigned concern and passing comments like "We'll look into it." But nothing happens.

The skyrocketing price of fuel has exacerbated the problem. Across the nation, thousands of towing companies are trapped in regulatory settings with antiquated rates and no practical avenue for prompt relief from soaring fuel prices. Profit margins, if any, are dwindling.

Against that backdrop, a Texas court ruling should be of interest to nonconsent towing firms. In January 2000, the City of Dallas enacted an ordinance setting the maximum allowable fee for a nonconsensual tow at $95.[1] In 2003, a newly-organized PPI tow company, VRC, LLC, sued the city under the Just Compensation Clause (JCC) of the Fifth Amendment to the U.S. Constitution. The JCC says that "private property [shall not] be taken for public use, without just compensation."[2] It is commonly invoked in cases of eminent domain or condemnation, such as when a state takes private property for a new highway. The property owner must be paid "just compensation."

Although the city had not physically taken any property from VRC, the towing company contended that the unreasonably low maximum rate interfered with its property — its tow trucks and the ability to use those trucks for any economically viable purpose — to such an extent that the city was depriving it of just compensation for its investment. VRC hired a financial expert who conducted a cost study showing that the per-tow rate required for it to make a reasonable rate of return was

$135. VRC wanted the city to reimburse it for the $40 loss it claimed to have suffered on each tow.

In a ruling issued on May 19, 2008, the Texas Court of Appeals agreed with VRC that there could be a violation of the JCC even though there had been no actual confiscation of its trucks. "[W]e recognize a regulatory taking if the governmental action unreasonably interferes with the owner's right to use and enjoy his property," said the court in the case of *City of Dallas v. VRC, LLC.*[3]

However, the court went on to say that whether a government's action (or inaction) is an unreasonable interference depends, in large part, upon the property owner's "distinct investment-back expectations." In other words, does the regulation impinge on what the owner expected in terms of value or earnings *at the time he invested in the property?*

The problem for VRC was that the $95 rate cap set in 2000 was in place before VRC applied for its license in 2002. Despite its discontent with the rate, VRC nevertheless obtained a nonconsent tow license and began towing at the $95 rate. Under those facts, the Texas appellate court held that Dallas' towing rate cap did not violate the JCC because "VRC had no reasonable investment-backed expectation of charging more than $95 when it began operations in Dallas."

Even though VRC lost its case, perhaps all is not lost. The Texas court decision seems to imply that, under the right set of circumstances, a towing company might successfully challenge a rate ceiling as unlawful under the JCC.

Assume, for example, that a towing company has performed private property towing for 15 years. During that time, there have been sporadic regulated tow rate increases that allowed the company to enjoy a reasonable rate of return on its investment. New equipment is purchased in anticipation of continued business and further rate increases.

However, despite an upsurge in fuel costs, the local government takes no action to increase the maximum allowable tow rate, which causes the tow operator to now suffer a below-reasonable rate of return. Unlike newcomer VRC, that established tow company might indeed have a reasonable expectation in a rate increase and, thus, have a legitimate JCC claim against the non-responsive municipality.

If fuel prices, and other operating costs, escalate, without corresponding rate adjustments by regulating government entities, more rate-capped nonconsensual towing companies may resort to filing JCC lawsuits — or bankruptcy petitions.

---

[1] City of Dallas (Tex.) Code § 48A-43(a)(1)(2007)
[2] U.S. Const., amend. V
[3] *City of Dallas v. VRC, LLC.*, 260 S.W.3d 60 (Tex. Ct. App. 2008)

§ 2:4 Drawing a Line in the Sand
Virginia high court okays territorial restrictions on impounds

It goes without saying that most private property impound (PPI) towing occurs within major metropolitan areas. That is where the shopping centers, apartment complexes, restaurants and bars with restricted "Customer Only" or "Resident Only" parking lots are located. And that is where vehicle owners routinely ignore those signs, park in violation of the restrictions and wind up having their vehicles removed.

Fairfax County, Virginia, an overcrowded suburb of Washington, D.C., is a hotbed for PPI towing. Thousands of commercial businesses in Fairfax County rely on PPI towing companies to rid their parking lots of unauthorized, trespassing vehicles.

Advanced Towing is in the business of PPI towing. Its storage lot is located in neighboring Arlington County, within a few miles of the Fairfax County line. But Advanced Towing cannot tow trespassing vehicles from PPI-rich Fairfax County to its storage lot in nearby Arlington County because of a provision in the Fairfax County towing ordinance requiring all PPI towing operators to "tow each vehicle to a storage site located within the boundaries of Fairfax County."[1]

A frustrated Advanced Towing, along with two other out-of-county towing firms, sued the county, contending that its ordinance requiring "in county" storage of PPI tows is unconstitutional. They claim that the territorial limitation in the ordinance illegally discriminates against out-of-county towing companies in favor of in-county companies. The case eventually worked its way all the way to the Virginia Supreme Court.

In the written decision filed in *Advanced Towing Company v. Fairfax County Board of Supervisors* on June 10, 2010,[2] the state supreme court first noted that the Equal Protection Clause of the U.S. Constitution[3] does not forbid all discrimination by governments. For example, laws prohibiting smoking in public places discriminate against smokers and laws restricting the issuance of driver's licenses to persons 16 years of age or older discriminate against wannabe drivers under age 16. But those discriminatory laws pass constitutional muster because they foster established governmental functions: health and safety.

Following long-standing case law precedent, the seven-judge appellate court in *Advanced Towing* wrote that it could not substitute its judgment or policies for those of the Fairfax County legislature, as long as that governing body's enactments have some legitimate underpinning. The Fairfax towing ordinance does not unlawfully discriminate if "there is any reasonably conceivable state of facts that could provide a reasonable basis for the [in-county storage restriction]," said the court.

The towing firms argued that there is, in fact, no legitimate justification for the territorial restriction. They pointed out that if the county's concern is the convenience of the vehicle drivers, i.e., distance to travel to pick up their vehicles, their out-of-county storage lots are more conveniently located to most of the high-volume tow-away sites than those of their closest in-county competitors. In other words, it is frequently more convenient for vehicle owners whose cars are towed from sites just inside the Fairfax County boundary to travel the short distance across the county line than to traverse a far greater distance to the closest Fairfax County-based storage lot.

According to the plaintiff towing firms, since their storage facilities are as conveniently located as the Fairfax County impound lots, the only purpose of the ordinance must be to protect the financial interests of the local towing companies. Economic protectionism of private businesses, they argued, is not a legitimate reason for Fairfax County to discriminate against their out-of-county businesses.

The county responded that, notwithstanding the convenience factor, there is another justification for the territorial storage restriction. The Fairfax County towing ordinance also contains a number of regulations regarding the safeguarding of impounded vehicles, including nighttime lighting, fencing, signage and the like. The county contended that the only way to ensure that its vehicle storage regulations are enforced is to confine the towing of PPI vehicles to in-county locations where county police officers have the authority to enforce those regulations.

The Virginia Supreme Court sided with Fairfax County, holding that the county's purported desire to maintain enforcement jurisdiction over PPI towing companies engaged in towing vehicles from within the county was a "reasonably conceivable state of facts" that provided a rational basis for the territorial restriction. In short, although the Fairfax County "in-county" vehicle storage rule plainly discriminates against out-of-county PPI towing companies, the court held that there was no constitutional violation because the county demonstrated a reasonable governmental purpose for the law.

The towing companies sought permission to present their arguments to the U.S. Supreme Court, but their request was denied without comment by that court on November 1, 2010.[4]

---

[1] Fairfax County (Va.) Code § 82-5-32(e)
[2] 694 S.E.2d 621 (Va. 2010)
[3] U.S. Const., amend. XIV
[4] 131 S.Ct. 524 (2010)(cert. denied)

Chapter 3   Safety and Safety Regulations

§ 3:1 Federal DOT Regulations: A Primer 89

§ 3:2 What You Don't Know Might Hurt You 91

§ 3:3 Size and Weight Exemptions 93

§ 3:4 Risky Business 96

§ 3:5 Hours of Service Rules for Tow Truck Drivers..................... 98

§ 3:6 Move Over, Buddy 100

§ 3:7 Tow Cars, Not People 102

§ 3:8 Duty of Care 104

§ 3:9 A Breakdown in Protection 106

§ 3:10 Proper Truck Maintenance Can Be the Best Defense 108

§ 3:11 Like a Moth to Flame 110

§ 3:12 Delay Causes Roadside Tragedies 112

§ 3:13 CDL Review 114

§ 3:14 Tough New CDL Rules.. 116

§ 3:15 Hidden Dangers 118

§ 3:16 Stranded Drivers Beware... 120

§ 3:1 Federal DOT Regulations: A Primer

The Federal Motor Carrier Safety Regulations (FMCSRs), Code of Federal Regulations, Title 49 pertain to all "commercial motor vehicles."[1] A commercial motor vehicle is defined as any motor vehicle with a Gross Vehicle Weight Rating (GVWR) or Gross Combination Weight Rating (GCWR) of 10,001 lbs. or more which is utilized for hire in interstate commerce.[2] The Federal Highway Administration (FHWA) has determined that a tow truck is a "combination vehicle," therefore if the combined weight of a tow truck and vehicle being towed exceeds 10,000 lbs., the operation of that tow truck falls within the scope of these federal truck safety rules.[3]

I often hear remarks like "I've been towing across state lines on a regular basis for 20 years and I have never had to stop at any scales or carry any log books or health cards!" That may be true, but the fact that the enforcement of the rules was lax or non-existent in the past does not alter the authority or deter the power that has nonetheless been vested in the federal government for over 200 years.

The basic laws on truck safety haven't changed much in over 50 years. What has changed are the laws relating to the enforcement of those safety rules. Perhaps the most important is the Motor Carrier Safety Act of 1984. One of the stated purposes of that law is "to assure increased compliance with the traffic laws and with the commercial motor vehicle safety and health rules, regulations, standards and orders."

Two important features of the federal motor carrier laws are: (1) that all commercial motor carriers (as indicated above, that term includes tow truck companies) must receive a safety fitness rating and (2) in order to qualify for federal highway funding, the states must enact commercial motor carrier safety regulations applicable to intrastate motor carrier operations which are at least as stringent as those in the FMCSRs. Congress even established a committee — the Commercial Motor Vehicle Safety Regulatory Review Panel — to review the state laws and decide whether specific state motor carrier safety laws are compatible with the federal regulations. Congress later provided for a large increase in the millions of dollars provided to the state departments of transportation to hire additional enforcement personnel and beef-up enforcement activities. That program is called the Motor Carrier Safety Assistance Program (MCSAP). In essence, Congress said, "The federal government has good truck safety laws on the books — the Federal Motor Carrier Safety Regulations. Let's make them apply to all trucking operations, interstate and intrastate, and let's get serious about enforcing them!"

TOWING and the LAW

As a result of the 1984 law and MCSAP, even if you only operate within one state and never cross a state line, your state DOT has truck safety regulations at least as exacting as the federal DOT rules for interstate commerce. In fact, most of the states have simply incorporated by reference the FMCSRs, meaning that those federal rules which previously only applied to towing operations crossing state lines are now also applicable to tow trucks operating wholly within a state.

---

[1] 49 C.F.R. § 390.3(a)
[2] 49 C.F.R. § 390.5
[3] Interpretive Ruling, Office of Motor Carrier Standards (March 23, 1989) (Michael Trentacoste, Director)

§ 3:2   What You Don't Know Might Hurt You

It has been said that under any set of circumstances, when a commercial motor vehicle is involved in an accident and, as a result of the accident, someone is seriously injured or killed there is no such thing as no liability.

While that may be an overstatement, studies bear out that there is an atmosphere of sympathy for injured persons and prejudice against trucking companies. A jury research report reveals that while plaintiffs in personal injury suits generally win 57 percent of the time, when the defendant is a trucking company, the study found that the plaintiff wins 80 percent of the time. To make matters worse, the average amount of damages awarded against trucking firms is significantly higher.

Of course, in most cases in which a commercial motor vehicle driver while acting within the scope of his employment causes an accident, the employer will also be sued under the theory of *respondeat superior*. In many truck accident cases, both the driver and his employer have solid or at least an arguable defense, such as contributory or comparative negligence. But any defense or mitigating factor can be torpedoed if an unsafe or incompetent driver was operating the truck at the time of the accident.

In most states, the owner of any vehicle may be held liable for the negligent entrustment of a vehicle to an incompetent driver. In a typical case, the vehicle owner, knowing of the driver's record of traffic offenses or habit of using drugs or alcohol while driving, nevertheless permits him to drive a vehicle.

Under the negligent entrustment theory, the owner becomes legally responsible for the use of the vehicle by the incompetent driver. Even where the vehicle owner is the employer of the driver and, therefore, liable under the theory of respondeat superior, a number of states allow the plaintiff to claim negligent entrustment as an additional ground of recovery and to demand punitive damages.

In Dallas, Texas, a trucking firm allowed a driver with four DUI convictions and four driving accidents to continue driving. After a rear-end accident that killed one woman and left another paralyzed, a jury awarded $623,000 in compensatory damages plus $1 million in punitive damages after finding the trucking company "grossly negligent" in entrusting its vehicle to its driver.

Now, you may be thinking, "I'm not aware of any driving history problems with any of my drivers. Their employment applications look good, they all denied any violations and all the MVRs in this state are clean so I can't be found responsible for punitive damages if he has an accident." WRONG!

A growing number of states have allowed plaintiffs to recover damages based on negligent hiring. Unlike negligent entrustment, actual knowledge of an employee's past driving record or other dangerous habits is not required. You may be liable for negligent hiring if you should have known about a driver's disqualifying record. A tow truck company subject to the Federal Motor Carrier Safety Regulations (FMCSR) has a legal duty to make inquiry about the background and driving record of prospective drivers.[1] In some instances, you may have a duty to go beyond the application and conduct a full scale background investigation to uncover if the driver falsified his or her driving history.

The FMCSRs require those companies subject to the rules to obtain driver's names, date of birth, Social Security number, CDL number, a list of accidents and moving violations, residence addresses and employers for the past three years and/or commercial driving experience for the past 10 years. Furthermore, the hiring company is specifically required to contact the driver's prior employers as well as the DMV in every state in which the driver held a driver's license during the previous three-year period. Unfortunately, in some companies the first truly thorough investigation of a driver is often conducted by a personal injury attorney.

---

[1] 49 C.F.R. § 391.23

§ 3:3　Size and Weight Exemptions

You receive a call from a truck repair shop located just a few blocks from your towing business. One of their customer's units has broken down on the interstate about 10 miles away.

The disabled unit is a tractor-trailer combination that had just been loaded and was hauling the maximum gross weight allowed by law. They ask you to tow the complete rig back to their shop.

Can you do it legally? That depends upon the state in which you are located. Obviously, a rescuing tow truck cannot hook-up and tow a complete, fully-loaded tractor-trailer unit, disabled by accident or mechanical breakdown, without the "new" vehicle combination of tow truck/tractor-trailer exceeding both the maximum weight and length regulations. Adding the gross weight and length of the tow truck necessarily results in an oversize and overweight vehicle combination.

There are, of course, alternatives to towing a complete tractor-trailer unit, but those options are sometimes impractical or dangerous. For example, the disabled tractor can be swapped-out or repaired at the scene of the breakdown. However, time, expense and traffic safety sometimes dictate that the complete unit be towed. Also, there are many situations in which the towing of a single disabled vehicle will result in an overweight or overlength violation once the tow truck is attached.

Recognizing that it is often in the public interest for tow trucks to remove disabled and wrecked heavy vehicles from the roadway even if doing so would ordinarily result in an oversize or overweight violation, most state legislatures have enacted laws exempting tow trucks from the size and weight laws when they are towing disabled vehicles from the site of a wreck or breakdown.[1]

Some states have enacted unlimited exemptions. If a tow truck is hauling a wrecked or disabled vehicle, it is completely exempt from the size and weight laws.

Other states are not as generous, imposing certain restrictions or limitations on the oversize/overweight movement. Typically, those laws limit the total distance which a tow truck is allowed to make an overweight or oversized movement. In Connecticut, the radius is 25 miles.[2] Illinois allows tow trucks to haul overweight up to a maximum of 20 miles, and overlength up to 50 miles, without a permit.[3] In New Jersey the permissible range for towing a loaded tractor-trailer combination is 75 miles from the point of disablement.[4]

In addition to mileage restrictions, several states impose further limitations on oversize towing. Many states allow the overweight/overlength tow only if the vehicle being towed is not already overlength or overweight. The justification for that restriction should be fairly obvious. Without it, truckers would have an easy way to avoid expensive overweight or overlength citations – simply call a wrecker and get towed past the weigh station. Virginia allows tow trucks to haul overweight and overlength disabled vehicles to any location designated by the operator of the disabled vehicle; however, the route cannot include passage over a weight-limit bridge.[5]

Exemption laws that are not specific with regard to the distance that a vehicle can be towed can be problematic for tow operators. Some state laws identify, in rather vague terms, a general location to which the oversized vehicle can be towed. For instance, Utah allows the movement to the "nearest safe area for parking or storage."[6] Wyoming law refers to the "nearest point of safekeeping."[7] Where might that be? Likewise, the Tennessee and Texas weight exemption authorize the towing of a combination of vehicles "directly to the nearest authorized place of repair."[8] "Authorized" by whom?

In the scenario presented in the opening paragraph, suppose there was another truck repair facility located between the point of disablement and your customer's repair shop. In Wyoming or Utah, you would have to drop the disabled vehicle there as the "nearest" location, even though the customer's desired destination might be only a few more miles up the highway. Certainly, the tractor might be separated from the trailer at that location and the tractor carried on to the customer's shop; however, the practical, logistical and business concerns in that situation should be fairly evident.

Vague exemption laws also invite second-guessing by law enforcement officers and courts with regard to what is "nearest," what is a "safe area" for storage, or what is a "repair facility." A good example is the former North Carolina statute that allowed oversize tows only to "the nearest feasible point for parking or storage." In 1994, I represented a North Carolina towing company in an extremely frustrating case in which the company was fined almost $4,000 for the overlength towing of a tractor-trailer loaded with gypsum. The unit broke down alongside an interstate highway. To complicate matters, the landing gear on the trailer was inoperable so the trailer could not be set down. The tow operator hooked up the complete rig and proceeded to tow it straight up the interstate about 20 miles to the trucking company terminal. The route took the towed combination by an interstate rest area. About five miles past the rest area the tow operator was stopped by a state trooper and cited for violation of the size and weight laws because he drove past the rest area, which the trooper had determined was "the nearest feasible point for parking or storage."

At trial, I argued that the movement fell within the statutory exemption for towing disabled vehicles because, due to the broken landing gear, it was not "feasible" to leave the combination unit anywhere but at the company's terminal. But the court disagreed, holding that, under the plain language of the North Carolina law, the tow operator was required to drop the disabled combination unit in the rest area parking lot, which was the "nearest feasible point for parking," rather than tow it a few more exits to the company's terminal.[9]

Correct ruling. Bad law.[10]

---

[1] Michael McGovern, *Size & Weight Exemptions for Tow Trucks*, Tow Times, July 1997, at p. 36
[2] Conn. Gen. Stat. § 14-262a
[3] 625 Ill. Comp. Stat. § 5/15-107(c)(6) and 5/15-111(d)
[4] N.J. Rev. Stat. § 39.3-84
[5] Va. Code Ann. § 46.2-1151
[6] Utah Code § 27-12-148(2)(e)
[7] Wyo. Stat. Ann. § 31-18-808
[8] Tenn. Code Ann. § 55-7-201(h) and Te. Code Ann. § 622.902(6)
[9] *State v. C & W Towing* (N.C. Super. Ct., Buncombe County, 1994)
[10] N.C. Gen. Stat. § 20-118(c)(7) was amended in 2005 to provide that a tow truck may tow a disabled vehicle combination "within 50 miles from the point [of disablement]." S.L 2005-248, § 1 (eff. August 4, 2005)

§ 3:4 Risky Business

Low-Price Towing is severely undercutting your pricing. He's towing for 25-50 percent less than your break-even rates. You've lost dozens of good accounts to him. He operates decent equipment, hires competent drivers and pays the same fuel and maintenance costs as you, so you've been wondering, "How can he charge those low rates?!"

One day at the local diner you are seated in the booth next to Low-Price Towing's insurance agent. While you are wolfing down your sandwich, you inadvertently overhear him telling his lunch companion, "I don't know how that guy at Low-Price Towing can sleep at night — he hardly carries any insurance."

"Ah-ha!" you say to yourself. "So that's how he does it!" Somehow, Low-Price Towing is flying under DOT's radar and is running underinsured. How frustrating. Especially if you comply with the DOT financial responsibility rules and are prudently carrying $750,000 or more of liability insurance to protect you, your accounts and their customers. You could complain to the state DMV, DOT or the state insurance commissioner, but that probably won't solve the problem. Low-Price may get a slap on the wrist. Even if he gets shut down, he, or somebody like him, will be right back in business operating with low limits of liability insurance which allows him to undercut your price.

So instead, after verification, you decide to take this new-found information directly to the customers that have been filched by this low-baller, hinting to them that their necks might be on the line if Low-Price causes an accident: "Hey, did you realize that Low-Price Towing has ridiculously low limits on its liability insurance? What if he damages one of your customer's vehicles or, worse, hurts somebody and his insurance won't cover it?"

In response, the service manager looks at you blankly and says, "So what? He hasn't dropped or damaged a car or truck yet. And even if he does, it's no skin off my nose. He's the one that's responsible. As long as he keeps charging me those cheap tow rates, I'm going to keep using him."

Generally, the employer of an independent contractor is not subject to legal liability for harm caused by the negligence of an independent contractor.

But what if the dealer or repair shop knew his tow contractor was underinsured? If Low-Price Towing caused an injury or property damage in excess of its insurance coverage, could the company that hired Low-Price to make the tow call — after having been informed by you of their deficit insurance status — be held liable for the amount of the claim in excess of Low-Price Towing's insurance coverage? Most likely, no.

The mere fact that a tow operator is underinsured has no bearing on his competency. It does not indicate that he is operating dangerously or that he is more likely to cause an injury than a company with higher liability insurance limits. Indeed, in my example above, Low-Price Towing had never had an accident, operated good equipment and hired good drivers. A towing contractor's insurance status or lack thereof, even if known to the employer, will not give rise to liability on the part of the employer for the negligent acts of the tow contractor.

But that is not to say that an employer of a towing company could never be held responsible for the acts of its chosen tow company. As with most "general rules," there are exceptions to the independent contractor rule. Employers of independent contractors can be liable for injuries caused by the independent contractor if the employer knew, or should have known, that the work to be performed would probably cause injury unless certain precautions were taken. If a foolhardy truck or auto repair facility continues to use a towing company which it knows to operate extremely unsafe equipment, e.g., faulty brakes or trucks that are operated by unqualified, inexperienced or underage drivers, and a towing accident happens, the repair facility could be found liable under a theory of negligent hiring. Under those circumstances, it would be foreseeable that the towing would have caused injury.

The exceptions to the general rule of "no liability for the acts of an independent contractor" are based upon a belief that as between two parties innocent of causing the actual harm — e.g., the dealer or repair shop hiring the tow truck and the hapless victim of the tow truck company's negligence — the risk of loss occasioned by the contracted work should be borne by the person for whom the job was done. If a dealership or garage knowingly uses an unsafe tow company, it certainly runs the risk that a judge or jury would hold it accountable for any damages caused by the negligent acts of the tow company. Of course, that's a risk that prudent dealers and repair shops can easily avoid by hiring only proven, competent towing firms.

§ 3:5 Hours of Service Rules for Tow Truck Drivers

As a commercial motor carrier — yes, that's what you are — you should be thoroughly familiar with the Federal Motor Carrier Safety Regulations (FMCSRs). Generally, those comprehensive truck safety regulations are applicable to all commercial motor vehicles (CMVs) with a Gross Vehicle Weight Rating (GVWR) greater than 10,000 lbs. operating in interstate commerce.

Almost all of the states have adopted some version of the FMCSRs, therefore many tow truckers operating *only in intrastate commerce* must comply with comparable truck safety rules. (See § 3:1). Furthermore, take heed that an *intrastate* tow trucker who only occasionally operates in *interstate* transportation is subject to the federal safety rules for eight consecutive days following any trip that takes him across state lines.

Since driver fatigue is a proven factor in many vehicle accidents involving long-haul truckers, one of the most important parts of the FMCSRs is the section restricting a CMV driver's time behind the wheel, known as the "Hours of Service" (HOS) rules.[1] Under the HOS rules for interstate drivers, effective January 4, 2004, the driver of a CMV may only drive for 11 hours following 10 consecutive hours of off-duty time, and may not drive beyond the 14th hour after coming on duty. In other words, under the rules applicable to interstate drivers, a tow truck driver who has been driving for 11 hours or been working for 14 hours, whether driving or not, is prohibited from driving his tow truck again until he has been off-duty for 10 straight hours. Again, remember that some version of those federal rules may, through adoption by the state, be applicable to tow truck drivers operating solely in intrastate commerce.

Recognizing the difference between "long-haul" and "short-haul" drivers, who spend a lot of non-driving time delivering property (tow truck drivers are a good example), the Federal Motor Carrier Safety Administration (FMCSA) included a provision in the HOS regulations that allows short-haul drivers to have an increased on-duty period of up to 16 hours once during a 7-day period.[2]

However, even with the "short-haul" exception, the HOS rule poses an obvious problem for towing companies with "on call" drivers who respond to after-hours or nighttime tow calls. If a tow truck driver works all day, then takes the tow truck home to respond to night calls, the 11/10 rule generally prohibits him or her from taking any tow calls for 10 hours. Even with the advantage of the "short-haul" exception, that nighttime "on call" driver could only respond to one after-hours call per week.

But there is another exception in the FMCSRs especially for tow truck drivers. Under the "Tow Trucks responding to emergencies" exception, promulgated in the early 1990s, a tow truck driver is relieved from the HOS rules if he or she is responding to a request from a federal, state or local police officer to move a wrecked or disabled vehicle.[3] Thanks to that exemption, the "on call" driver is permitted to respond to a nighttime police emergency call, even if they have not had the required 10 consecutive hours of off-duty time, and even if they have already used their "short haul" exception for the week.

But the "emergency response" exemption is by no means a free pass for off-hours tow calls. Its scope is extremely limited. First, the exemption does not apply to calls received from motorists, commercial accounts, auto clubs, etc. Nor does it apply to a call from a law enforcement official for anything other than "to move" a vehicle. Thus, a tow truck driver who has worked an all-day shift might be violating the HOS rules if he responds to a motor club call at midnight or to a police call for any type of roadside service other than a tow. Second, there is a time limit on the exemption. The relief from the HOS rules is not to exceed the length of time the driver spends on the police call, including travel to and from the scene or 24 hours from the time of the initial request, whichever is less.

Unquestionably, there are some ambiguities in the "emergency response" exemption for tow truckers. Towing company owners and their drivers are well-advised to become familiar with the FMCSRs and any state HOS rules applicable to their operations.[4] The financial fines and penalties for violations can be severe.

---

[1] 49 C.F.R., Part 395
[2] 49 C.F.R. § 395.1(e)
[3] 49 C.F.R. § 390.23(a)(3)
[4] See Notice of Proposed Rulemaking, Docket No. FMCSA 2004-19608, 75 Fed. Reg. 82,170 (December 29, 2010)

§ 3:6 Move Over, Buddy

I don't know about you, but I'm sick and tired of reading reports in the trade publications, on towing websites and in the general media about tow truck drivers, while in the process of hooking-up disabled vehicles on the roadside, being struck by other vehicles. To be more accurate, I am mad as hell and equally frustrated by the senseless tragedies. Almost every week a news story appears somewhere relating the death or serious injury of a driver caused by a motorist slamming into his or her roadside work site.

Although it has been many years since I drove a tow truck for pay, I still vividly recall the anxiety of handling a service call or tow from the emergency lane of a high-speed interstate highway. In those "pre-wheel-lift" days, I would often find myself flat on my back shimmying up to an axle with a J-hook in my hand, my head only inches away from the travel lane of Interstate 40 and oncoming traffic whizzing by at 70+ miles per hour. Fortunately, I was never hit, but the thought regularly crossed my mind that the slightest incident — a tire blowout, a small piece of debris in the road or even a hard sneeze — could send a passing motorist crashing into me. Lying on my back or standing between the vehicles, I would have been completely vulnerable.

Of course, the dangers associated with roadside assistance are not unique to the towing industry. Law enforcement officers, highway maintenance personnel and ambulance/rescue squad drivers face similar risks.

Common sense should oblige a traveling motorist approaching an emergency vehicle in the service lane of a highway to slow down and/or move-over wherever practical. But they often do not. In the U.S., we tend to legislate in matters of common sense, i.e., to criminalize imprudent conduct. Consequently, in recent years most states have put so-called "move-over" laws on their books.[1]

Those laws generally require a motorist on a highway with two or more lanes of traffic proceeding in the same direction as a roadside tow truck, police car or other emergency or maintenance vehicle, which is operating flashing lights, to make a lane change into the lane of traffic which is not adjacent to the working vehicle, if traffic conditions permit. If traffic conditions do not permit a lane change, the motorist is then required under the law to proceed with due caution and reduce his speed while maintaining a safe speed for road conditions. Violations of the law are minor misdemeanors, typically calling for fines of less than $100. But some of the laws call for enhanced punishment if a violation results in an injury or death.

On paper, the move-over laws look terrific. The drawback is in the enforcement: How do you catch violators? Most roadside highway tow calls do not involve a law enforcement agency, so move-over law violations can occur unchecked. Even if a law enforcement officer is on the scene of a roadside tow, he is most likely busy with an accident report or has a driver in custody, so he is unavailable to give chase to a move-over violator. On a road trip to Nashville, I observed four flagrant violations of Tennessee's move-over law during my 200-mile drive.

The enactment of the move-over laws is a good start, but it will take some time for the full benefit — saved lives — to be realized. Public education is critical. What good is the law if the motoring public isn't aware of it? Highway billboards and public service announcements would help. Occasional law enforcement crackdowns with two on-scene police cruisers, one dedicated to enforcing the move-over law, would go a long way toward increasing public awareness. Emphasizing the laws in high school driver education classes is also essential.

Realistically, though, even full compliance with the move-over laws will only eliminate roadside collisions resulting from mistakes — moments of inattentiveness by otherwise competent and law-abiding drivers which cause their vehicle to move a few feet or more off the roadway. The move-over laws, helpful as they may be, do not eliminate your exposure to intoxicated or overly fatigued drivers. A driver who is drunk or asleep could care less about moving over. Indeed, even if in apparent compliance with a move-over law by traveling in a lane of traffic not adjacent to the break-down lane, an impaired driver will often veer across two or three lanes of traffic and strike a roadside assistance vehicle.

Unfortunately, only full compliance by motorists with all highway traffic laws, including the DUI laws and the "sleepy driver" and move-over laws, can ensure a safe roadside working environment. Given the unlikelihood of that, all tow truck drivers should continue to remain vigilant and exercise all due precautions while working roadside.

---

[1] *Move Over Laws*, Tow Times, July 2007, at p. 26

§ 3:7   Tow Cars, Not People

I was driving to my office this morning when I was passed by a wheel-lift tow truck. The tow truck had a passenger vehicle suspended from the wheel-lift in tow. In the car that was being towed were three people, two in the front seat and one in the back seat. They were all grinning and seemed to be having a grand time whizzing down the interstate with the front end of their car lifted up in the air behind the tow truck.

While I watched the tow truck and its happy cargo drive out of sight, two questions came to my legal mind: First, is it legal to carry passengers in a vehicle being towed? And, second, even if it's legal, is it advisable?

Several states have laws or regulations that specifically prohibit tow truck operators from allowing customers to ride in towed vehicles. New Hampshire and Washington have enacted laws making it illegal for anyone to occupy a vehicle while it is being towed by a tow truck.[1] The fines and penalties are imposed on the tow truck driver, not the passenger. Although they do not address the towing of automobiles with passengers inside, the Federal Motor Carrier Safety Regulations provide that, absent special circumstances, no disabled bus with passengers aboard shall be towed.[2]

Even in those states without specific laws directed at tow truck operations, the practice may be indirectly proscribed. There are statutes in most states that prohibit passengers from riding in a trailer (e.g. a house trailer or camping trailer) while it is being towed on a public highway. A careful reading of the definition of trailer may lead a court to conclude that a disabled vehicle in tow falls within definition of "trailer" and that riding in such vehicles is thus forbidden. For example, the Florida statute that makes towing an occupied vehicle a crime defines a trailer as any vehicle without motive power designed for carrying persons or property being drawn by a motor vehicle.[3] Isn't a disabled or wrecked car or truck a vehicle without motive power designed for carrying persons?

The traffic regulations for the national park system forbid a person from operating a motor vehicle while allowing another person to ride within any vehicle, trailer or other mode of conveyance towed behind the motor vehicle.[4] Again, although that traffic rule of the National Park Service was probably intended for recreational campers and trailers, a literal interpretation of that federal law would prohibit tow trucks from towing vehicles within the park system with a passenger in the towed vehicle.

Even if there is no law in your state that directly or impliedly prevents you from carrying passengers in a vehicle being towed, is it a smart practice? I am aware of two incidents — one in Rangely, Colo. and one in Pullman, Wash. — in which passengers in towed vehicles were killed after the vehicle in tow broke loose from the tow truck and crashed. In New Jersey, an armored car slammed into the side of a vehicle being towed, seriously injuring the customer riding inside. I am certain there have been other, similar episodes.

One might contend that a passenger riding in a towed vehicle is no more at risk than one riding in the cab of the tow truck; after all, the tow truck itself might become involved in a wreck and the armored car might just as likely have struck the passenger side of the tow truck cab as the vehicle in tow. On the other hand, it can be argued that whenever you are towing a vehicle behind a vehicle on a conventional sling or wheel-lift there is an increased risk factor: tow bars might fail, safety chains can break and defects in the towed vehicle might come into play. Of course, it is simply good business practice to avoid foreseeable risks and lessen your exposure to liability.

There will be exceptional circumstances in which a tow operator has no choice but to carry passengers in a towed vehicle. You wouldn't leave a family of six stranded out in the middle of the Arizona desert in August. The New Hampshire statute even provides an exception to the general rule against persons occupying towed vehicles when the tow operator is directed to do so by a police officer.

If the occasion arises in which there is no choice but to allow customers to ride in a vehicle being towed, it would be prudent to use a car carrier rather than a conventional tow truck or wheel-lift, if possible, and to limit the distance in which the passengers ride in the towed vehicle. Take the passengers to the nearest safe haven and then continue the tow with the passenger-less vehicle.

---

[1] N.H. Rev. Stat. § 265:154 and Wash. Rev. Code § 46.61.625(2)
[2] 49 C.F.R. § 392.63
[3] Fla. Stat. §§ 316.003(59) and 316.2014
[4] 36 C.F.R. § 4.22(b)(4)(i)

§ 3:8 Duty of Care
A fine line of legal responsibility

As a tow truck driver, you have a responsibility to use reasonable care to refrain from conduct that will foreseeably cause harm to your customers. The law calls it a "duty." Duty is the legal obligation to conform your conduct to that of a reasonable person in a similar situation. If you fail to meet that legal standard of care and some harm occurs to your customer, you can be held liable for any injury or loss.

For example, if you knowingly allow a customer to linger between the back of your tow truck and his vehicle during a winch-out operation and the customer is injured when the cable snaps, you would likely be held accountable. That is because a reasonable tow operator should take steps to protect the customer from the clearly foreseeable risk of a winch cable break. In other words, you did not comply with your legal duty.

On the other hand, if you drop off a customer and his vehicle at a repair facility and then, a few minutes after you depart, the customer is struck by a vehicle while crossing the street to a donut shop, you should not be liable. Your duty to the customer ended when you left the repair facility.

However, as demonstrated by a 2006 Tennessee court ruling, determining when your legal duty begins and when it ends can sometimes be a difficult task.

On November 10, 2002, at about 11:30 p.m., young Carrie Hurd was traveling eastbound on Interstate 40 when she pulled her Saab vehicle onto the shoulder of the highway in Smith County. It became stuck in the mud. A sheriff's deputy arrived shortly thereafter and called dispatch for a tow truck. Doug Clemons, of Clemons Wrecker Service in Carthage, responded and winched the Hurd car from the mud.

Ms. Hurd did not have sufficient cash to pay the bill and Clemons was unable to process her credit card at the scene. Clemons and Hurd discussed the location of an ATM and decided that the nearest one was at a restaurant located at the last exit behind the site of the pull-out. They agreed to meet at that ATM to settle-up the tow bill.

Clemons returned to his tow truck and continued eastbound on I-40. Ms. Hurd followed behind. Approximately two miles from the scene of the pull-out, Clemons turned left into an emergency vehicle crossover between the eastbound and westbound lanes of I-40. Ms. Hurd did not follow him. Instead, she steered to the right and stopped on the eastbound right-hand shoulder adjacent to the crossover. After a few minutes, and without explanation, Ms. Hurd suddenly turned left into the eastbound lane of traffic directly in the path of another vehicle. A violent collision occurred resulting in the death of Ms. Hurd and the driver of the other vehicle.

Ms. Hurd's parents sued Clemons Wrecker Service, contending that "Clemons took the responsibility of leading [Hurd] to the [restaurant ATM] in order to ensure that he would be paid." As such, according to Hurd's parents, Clemons "took upon himself the duty to guide [Hurd] to the restaurant." In 2005, the trial judge dismissed the case against Clemons. An appeal ensued. On June 13, 2006, the Tennessee Court of Appeals confirmed the trial court's dismissal, finding that Clemons had no duty of care at the time of the accident.[1]

The court found it important that Clemons never expressly told Ms. Hurd to follow him to the ATM at the restaurant nor did he inform her of the safest route. Furthermore, Clemons never signaled or motioned for Hurd to turn from the right-hand emergency lane into the path of the oncoming vehicle. Had he done so, and thereby assumed responsibility for her safety, the result in the case may have been quite different. As it was, the court of appeals held that Clemons was not liable:

[Clemons] owed no duty of care under the facts of this case. While the risks associated with using an interstate crossover are great and the safer course of action would have been to use the next available interchange, Clemons could not foresee that [Hurd] would stop her vehicle on the shoulder of the interstate and then turn into the path of an oncoming vehicle. When a defendant could not have foreseen the resulting injury, no duty of care is held to arise.

The Hurds also asked the court to adopt a blanket rule that a tow truck driver owes a duty of care to ensure that all assisted customers arrive safely at their destinations. The court said that such a rule would "place too heavy of a burden on the [tow truck] defendant in this case, making him the insurer of the [motorist's] safety for the entire journey," and rejected the suggestion.

The court properly determined that Clemons was not responsible for this tragic accident. But the ruling highlights the extremely fine line that a tow truck driver treads upon when it comes to responsibility for customer safety.

---

[1] *Hurd v. Flores*, 221 S.W.2d 14 (Tenn. Ct. App. 2006)

§ 3:9 A Breakdown in Protection
Does law enforcement share the blame for roadside accidents?

The Wall of the Fallen Memorial at the International Towing & Recovery Hall of Fame and Museum in Chattanooga, Tennessee, is dedicated to tow operators who have been killed while performing their work duties. The fact that such a memorial has even been created highlights the danger that exists in the towing industry and the need for continuing education and legislation directed towards reducing these tragedies.

Roadside tow truck driver fatalities or injuries are often followed by the question: "Who is to blame?" Certainly, the driver of the vehicle that strikes the tow truck operator carries most, if not all, of the blame, especially if he or she is driving recklessly or under the influence of drugs or alcohol. But others may be partially responsible. A 2006 court ruling in California considered whether on-site law enforcement officers carry a responsibility to protect tow operators from harm at the scene of an accident recovery.

Around noon on a winter day in 2003, in Tehama County, north of San Francisco, the driver of a Volkswagen Jetta lost control of the vehicle on a rain-slick, two-lane road. The Jetta was upside down in a ditch next to the southbound lane.

The California Highway Patrol (CHP) investigated the accident and dispatched J & L Towing to recover the vehicle. The driver sent to the call, Troy Minch, rolled the Jetta over, extracted it from the ditch, hooked it up and pulled forward about 15 to 20 feet onto the southbound shoulder of the road.

He parked the tow truck with its driver-side wheels resting on the solid white fog line. Ahead of him, the road curved such that northbound traffic would be coming around a blind curve shortly before the accident site. A CHP officer had positioned himself in that curve, using hand signals to warn northbound traffic to slow down.

Minch spoke with the vehicle owner about insurance and other things, then went to the cab of the tow truck to get his receipt book. He approached the truck on the driver's side, i.e., traffic side. Although Minch had been trained to stay on the non-traffic side of the truck for safety purposes, he went to the traffic side because the passenger door had automatically locked and he had forgotten to unlock it.

While Minch was approaching the cab of his tow truck, despite the signaling efforts of the CHP officer, an inattentive driver in a pickup truck, surprised by the brake lights of a vehicle in front of him, swerved to the left and hit Minch. Minch suffered severe personal injuries.

Minch sued the CHP contending that the officers had a duty to protect him at the scene of the vehicle recovery and that they failed to exercise reasonable care in performing that duty. The CHP defended on the basis that, under the circumstances, it owed no legal duty to Minch. On June 22, 2006, in a written opinion issued in *Minch v. California Highway Patrol,* the California Court of Appeals agreed with the CHP and dismissed Minch's case.[1]

The appellate court focused on the fact that Minch had already completed the recovery and that he remained at the scene only for "business purposes."

"The officers successfully protected [Minch] as he extracted the Jetta. [Minch] was not injured during that process," the court noted. "Rather, his injury occurred after he had extracted the Jetta and while he had parked the tow truck, with the Jetta in tow, for business purposes."

The court found it significant that the CHP officers did not direct Minch to remain at the scene, they did not direct him where to park and they did not lock the passenger door of the tow truck forcing Minch to walk on the traffic side. The court concluded that Minch "was not in a position of dependency on the officers, and they did not say anything to indicate that they would guarantee his safety."

Minch also argued that the officers violated the CHP Officer Safety Manual, which was proof that they failed to exercise due care. According to the court, however, the manual does not have the force of law so any failure of the officers to comply with its directives did not establish a legal duty. In any event, said the court, Minch did not demonstrate that the officers violated any provision of the manual.

Although the court did not directly address the issue, one could imply from this ruling that law enforcement officers on the scene of an accident or breakdown, at least in California, have a legal duty to protect tow truck drivers who are in the actual process of performing roadside extractions or hook-ups.

However, the most important lesson to be derived from this case, by far, is that tow truck drivers must continue to take primary responsibility for their own safety and, regardless of the circumstances, never rely solely upon others for their protection. Obviously, when the first opportunity presents itself to leave a dangerous work zone, the prudent tow truck driver should take it. After all, the ultimate goal is not to assign blame after a roadside accident; it is to avoid having your name inscribed on the Wall of the Fallen.

---

[1] 44 Cal. Rptr.3d 846 (Cal. Ct. App. 2006)

§ 3:10 Proper Truck Maintenance Can Be the Best Defense

It is a tow truck company owner's worst nightmare: A heavy-duty tow truck is hauling a disabled cement mixer. The tow truck driver applies the brakes as he approaches a stop signal at a major highway intersection, but the brakes fail, sending the tow truck-cement mixer combination hurtling into crossing traffic. A horrific collision occurs killing or seriously injuring several motorists and passengers. A post-accident inspection of the tow truck reveals that the brakes on three wheels were either completely inoperable or severely out of adjustment. Inevitably, multi-million dollar lawsuits will be filed against the tow truck driver – and the towing company that employed him.

The law imposes on every tow truck driver a duty to operate his or her tow truck in a responsible manner. Included in that duty is the obligation to operate mechanically safe vehicles. Driving a tow truck with mechanical defects which the driver knew about, or reasonably should have discovered, will most certainly result in civil, if not criminal, liability to the driver should an accident occur as the result of that inadequate vehicle maintenance.

Under the common law concept of *respondeat superior*, an employer is responsible for damages or injuries caused by his employee while that employee is acting within the scope of his employment. Thus, in the unfortunate intersection accident described above, the employer would have legal liability if his driver was determined to be negligent.

Furthermore, the Federal Motor Carrier Safety Regulations (FMCSRs) impose statutory obligations with regard to vehicle inspection and maintenance on both tow truck drivers and the companies that employ them.[1] Parts 392, 393 and 396 of the FMCSRs set forth specific legal duties concerning vehicle safety inspections. Most states have adopted those sections of the federal motor vehicle safety rules to apply equally to intrastate motor carrier operations. The duties set forth in those regulations include maintaining a systematic program for truck inspection, repair and maintenance and keeping records documenting that program.

Failure to meet the inspection standards, failure to monitor employee-driver compliance with their duties under the regulations (including completing and filing vehicle inspection reports) or failure to keep the required maintenance and inspection records may result in per se liability on the part of a towing company. Per se liability is imposed when the breach of a legal duty causes damage or injury. That legal concept is significant because in a per se case the plaintiff does not have to show actual negligence on the part of a defendant (i.e., that the defendant acted unreasonably under all the circumstances); liability is imposed upon the mere showing that the defendant failed to comply with the FMCSRs and that failure resulted in an accident or loss.

For example, FMCSR 396.13 imposes a duty on a tow truck driver to inspect a tow truck before driving it.[2] The driver must be "satisfied that the motor vehicle is in safe operating condition." In my example, if the driver had failed to perform the mandated inspection and that inspection, if performed, would have revealed the brake problem, the tow truck driver would be per se liable for the personal injuries resulting from the accident.

Under the FMCSRs, tow truck company owners have a separate responsibility for the inspection and maintenance of their tow trucks.[3] They also have a duty to ensure that the drivers employed by them observe the duties imposed upon them by the FMCSRs. Again, a failure to comply with the rules can lead to dire consequences should such a failure result in property damage or personal injury.

Violations of the federal truck safety rules are increasingly used to form the basis for liability in cases against motor carriers. An article in a personal injury lawyer's magazine urged its readers to utilize a motor carrier's own FMCSR records, especially any inadequacies or omissions therein, in prosecuting motor vehicle accident cases involving trucks. In other words, personal injury attorneys are rooting through truck maintenance records looking for the "smoking gun" failures of the company to comply with the FMCSRs truck maintenance and inspection rules.

Studies show that every company that operates trucks as a principal part of its business operations will experience at least one accident over every two-year period. In light of that reality, it is simply a sound business practice to develop and sustain a thorough tow truck maintenance program, including strict compliance with the vehicle maintenance rules set forth in the FMCSRs. Obviously, good truck maintenance can prevent accidents from occurring in the first place. Additionally, in the event of the unavoidable accident, good truck maintenance records can be your best defense to a multi-million dollar lawsuit.

---

[1] 49 C.F.R., Part 396
[2] 49 C.F.R. § 396.13(a)
[3] 49 C.F.R. § 396.3(a)

§ 3:11 Like A Moth To Flame

In the dead of night, when your tow truck is parked on the apron of the highway and you are hooking up a disabled vehicle, do you switch on your flashing light bar? Does it make you feel safe and secure when those oscillating rays of amber light pierce into the dark like the sweeping beam of a seaside lighthouse? Does it seem as though that flashing light bar atop your tow truck is a guarantee that passing traffic will reduce their speed and make a slow, wide path around your work area?

Did you ever think that, instead of protecting you, your beacon warning light might be the very thing that could get you killed?

Tow truck light bars and warning lights are intended to alert oncoming motorists of a hazardous situation ahead. Being so warned, it is assumed that those motorists will respond by increasing their attention to the upcoming situation and exercising extra caution. Unfortunately, science and experience tell us that we cannot always count on such a response to tow truck warning lights. In fact, they tell us that in some situations, tow truck warning lights are themselves the hazard.

The towing industry's long-standing faith in flashing beacon lights as a safety device was shaken in the early morning hours of February 11, 1979. It was then that Alain Desouches was driving on a southern California freeway in his antique Mercedes Benz. The vehicle experienced a mechanical failure and Mr. Desouches pulled his vehicle to the shoulder of the freeway, out of the lanes of traffic. A highway patrol trooper came along and dispatched Anderson's Tow Service to the scene. Upon arrival, the tow truck driver stopped his tow truck on the shoulder in front of the disabled vehicle, turned on his rearward flashing amber lights, then went to the back of the disabled vehicle where he began making some roadside repairs. Mr. Desouches stood with his back to passing traffic, watching the tow truck driver work on his car. He was struck by an oncoming vehicle and seriously injured, including the loss of one leg.

In what is perhaps the leading case on this issue, Mr. Desouches and his family sued the towing service contending that the tow company driver was negligent, in part, for turning on the tow truck's flashing amber lights. Relying upon scientific evidence, the plaintiff contended that rather than protecting the tow truck driver and his customer, the flashing lights actually created a hazard. His expert testimony demonstrated that, instead of diverting nighttime drivers away from the scene of breakdowns, flashing tow truck lights actually attract tired, intoxicated or otherwise impaired nighttime drivers "like a moth to flame." The plaintiff received a substantial settlement before trial.

For as long as I have been involved in the legal aspects of the towing industry, I have heard the debates about light bars. There are two primary questions: 1) What is the most appropriate color for tow truck warning lights? and 2) When should tow truck warning lights be operated? Of course, underlying the debate is the question of safety and potential legal liability.

What color? Amber? Red? Blue? Some physiological studies show that amber is the color most likely to "pull" a motorist towards a tow truck. Yet many state laws prohibit any lens color other than amber on tow trucks so they are not confused with fire, rescue or law enforcement vehicles.[1] A few state statutes require both amber and red lights on tow trucks: amber for merely cautious situations and red for truly hazardous situations, for example, where a tow truck is partially blocking a roadway during a recovery operation.[2]

The actual operational practices of light bars and beacon lights by tow truck operators, regardless of the color of the lights, raises more questions. When should the lights be utilized? Is it reasonable for a tow truck driver to operate the warning lights during a normal tow when the vehicle is tracking properly behind the tow truck with no protruding parts? Few would argue that it would be prudent for the driver of a tow truck which is stopped and partially blocking a lane of traffic in the process of a recovery to activate the truck's emergency beacon lights. But what about the situation like that faced by the Anderson's Tow Service driver who responded to the Desouches call alongside a California freeway at 2 o'clock in the morning? If both the tow truck and the disabled vehicle are out of the travel lanes, is it unreasonable, i.e., negligent, for the tow truck driver to switch on the light bar? Is the tow operator in that situation exposing himself and his customer to a known or foreseeable risk of injury due to the "moth to flame" phenomena? Some experts think so. And so might some juries.

---

[1] *State Guide: Authorized Warning Lights for Towing Vehicles,* Tow Times, February 1998, at p. 42

[2] *See, e.g.,* Wis. Stat. Ann. § 347.26(6)b

§ 3:12 Delay Causes Roadside Tragedies

Shortly after 5 p.m., Mr. Alba's vehicle broke down on I-95 near Canton, Massachusetts. He pulled over onto the right-side emergency stopping lane. Mr. Alba was a member of an auto club. At 5:15 p.m. he called the club's toll-free number from his car phone and requested towing service. He was told by the dispatcher to wait with the vehicle, so Mr. Alba waited . . . and waited . . . and waited.

The towing service never arrived and dusk was beginning to fall, so Mr. Alba walked to a nearby mall and called his brother. His brother went to the mall, picked up Mr. Alba and the two of them, in the brother's car, returned to Mr. Alba's car on I-95. They pulled behind the disabled vehicle, in the emergency lane, and waited . . . and waited . . . and waited. An hour and twenty-five minutes later and still no tow truck.

The tow truck never arrived but a drunken driver did, slamming into the rear of the brother's parked car which exploded into a flaming inferno. Mr. Alba died and his brother was seriously injured.

In another incident, two teenage boys sat in a disabled car on the side of a California freeway for over an hour waiting for a tow truck dispatched by the Automobile Club of Southern California. A drunken driver crashed into the parked vehicle, killing 16-year-old Seth Bloomberg.

Certainly the reckless or drunken drivers who caused the collision carry the bulk of the responsibility. But the accidents would never have happened — the disabled vehicles wouldn't still be in a position to be hit — if the tows had been performed in a timely manner. So should the towing companies and automobile clubs share in some of the blame — and some of the financial liability? Many people think so.

In the Alba case, the towing company that was dispatched to the call by the auto club was located less than five miles from the accident scene. The dispatch records maintained by the auto club show that they were given an estimated time of arrival (ETA) of 30 minutes. The towing company representatives claim they did respond to the call but were given the wrong location by the auto club dispatcher. In the California case, the towing company got lost on the way to the call.

As a general rule, the law requires people to conduct themselves reasonably considering all the circumstances facing them. To not act reasonably is to act negligently. We are responsible for any injuries that might occur as the foreseeable consequence of our negligent actions or inactions.

In the situations described above, were the towing companies' actions, or inactions, reasonable under all the circumstances? Did they act the same way a reasonable towing company might have? What if, instead of a wrong location, the response time delay was the result of a tow company's practice or policy to take all commercial account tows first, giving low-priority to low-paying auto club calls? Was there anything they could have, or should have, done to facilitate the tow and thus avoid the accident?

Some of the same questions are applicable to the auto clubs: did they act reasonably? Does their responsibility end when the call is given to the towing company or do they have a duty to confirm that the call information given is accurate and to follow-up on the status of the call?

These questions are important because it can hardly be disputed that such roadside accidents occur all too frequently. In the California case, the court said, "It is not uncommon and therefore foreseeable for intoxicated or speeding drivers to lose control and crash into poles, buildings or whatever else may be standing alongside the road they travel."[1] The court said that the teenagers in that case "relied" on the auto club to come to their assistance. So, with the knowledge that such accidents are a foreseeable risk when disabled vehicles are sitting by the roadside, and that the club members are depending on prompt service, what is the legal duty of towing companies and auto clubs called to respond to roadside breakdowns?

Many auto club calls still involve a third party (the auto club dispatcher) in the transmission of service call information. That process can and does result in delays in the relay of call information and increases the potential for miscommunications and liability.

---

[1] *Bloomberg v. Interinsurance Exchange,* 207 Cal. Rptr. 853 (Cal. Ct. App. 1984)

§ 3:13 CDL Review
Commercial driver's license basics

I spoke at a towing convention about several legal issues affecting the towing industry on a federal level, including the then-new changes to the Commercial Driver's License (CDL) regulations. From the feedback from the attendees, I realized that there remains some confusion about the basics of the CDL program.

The CDL originated in the Commercial Motor Vehicle Safety Act of 1986.[1] The goal of that federal legislation was to improve highway safety by ensuring that drivers of large trucks are qualified to operate those vehicles and to remove unsafe and unqualified drivers from the highways. The Act established minimum national standards which the states must follow when licensing commercial motor vehicle (CMV) drivers. Among other things, the Act made it illegal for a CMV driver to hold a license issued by more than one state and required states to adopt licensing standards for truck drivers that include both written knowledge tests and skills (driving) tests. Successful applicants are issued a CDL.

In addition to the basic CDL, drivers who operate CMVs under special conditions must pass additional tests and obtain an "endorsement" to the CDL. For example, drivers of double/triple trailers, passenger vehicles, tankers and vehicles containing hazardous materials must have endorsements for such specialized activities.

The CDL regulations are found in Part 383 of the Federal Motor Carrier Safety Regulations.

Tow truck drivers need a CDL if they drive a wrecker or tow truck that meets one of the following classes defined in the law:

Class A: A combination of vehicles with a gross combination weight rating (GCWR) of 26,001 lbs. or more if the gross vehicle weight rating (GVWR) of the vehicle being towed is more than 10,000 lbs.

Class B: A single vehicle with a GVWR of 26,001 lbs. or more.

The Federal Motor Carrier Safety Administration (FMCSA) has determined that, for purposes of the CDL regulations, a conventional wrecker/tow truck with a vehicle in tow is treated the same as a tractor-trailer rig, i.e., a combination of vehicles.[2] Thus, whether a CDL is required and, if so, what class of CDL is required, depends not only on the GVWR of the tow truck being operated by the driver but also the GVWR of any vehicle that might be towed with that tow truck. Obviously, heavy-duty tow truck operators are all Class A drivers.

But the ever-increasing GVWRs of Class 5 and 6 tow truck chassis are putting more light-duty drivers in the Class A CDL category.

Consider a Ford F-650 wrecker/wheel-lift unit with a GVWR of 20,000 lbs. The towing of a standard-sized automobile of 4,000 or 5,000 lbs. GVWR does not impose a CDL requirement on the tow truck driver because the GVWR of the tow truck is less than 26,001 lbs. and the GVWR of the vehicle being towed is less than 10,001 lbs. But if the driver of that F-650 tow truck hooks to a vehicle with a GVWR of 10,001 lbs. or more — for example, a small box truck on a Chevy W-Series chassis (12,000 lbs. GVWR) — he or she becomes a Class A (combination vehicle) CDL driver: The vehicle being towed has a GVWR in excess of 10,000 lbs. GVWR and the combination of tow truck and towed vehicle exceeds 26,000 lbs. GCWR.

Drivers of car carriers or rollbacks may avoid the CDL licensing requirements if the carrier is not equipped with a tow bar. For example, a Freightliner M2 two-car carrier (25,500 lbs. GVWR) without a tow bar is a single vehicle, therefore a Class A (combination vehicle) CDL would be inapplicable. A Class B (single vehicle) CDL would not be required for the driver of that Freightliner because the GVWR is less than 26,001 lbs. But if the GVWR of a car carrier is over 26,000 lbs., the driver must have at least a Class B license. If the carrier is equipped with a tow bar, and vehicles in excess of 10,001 lbs. GVWR will be towed behind the carrier, a Class A (combination vehicle) license is required.

What about the endorsements? According to the FMCSA, as long as the tow is an emergency "first move" from the site of a breakdown or accident to the nearest appropriate repair facility, no endorsement is required.[3] Thus a tow truck driver towing a disabled vehicle containing hazardous materials, a bus, a tanker, or a tractor-trailer combination (thus creating a "double/triple trailer" combination) does not need an endorsement. An exception to that rule is that a tow truck driver never needs a passenger vehicle endorsement when towing a bus or other passenger vehicle. Also, note that the "emergency move" exception is only for the endorsements, not the CDL itself.

Considering that driving a tow truck without the proper license exposes both the driver and his employer to substantial fines, and can result in the driver being placed out of service, the prudent towing employer might require all tow truck drivers to hold a Class A CDL.

---

[1] 49 U.S.C. § 2505(a)
[2] 49 C.F.R. § 383.91, DOT Interpretation, Question 5
[3] 49 C.F.R. § 383.93, DOT Interpretation, Question 10

§ 3:14 Tough CDL Rules
Non-commercial driving record now scrutinized

If you drive a medium- or heavy-duty tow truck, you should have a Commercial Driver's License (CDL). If you have a CDL, you should be familiar with the CDL standards.

The CDL licensing system was implemented by Congress in 1986 and is found in Part 383 of the Federal Motor Carrier Safety Regulations (FMCSRs) or at www.fmcsa.dot.gov. (See § 3:13). Over the years the federal government has occasionally tweaked the CDL regs hoping to improve highway safety by ensuring that drivers of commercial motor vehicles (CMVs) are qualified to operate those vehicles.

One of those adjustments was the Motor Carrier Safety Improvement Act (MCSIA), which went into effect on September 30, 2005.[1] The MCSIA made radical changes to the rules regarding commercial driver disqualification. "Disqualification" is the feds technical term for "find another job" and is determined by the nature and number of a driver's traffic violations.

Traffic violations that can cause problems for CDL drivers are divided into two categories: Major Traffic Offenses (MTOs), those which Congress has deemed to be especially high-risk,[2] and the lesser Serious Traffic Offenses (STOs).[3]

The following offenses have always been MTOs if committed while driving a commercial vehicle: DUI, driving a CMV with a blood alcohol content (BAC) of .04 or higher, refusing to take a breathalyzer test (BAT), and leaving the scene of an accident. A conviction for any of those driving crimes calls for a one year suspension of the driver's CDL. A second MTO conviction results in a lifetime disqualification.

Serious Traffic Offenses include the following violations committed while driving a CMV: speeding in excess of 15 mph over the posted speed limit, reckless driving, improper lane change and following too close. The sanctions for STOs are not as severe as those for MTOs. Two convictions for any combination of STOs within a three-year period results in a 60-day suspension of a CDL. Three or more STO convictions within three years mandates a 120-day suspension.

The MCSIA includes some very important changes concerning driver disqualification. First, it added more MTOs and STOs. New Major Traffic Offenses are: (1) driving a CMV while a CDL is revoked, suspended or cancelled and (2) causing a fatality during the negligent operation of a CMV. Additions to the list of Serious Traffic Offenses are: (1) driving a CMV without first obtaining a CDL, (2) driving a CMV without a CDL in the driver's possession and (3) driving a CMV without the proper class of endorsement.

Second — and certainly the most significant change in the CDL rules — the Major Traffic Offenses for drugs, alcohol, leaving the scene of an accident and felonies in a personal vehicle will count the same as if the violation occurred in a CMV. Serious Traffic Offenses committed in a personal vehicle now count towards CDL sanctions if the violation separately results in suspension or revocation.

Under the previous CDL rules, convictions for traffic offenses in personal vehicles did not affect a driver's CDL status. For example, a conviction for a DUI that occurred while driving a personal vehicle did not count as a Major Traffic Offense for the holder of a CDL. Many truck drivers convicted of DUI in their personal vehicles, resulting in a suspension of driving privileges under state law, continued to drive CMVs on restricted or "work permit" CDLs. Not anymore. For CDL sanction purposes, a DUI while operating a personal vehicle is treated the same as a DUI while operating a commercial vehicle.

Note that violations that were not considered MTOs or STOs prior to September 30, 2005, are not counted towards the new CDL sanctions. So no need to worry about that reckless driving charge you picked up in your hotrod Mustang in December 2003.

Possible real-world scenarios:

A CDL tow truck driver is convicted of leaving the scene of an accident in his personal vehicle. One year suspension of CDL. Turn in the truck keys.

A driver in a 17,000-lb. GVWR wheel-lift towing a 12,000-lb. GVWR box truck is cited by a DOT officer for operating a combination vehicle without a Class A CDL. Her employer begrudgingly pays the fine and sends her off to get her CDL. Nine months later, that same tow truck driver receives a citation in her personal vehicle for excessive speeding in a work zone that results in a 30-day suspension of her driver's license. Because the second STO in her personal vehicle occurred within three years of the first STO and resulted in a suspension of her license, it draws a CDL sanction. She can reinstate her non-commercial driving privileges after 30 days, but she must hang up the gloves and chains for 60 days.

A CDL driver, who has been working as a heavy-duty tow truck driver for the last few years, previously drove a tractor-trailer over the road. In 1997, he was convicted of driving his rig with a BAC of more than .04. At that time, his CDL was suspended for one year. In 2006, he is stopped on suspicion of DUI while driving his personal vehicle and refuses to take a breathalyzer test. If he is found guilty of refusing to consent to a BAT, he will be looking for a new career. That would be his second MTO, which calls for a lifetime CDL disqualification.

An employer who knowingly allows a disqualified driver to operate a CMV is subject to a fine of $2,750 to $11,000.[4] With the advent of the MCSIA, employers should be especially cautious.

---

[1] Public Law 106-159, 113 Stat. 1748-1773
[2] 49 C.F.R. § 383.51(b)
[3] 49 C.F.R. § 383.51(c)
[4] 49 C.F.R. § 383.53(b)(2)

§ 3:15 Hidden Dangers
Defective parts on towed vehicles can lead to disaster

On January 21, 2009, a disabled delivery truck was being hauled behind a conventional-type tow truck on Interstate 495, the Washington, D.C. Beltway. The vehicle in tow was hoisted on the tow bar with two wheels on the road. Somewhere in Prince George's County, Maryland, one of the rolling wheels broke loose from the delivery truck, bounced into the center guardrail, ricocheted across the median into another guardrail, then careened into a tractor-trailer. That impact launched the large wheel and tire back across the median where it landed on top of a Honda Civic, crushing the roof and killing the driver. A tragic accident.

Unfortunately, there have been numerous other reported incidents in which a wheel has broken loose from a vehicle in-tow, resulting in property damage or personal injury. In fact, in 2000 a wheel broke loose from a towed car on Highway 80 in West Paterson, New Jersey, and struck a vehicle traveling in the opposite direction, injuring the driver. There have also been lawsuits in Texas and Pennsylvania involving breakaway wheels or parts.[1] In east Tennessee a person was injured when a steering part broke on a vehicle being towed from the rear, causing the towed vehicle to swing out into oncoming traffic.

Clearly, a towing company owner must be concerned about his or her liability if a wheel or other critical part breaks on a vehicle that has been placed in their care and custody. However, just because the vehicle is in the tow operator's possession when the equipment fails or the part breaks off does not automatically make the tow operator liable for any damage or injury caused.

As a general rule, the law requires people to conduct themselves *reasonably* considering all the circumstances facing them. To not act reasonably in the face of a *foreseeable* danger is to act negligently. For example, it would be negligent for a person to drive a car at an excessive speed on a curvy, rain-soaked road because to a reasonably prudent person it would be clearly foreseeable that the car might slide off the roadway. A negligent person is liable for all personal injury and property damage that was a foreseeable consequence of his negligent action.

In determining whether a tow truck driver is legally responsible for injuries caused by a wheel or part ejected from a towed vehicle, i.e., whether he was negligent, the principal inquiry is whether the incident was foreseeable. In other words, would it have been foreseeable to a reasonably prudent tow truck driver, operating under the same set of circumstances, that the equipment failure would have occurred while the vehicle was in tow?

Consider the following exaggerated scenario: A tow truck driver operating a wheel-lift tow truck (not a car carrier) is dispatched to a breakdown call. Upon arrival, the vehicle owner tells him that the problem seems to be the right front wheel bearing. The driver notices that, indeed, the right front wheel is tilted slightly inward. Nevertheless, because the car is rear-wheel drive, the tow truck driver hoists the vehicle from the rear and starts down the road with a noticeable high-pitched squeal emanating from the front of the car. Unquestionably, if the right front wheel broke loose in transit and caused an injury, the tow operator would be held accountable. That is because, under my theoretical, it was obviously foreseeable that the wheel might disengage from the vehicle while it was in tow. It would, therefore, be negligent for the driver to tow the vehicle with the front wheels down.

But most accidents of this nature do not involve a problem that was evident to the tow truck driver beforehand. Defects are usually latent, meaning they are not visible to the tow truck driver. For example, if a wheel bearing is bad, a steering box is about to fail, or a spring hanger is broken, that structural problem is usually unknown to the tow truck driver. If a tow truck driver had no actual notice of a defect, and a reasonable pre-tow inspection of the vehicle would not have revealed any potential equipment failure, a breakaway part would not be foreseeable, and the tow company should not be legally liable for any resulting injury or damage. An injured party might look to the vehicle owner, the vehicle maintenance facility or perhaps the part manufacturer for reparation.

The good news is that the increased use of car carriers and lowboy trailers for towing wrecked and disabled vehicles makes these types of accidents increasingly rare. Nevertheless, all tow operators would be well-advised to adopt a company policy calling for a thorough pre-tow inspection of the rolling components of all vehicles towed on the ground – and always carry adequate liability insurance.

---

[1] *Parker v. Leach*, 274 S.W.2d 721 (Tex. Ct. App. 1955) and *Dobb v. Stetzler*, 87 A.2d 380 (Pa. 1952)

§ 3:16 Stranded Drivers Beware
Snow pull-outs not a job for amateurs

When wintertime rolls around, that means freezing temperatures, sleet, snow and ice in many parts of the nation. During an ice or snow storm, many hapless motorists find themselves in an awkward position – off the road, sideways or tilted. Ideally, a professional tow truck operator will safely winch the vehicle back onto the roadway, charge a reasonable fee, then send the uprighted motorist along his or her treacherous way.

But winter storms tend to bring out four-wheel drive (4WD) vehicle owners who decide to be "tow truck drivers for a day." They roam the snow-covered highways in search of stranded vehicles, hoping to filch retrieval jobs from professional tow truck operators. Some 4WDs are equipped with electric bumper winches, but the technique preferred by most of these "wannabe" tow operators is to attach a slap chain or nylon rope to the stuck vehicle, rev the engine on the 4WD, then pop the clutch and jerk the vehicle from the snow bank or ditch. Most 4WD jockeys charge a fee for the pull-out. Some do it for free – "just for the fun of it."

Motorists should beware that having an amateur perform a pull-out may be unlawful and, more importantly, can be quite dangerous.

Many states, including Arizona, Texas, Oklahoma, Colorado and Connecticut, have laws making it illegal for nonprofessionals to perform vehicle extractions for compensation. That is because the business of for-hire towing requires a license.[1] Anybody who desires to engage in the towing business for profit must comply with certain minimum safety standards, including equipment specifications, company identification and minimum liability insurance requirements much greater than those required of private vehicle owners. Some state laws also mandate certain operational standards for vehicle recovery operations, such as the use of flashing warning lights and other scene management devices.

Virtually all 4WD bandits operate without a towing license, without training in proper vehicle recovery and without adequate insurance. The driver of a 4WD vehicle who offers to perform vehicle retrieval services without complying with applicable licensing requirements is breaking the law.

Furthermore, permitting amateurs to perform pull-outs creates an undue risk of damage to the vehicles, and serious injury to the person performing the pull-out, the owner of the stuck vehicle and anyone who might be standing nearby. The hazards of unskilled vehicle recovery are perhaps best illustrated by an incident in Minnesota in which a member of a 4WD enthusiasts club, driving his

Chevrolet pickup 4x4, attempted to retrieve a fellow club member's Ford truck that was front-stuck and mired up to its hubcaps in an exposed portion of the Mississippi River bottom. He attached a J-hook and a nylon rope to the rear frame rail of the stuck pickup truck. When he gunned the Chevy's engine and engaged the clutch, the J-hook ripped loose from the rear frame of the stuck Ford. The J-hook sailed like a missile through the rear window of the Chevy truck, striking the driver in the head and causing severe brain damage.

In the inevitable lawsuit that followed, an expert witness testified that with the buildup of kinetic energy in stretched nylon tow straps, the velocity of an attached J-hook when straps are torn loose can be in excess of a speeding bullet. The jury awarded the Chevy driver millions of dollars in damages against Ford Motor Company based on the faulty design of the rear frame rail on the Ford pickup, which caused the strap to come loose. Significantly, though, the driver of the Ford pickup who requested the pull-out was also assessed partial responsibility.[2]

The Minnesota case should serve as a warning to any ditch-bound motorist who is solicited by the driver of a non-commercial 4WD vehicle for a free or low-cost pull-out. In the event of an accident or injury caused by the amateur 4WD driver, they might find themselves trying to explain to a judge or jury why they did not use a professional towing company.

---

[1] Ariz. Rev. Stat. § 28-1108; Tex. Occ. Code Ann. § 2308.101; Okla. Stat. tit. 47, § 953; Colo. Rev. Stat. § 40-13-103; and Conn. Gen. Stat. § 14-66.
[2] *Gross v. Running,* No. 455690 (Ramsey County (Minn.) District Ct., March 3, 1986), *aff'd* 403 N.W.2d 243 (Minn. Ct. App. 1987)

TOWING and the LAW

Chapter 4   Vehicle Impounding and Possessory Lien

§ 4:1   You Gotta Know When to Hold 'Em 123

§ 4:2   Police Department Holds 125

§ 4:3   Vehicle Forfeiture: Who Really Loses 127

§ 4:4   When Nikki Wants her Nikes 129

§ 4:5   A "Good Faith Effort" 131

§ 4:6   Care Custody and Control 133

§ 4:7   Gate Crashers 135

§ 4:8   Lien Sale Theft Case Trumped by Federal Deregulation 137

§ 4:9   Damage Release Forms 139

§ 4:10 The Bankruptcy Quandary 141

§ 4:1 You Gotta Know When to Hold 'Em

It is a common practice of the towing industry to refuse to release vehicles that have been towed and placed in storage until all towing and storage fees have been paid. The "no pay, no release" policy is defended on the grounds that nobody would pay if they were allowed to retrieve their vehicles first, then pay later.

Generally, it is unlawful to take or detain someone's property without their consent or without some legal basis. In the towing business you frequently tow and impound vehicles in direct opposition to the vehicle owner's wishes, for example, private property removals. Therefore, if you do not have consent, in order to lawfully withhold the vehicle in lieu of payment there must be some other legal basis. Ordinarily that legal basis is a statutory lien granted by the state legislature. Absent a statutory lien or the vehicle owner's consent, you have no legal right to retain a vehicle as security for payment of towing and storage charges.[1]

In that situation, you are required by law to release the vehicle and attempt to collect your tow bill later. Additionally, your failure to release the vehicle upon the demand of the vehicle owner could result in a criminal prosecution against you for theft of a vehicle. Think I'm kidding?

In 1984, a tow operator in Phoenix, Arizona, was charged with felony theft for refusing to release a private property tow-away vehicle until he was paid his towing and storage bill. The case wound up in the Arizona Supreme Court where the court ruled that, yes, the tow operator was guilty of felony theft because there was no consent and no lien statute.[2] But, because it was a case of "first impression," the ruling would be applied only in future cases.

In 1990, a Connecticut court found a Hartford towing company liable in a class action lawsuit based on the Connecticut Unfair Trade Practices Act (CUTPA). Following a long line of previous court decisions, the Connecticut court said, "No lien in favor of the defendant exists at common law or by statute, and this court cannot change the law in regard."[3] After consideration of all the evidence and applicable law, the court concluded that the towing firm's no pay/no release policy was an unfair trade practice under CUTPA. Specifically, the court concluded that the practice constituted in each individual case an intentional conversion (theft) of the vehicle by the defendant towing company.

Fortunately, most states have enacted lien laws which give towing companies a possessory lien when towing and storing vehicles in non-consent situations. The legislatures in both Arizona and Connecticut, and many others, have taken remedial action.

Obviously it would be difficult for a towing firm to function without such legislative protection.

When I read the May 1997 letter opinion of the Idaho Attorney General regarding possessory liens it was as if a scab had been torn from an old sore. In response to an inquiry from a city official, the attorney general said that Idaho law does not give tow operators there a possessory lien "unless they have first obtained consent for such lien from the registered legal owners of the vehicle."[4] Without the owner consenting to his vehicle being held — which, of course, is absurd — Idaho tow operators must release vehicles upon demand and, in the words of the attorney general, resort to a "collection proceeding." The attorney general went on to warn that failure to release vehicles upon demand could expose the tow operator to prosecution for theft.

Do you have the legal right to maintain possession of vehicles towed into your storage yard until the outstanding charges are paid?

---

[1] Michael McGovern, *Possessory Lien Review*, Tow Times, June 1991, at p. 23

[2] *Capson v. Superior Court of State of Ariz.*, 677 P.2d 276 (Ariz. 1984)

[3] *Halloran v. Spillane's Servicecenter, Inc.*, 587 A.2d 176 (Conn. Super. 1990)

[4] Letter from Matthew J. McKeown, Deputy Attorney General, Intergovernmental and Fiscal Law Division, Idaho Attorney General, to Rick Carnaroli, Chief Civil Deputy, City of Pocatella Legal Department, May 28, 1997 (copy on file with author)

§ 4:2 Police Department Holds

"Oh, by the way, put a hold on that vehicle," says the arresting officer as you pull away with a vehicle being impounded as a consequence of suspected criminal activity. You know what that means: Nobody can retrieve the vehicle, get anything out of it, touch it or even look at it, without an okay from the arresting officer.

A "hold" on an impounded vehicle can serve a useful purpose. Often a vehicle is, or contains, evidence of a crime. For example, blood and hair samples or fingerprints may need to be taken from a vehicle. It is usually impractical to perform such criminal investigative procedures at the scene of a crime because of time, weather or darkness. It is more convenient to impound the vehicle, then gather such evidence at the vehicle storage facility. Without the ability to place "holds" on impounded vehicles, the vehicle could be immediately retrieved by the suspected criminal or his cohorts and the evidence lost forever. In other cases, for example, a driver fleeing the scene of an accident or a vehicle operated without proper registration, the police want to hold the vehicle "hostage" as a means of obtaining proof of ownership or to determine the driver's identity.

Police "holds" are normally honored by towing companies as a courtesy to the police agency, but "holds" raise two very important questions: First, what legal authority does a towing company have to deny the vehicle owner possession of his vehicle if he comes, money in hand, to get his car? Second, assuming that the towing company does have the legal authority to maintain custody of a vehicle despite the vehicle owner's demand for possession, who is responsible for payment of storage fees during the period the "hold" is in effect?

A towing company's authority to maintain possession of a vehicle under a "hold," in spite of the vehicle owner's demand and willingness to pay accrued towing and storage fees, is only as good as the authority of the police department which ordered the "hold." The U.S. Constitution forbids the confiscation of any person's property without probable cause.[1] Ordinarily, a court order is required. Even without an order, police agencies have the right to immediately seize easily transportable property which they have probable cause to believe is evidence of a crime. Under those circumstances, a police agency, and therefore the impounded towing firm as its agent, has authority to retain possession of an impounded vehicle for the amount of time reasonably necessary to conduct the forensic investigation or preserve the evidence. Ordinarily, that process should take only a few days, maybe a week. After that, absent a court order, the "hold" must be immediately released and the vehicle made available to its owner.

Even in cases in which the vehicle itself is evidence of a crime, a photograph of the vehicle can be taken, then the vehicle released to the owner. A police officer may not intentionally refuse to release a vehicle "hold" after a completed investigation just to punish the vehicle owner or operator ("curbside justice") or for any other improper purpose.

So who pays the storage fees incurred during the period of a "hold?" Is it fair to make the vehicle owner or his insurance company pay those storage charges? After all, "hold" vehicles are stored for the convenience of the police agency, not the vehicle owner. In a case out of Baton Rouge, La., a car driven by a suspected burglar was impounded by the city police department. The vehicle was left under a "hold" for about ten (10) weeks, even though the investigation was completed in three (3) weeks. The car owner sued the city and the towing company. Finding that the vehicle owner "was unreasonably denied access to his vehicle for a period of approximately seven weeks," the state court of appeals held that the defendant/vehicle owner was not responsible for any storage fees from the time the investigation was completed until the "hold" was released.[2]

If a vehicle owner can't be held to pay the fees for such unjustified storage, who does pay for the period of time that is actually necessary for the police investigation, for example, the three-week period in the Louisiana case? Shouldn't the impounding police agency pay the storage fees accrued during a "hold" as an ordinary cost of investigation? Some law enforcement agencies may voluntarily accept their obligation to pay "hold" storage fees.[3] Others will not. If the vehicle owner cannot be compelled to pay, and the investigating agency does not willingly step up and pay the storage fees, the towing firm is constrained to either write-off the fees or attempt to collect them from the impounding police department or district attorney.

I appreciate the practical, and political, problems that can arise by billing police agencies for vehicle storage charges. The prudent tow operator will negotiate a contract in advance with local law enforcement agencies regarding storage fees on "hold" vehicles. Indeed, both the Missouri Court of Appeals and the California Attorney General have issued opinions stating that law enforcement agencies in those states can be held accountable for storage fees on "hold" vehicles only if there is a pre-existing agreement between the police agency and the impounding towing firm that complies with those states' public contract laws.[4] Without such an agreement, a tow operator stores "hold" vehicles at his own risk.

---

[1] U.S. Const., amend. IV

[2] *Jordan v. City of Baton Rouge*, 529 So.2d 412 (La. Ct. App. 1988) writ denied 532 So.2d 152 (La. 1988)

[3] *See, e.g.*, Fla. Stat. § 323.001

[4] *Allen v. Butler County*, 743 S.W.2d 527 (Mo. Ct. App. 1987) and Cal. Atty. Gen. Op. 84-106 (68 Ops. Cal. Atty. Gen. 94 (1985)); see also Cal. Atty. Gen. Op. 85-104 (69 Ops. Cal. Atty. Gen. 36 (1986))

§ 4:3 Vehicle Forfeiture: Who Really Loses?

Like most states, Tennessee has enacted a vehicle forfeiture law.[1] Pursuant to the provisions of that law, motor vehicles driven by persons in possession of drugs, or by drunk drivers with a prior DUI conviction, are subject to being forfeited to the arresting law enforcement agency. In the event of a DUI or drug arrest, the vehicle being operated by the suspect is seized and impounded. The owner is notified that the state intends to take his vehicle and, after an administrative hearing, ownership of those vehicles can be, and usually is, forfeited to the government. Those vehicles can then be used by the government in law enforcement activities, or the vehicles can be sold at auction with the sale proceeds allocated to DUI and drug interdiction programs. As a practical matter, most vehicles subject to forfeiture are low-value vehicles that will be auctioned.

But when the police seize vehicles, where are they stored pending the sometimes lengthy administrative process? And who pays for that storage? Also, after the legal forfeiture process is completed, how and when are the vehicles auctioned? Those questions — important to the towing industry — were at the center of a 2002 ruling by the Tennessee Court of Appeals.

In 1996, Freddie Trew of Trew's Wrecker Service approached his local sheriff's department with a verbal proposition regarding the county's "forfeiture vehicles." Trew would tow forfeiture vehicles and store them in his impound facility for a flat "per vehicle" fee. Trew would be paid when the car was either auctioned or picked up by the sheriff's department for its own use. In what would prove to be a costly mistake, the agreement was never reduced to writing. The sheriff accepted Trew's offer and within a few days Trew's Wrecker Service began receiving calls from the sheriff's department to tow and store the DUI and drug arrest vehicles.

Trew was impounding dozens of forfeiture vehicles and was looking forward to a boost in cash flow. But to Trew's surprise, the drug and DUI impound vehicles weren't going anywhere. Trew towed the vehicles into his yard and there they sat . . . and sat . . . and sat. Before long, Trew had over 80 forfeiture vehicles in his storage facility. Despite repeated pleas from Trew, almost four years went by without an auction being held by the sheriff's department.

Faced with a terrible cash crunch and an impound yard overflowing with non-revenue-generating vehicles, Trew demanded payment from the sheriff's department of his flat fee, plus a $10 daily storage fee on every vehicle held more than 30 days. Needless to say, the sheriff did not pay. Trew's Wrecker filed a lawsuit.

The terms of the oral contract were hotly disputed at trial. Trew contended that the sheriff agreed to pay a $100 per vehicle towing fee and that the sheriff had also promised to sell or retrieve each impounded vehicle within 30 days. Trew admitted, however, that there was never any discussion about what would happen if the vehicles were not sold or removed within 30 days and there was no agreement regarding daily storage fees after the first 30 days.

The sheriff testified that the flat fee agreed upon was $45 to $65, depending on the difficulty of the tow, and that he never agreed to move the forfeiture vehicles within 30 days. To the contrary, the sheriff said he told Trew that the state's vehicle forfeiture process was complicated and lengthy. He also said he advised Trew that it might take years for enough vehicles to accumulate to make it cost effective to conduct an auction sale.

The trial judge determined there was a binding oral agreement, but he only awarded Trew's Wrecker the sum of $45 on each of 83 vehicles towed and stored. The court did not allow for payment of any additional storage fees.

On appeal, the appellate court affirmed the trial court, finding that although Trew did not agree to store the forfeiture vehicles for an indefinite period of time, the evidence showed that the towing company did agree to store the vehicles until it was feasible to conduct a sale. Relying upon the testimony of an attorney for the Department of Safety concerning the vehicle forfeiture process, and noting the absence of any deadlines imposed by the state forfeiture laws, the court held that it was not unreasonable for the sheriff to stockpile vehicles until he felt it was cost-efficient to conduct a sale.

In its opinion in *Trew v. Haggard*,[2] the appellate court also emphasized that Trew and the sheriff "never discussed the issue of whether Trew's Wrecker Service would charge a storage fee after the initial 30-day storage period." The court concluded that Trew's was not entitled to any storage fees other than those that might have been included in the $45 flat fee. Bottom line: after towing and storing 83 vehicles for almost four years Trew's was paid about $3,700.

This case highlights the problem that arises when no provision is made for the cost of storing the impounded vehicles while the forfeiture process is pending. It is a matter that needs to be addressed by the legislatures in Tennessee and elsewhere. And one other thing — get your storage contracts in writing.

---

[1] Tenn. Code Ann. § 55-10-403(k)
[2] No. E2001-02183-COA-R3-CV, 2002 WL 1723686
(Tenn. Ct. App. 2002)

§ 4:4 When Nikki Wants Her Nikes
Withholding items to compel payment

If you are in the towing business, you are probably also in the vehicle impounding business. When a vehicle is impounded, the personal items in the vehicle — tools, guns, jewelry, electronic equipment, music CDs, cash, sporting goods, etc. — are impounded, too.

Releasing personal items from an impounded vehicle ordinarily poses no problem. The prudent towing firm will obtain identification from the person removing the property, get a signed authorization and release form, and inventory the items taken from the vehicle.

Things get a bit testy, however, when it is obvious that the towing and storage fees will not be paid. Uninsured totals and abandoned vehicles are generally worth less than the outstanding charges due and are likely candidates to be dumped on the towing firm. In those situations, if the vehicle owner comes to claim his personal belongings, the towing firm will often try to hold those items as "hostage" to secure payment.

For example, assume that a rusty 1986 Buick Century is towed from an apartment complex for violating the community parking rules. After two or three weeks the tow bill and accrued storage fees charged against the derelict vehicle are about $400. The owner shows up looking for his Snap-On® tools in the trunk.

"I want to get some things out of my car," he says.

Knowing that as he leaves with his tools the guy is going to kiss goodbye his old Buick and the tow bill, the tower replies, "No problem — just as soon as you pay me the $400 bill."

"You can't make me pay $400 just to get my stuff!" exclaims the car owner. Most likely, he is right.

In legal terms, the tower is attempting to exert a possessory lien over the personal property as security for the payment of the towing and storage bill. Possessory liens, or the right to hold property in lieu of payment for services provided, exist only under grant of state law. Examples of statutory liens are warehouseman's liens, innkeepers (hotel) liens and mechanics liens. Under those laws, a warehouseman has the right to hold the stored goods until the rent is paid, and an auto mechanic or shoe repairman can maintain possession of a vehicle or pair of boots until the repair bill is paid.

The majority of state codes also include a law that gives towing companies a possessory lien on impounded vehicles until they are paid a reasonable fee for their services. Importantly, however, in most states the law only grants a lien against the *vehicle*. The law is silent with regard to the *contents* of the vehicle. In the absence of statutory language extending the lien against the contents of the vehicle, it would be unlawful for a towing company to withhold personal property from a vehicle owner until a bill is paid. In some states, for example, California, Wisconsin, Florida and Nebraska, the law specifically directs towing firms to release all personal items upon demand, without payment of the towing fee.[1] (If the items are sought after-hours, however, a reasonable access, or "gate," fee might be charged.)

On the other hand, the tow operators in Arkansas, Missouri, South Dakota and a few other states have successfully petitioned their legislatures to add the phrase "and its contents" after the word "vehicle" in the lien statutes.[2] That gives the towing companies in those states the legal right to retain possession of the personal items within a vehicle to secure payment of tow bills. Typically, those "content" liens exempt essential personal items such as prescription medicines and eyeglasses, wallets and purses, house keys, food or food stamps, legal papers, child car seats, schoolbooks and tools of trade. Those indispensable items can always be retrieved by their owners without having to first pay the tow bill. But anything else, including clothing, jewelry, golf clubs, a boom box, or a personal CD player, stays put unless the bill is paid.

Oregon has a unique manner of dealing with the issue. The Beaver State law gives the owners of vehicles towed from public property a 15-day "grace period" in which to retrieve their personal belongings before the possessory lien attaches.[3]

Readers are encouraged to determine the status of the possessory lien law in their state. Also take note that if an item is permanently affixed to the vehicle such that tools and some labor are necessary to remove it — for example, wheels, tires or an installed stereo system — it would be considered to be part of the "vehicle" and not contents. Even if the lien law only extends to the "vehicle," a towing firm may retain possession of those items as security for payment of its outstanding charges.

---

[1] Cal. Veh. Code § 22651.07 and 22851; Wisc. Stat. Ann. § 349.13(5)(b)2 and 3; Fla. Stat. § 713.78(10); and Neb. Rev. Stat. § 60-6,165(2)

[2] Ark. Code Ann. § 27-50-1101(a)(3)(B)(ii); Mo. Rev. Stat. § 304.155; and S.D. Codified Laws § 32-30-18

[3] Or. Rev. Stat. § 819.160

§ 4:5 A "Good Faith Effort"
Laws on Processing Unclaimed Vehicles Leave Doubts

A 1999 Mercedes breaks down in the middle of the road in Florida. The vehicle owner, an elderly retiree suffering from dementia, walks away, leaving the vehicle where it sits. A local towing company is dispatched by the sheriff's department to remove the vehicle from the roadway. Because it is a disabled vehicle, not an accident or arrest, the standard law enforcement tow-in report, which includes the vehicle ownership information, is not provided to the tow operator. The vehicle is impounded.

A week passes with no contact from the owner of the vehicle, so the towing company starts the process under the Florida unclaimed vehicle laws. First, he seeks owner and/or lienholder information from both the tax collector's office and the sheriff's department by providing them with the correct Vehicle Identification Number (VIN) and the out-of-state license plate number. Those requests are returned "No Record Found." A search of NCIC indicates that the vehicle has not been reported stolen. A physical search of the vehicle reveals no owner information.

In accordance with state towing lien law, the towing company then advertises a lien auction sale of the Mercedes. The ad is published in a local newspaper of general circulation. About two months after the impound, the Mercedes goes on the auction block. Nobody appears for the sale so, as he always does when there are no bidders, the tow operator submits his own bid and obtains a certificate of title for the vehicle.

Routine lien sale, you say? If you are in Florida, Missouri or Mississippi, perhaps not. Because of the towing laws in those states, under those circumstances a tow operator might find himself in civil court defending a lawsuit brought by the owner or lienholder for the full value of the vehicle plus punitive damages or, worse, in a criminal court defending a felony indictment for stealing the Mercedes. Indeed, in 2005 I represented a Florida tow truck operator in a trial in which he was charged with grand theft on essentially the facts set forth above.[1]

The typical state statute dealing with unclaimed impounded vehicles imposes an obligation on a tow operator to send a certified notice to the owner/lienholder advising of the towing lien, the charges and the possibility of sale if the vehicle is not retrieved within a stated period of time. Usually, the ownership information is obtained by providing the DMV of the state of registration with the license tag number, if one, and the VIN.

If no owner/lienholder information is located by that computer search, the tow operator must place a newspaper advertisement giving public notice of an auction sale of the vehicle to satisfy the towing and storage lien. If a buyer appears for the sale and the vehicle sells for more than the towing/storage bill, the tow operator deducts his bill from the sale proceeds and sends the balance to the state treasury to hold in escrow for the owner or lienholder. On the other hand, if no buyers appear for a properly-advertised auction, the tow operator may lawfully submit a bid in the amount of his bill and obtain title.

But the laws in Florida, Mississippi and Missouri impose an additional requirement on tow operators when a computer check of the VIN and license tag fails to produce ownership information. Before scheduling a vehicle for auction, those laws require that a towing company first use a "good faith effort" to locate a vehicle owner.[2]

Here's the problem: What constitutes a "good faith effort"? If a physical search of the Mercedes uncovered a laundry receipt from New Jersey and a 2009 parking sticker from the University of Tennessee, does the "good faith effort" law require DMV searches in New Jersey and Tennessee? A request to the university to check parking permits issued to all Mercedes in 2009? Should the car be dusted for fingerprints to be run through the FBI database?

There are no cut-and-dry answers to those questions. That is the point. Every time a DMV computer check is returned "No Record Found," a tow operator must make a judgment call regarding how much further effort to take in locating the vehicle owner. Laws requiring a tow operator to use a "good faith effort" are fodder for litigation and invite second-guessing by vehicle owners, lienholders and — as demonstrated by the Florida case — criminal prosecutors. Scrutiny is obviously heightened when a high-valued vehicle is sold at auction for little or nothing to the impounding firm which then obtains a "windfall profit" on the re-sale of the vehicle.

Fortunately, the jury acquitted the Florida tow operator of grand theft of the Mercedes. But faced with a similar situation, a tow operator in Florida, Missouri or Mississippi, using a reasonable, though unsuccessful, effort to locate and contact the vehicle owner before a lien sale, can never be certain that he did enough — that he used a "good faith effort" — until the judge's gavel falls.

---

[1] *State v. Michael Viera*, No. 2003 CF 009838 NC (Fla. 12th Circuit Ct., June 30, 2005)

[2] Fla. Stat. § 713.78(4)(d); Miss. Code Ann. § 85-7-251(2); and Mo. Rev. Stat. § 304.156

§ 4:6 Care, Custody and Control
Duties and liabilities of a bailee for hire

The word "bailment" is derived from the French word "bailler," which means "to deliver." Generally, a "bailment" is created whenever personal property is delivered by one person to another for a specific purpose with an understanding, either express or implied, that the special purpose will be accomplished, and that the property will be returned or duly accounted for when the person owning the property reclaims it.

In the towing business, a bailment is established every time a motor vehicle belonging to someone else is placed in your possession. The vehicle owner is the "bailor" and the towing company is the "bailee for hire." The purpose of the bailment, of course, is the safekeeping of the vehicle until such time as the vehicle owner, or their representative, reclaims the vehicle. The bailment contract is usually implied, meaning there is no specific written agreement regarding the parties' rights and duties.

As a bailee you are legally responsible for all vehicles that are placed in your care, custody and control. The law requires you to exercise reasonable diligence in safeguarding all impounded vehicles from damage or theft. If some loss or damage occurs to a stored vehicle, the vehicle owner has a significant legal advantage should a lawsuit be filed. He or she need only prove the condition of the vehicle at the time you towed it in and that the vehicle's condition was changed upon redelivery.

For example, the owner can testify that the vehicle did not have a dent in the fender when it was towed, but when it was delivered or picked up at the tow lot there was a dent in the fender. Unlike other non-bailment cases for property damages, the owner of a vehicle damaged or stolen in a storage yard does not have to prove how the theft or damage occurred or that the loss occurred because of some negligence of the tow operator. Under bailment law, it is *presumed* that the bailee's negligence caused the loss.

That does not mean that you are legally liable every time a vehicle suffers damage or a loss occurs in your storage facility. A bailee has the right to *rebut* the presumption of negligence by showing that he exercised reasonable care under all the circumstances. I once represented a towing company sued for the loss of a CD player and some stereo speakers. Those items had been stolen late one night out of a disabled vehicle that had been impounded at my client's storage yard. Although the storage facility was not staffed at night, it had an 8-foot high chain link fence completely surrounding the lot, floodlights covering the entire storage area, and was regularly checked by the local police department. The thieves cut through the fence with bolt-cutters and broke the window out of the vehicle. I argued that my client had taken reasonable precautions to protect the vehicle and was, therefore, not negligent. The judge agreed and dismissed the claim.[1]

What about items concealed in the locked trunk of a stored vehicle? It is curious how many people, particularly those whose vehicles are impounded for parking violations or an arrest, say that they have left valuables such as jewelry, cash, priceless collectibles or the like, in the trunks of their vehicles. Amazingly, they will report the items missing before they even examine the contents of the truck. Here the law helps the tow lot operator: your duty as a bailee does not extend to property that is concealed from you or property which you are unaware is in your control and possession. If you have no knowledge of the tools, guns or wedding gifts locked in the trunk or glove compartment, you cannot be held liable *as a bailee* for loss or damage to such property.[2]

Vehicle storage can be financially lucrative but it has its price. That price is bailment liability. You can reduce that liability by taking steps to ensure that your lot is secure, establishing a thorough and regular property inventory system, and training and supervising employees with an emphasis on the protection of stored vehicles and known contents.

---

[1] *Gilland v. Jimmy Collins d/b/a Casper's Body Shop,* No. 42168 (Greene County (Tenn.) General Sessions Court, August 17, 1995)

[2] *Lanman v. Nick's Sunoco Station, Inc.,* 6 Conn. L. Trib No. 26 (March 28, 1980)

§ 4:7 Gate Crashers
Sometimes they make it; sometimes they don't

If you impound vehicles, especially those towed for illegal or improper parking, you have probably faced situations in which vehicle owners have snuck into your lot, got into their vehicles and attempted to drive out without paying. They might hide in the vehicle and wait for an opportune moment when the security gate is open to drive out.

Depending on their level of intoxication, others will brazenly try to crash through the gate. Sometimes they make it; sometimes they don't. When I was working at my family's towing business, I remember a few incidents in which an individual scaled the security fence and attempted to flee in their car. Late at night an engine unexpectedly cranks up out in the lot, the headlights pop on and come barreling towards the gate, the engine is revving and the gravel flying ...

So while Tony Joiner was certainly not the first person to sneak a vehicle out of a towing impound lot, he may be the most famous. In October 2007, Joiner, a strong safety on the University of Florida Gators football team, went to the impound yard of Watson's Towing in Gainesville at about 4:30 a.m. to retrieve his girlfriend's car. Her car had been impounded earlier that evening for illegal parking. Watson's impound lot was closed. Joiner forced opened the electric gate, went into the lot and drove out with his girlfriend's car. A witness called the police and Joiner was charged with burglary. The Gators' head coach immediately suspended Joiner from the team.

For those of you who do not live in the South, you may not appreciate the significance of such an event. Accusing a star player on the defending national championship football team of a crime, which results in him getting kicked off the team, is tantamount to calling Robert E. Lee a sissy. The owner of the towing firm, Stan Forron, received more than 200 threatening phone calls, including a dozen death threats. Several callers — Gator fans, no doubt — offered to pay the $76 tow bill if Forron would drop the charges against their beloved Joiner.

Turns out, according to Forron, it was all a big misunderstanding. He says that Joiner had made prior arrangements to pay the tow bill, but when he arrived at the impound lot nobody was there to take his money. So he took the car, intending to return later to pay the towing fees. (Yeah, right.) The criminal charges against Joiner were dropped, he was reinstated to the team, and the Gator Nation was happy once again.[1]

The Joiner case reminded me of a far more serious gate-crashing event that occurred in Indiana in 2005. David DeWhitt improperly parked his Ford Expedition at Fort Benjamin Harris in Indianapolis. It got impounded at Lawrence Towing. DeWhitt went to the tow yard, but instead of going into the office, he went straight into the impound yard. Two employees confronted DeWhitt, telling him that he needed to pay and fill out some paperwork first, but he refused to comply. He got in his vehicle and began to drive out "pretty fast," according to witnesses. One of the tow truck drivers attempted to shut the gate but before it was completely shut, DeWhitt hit it. He drove through the gate and struck the employee in the leg with the bumper of the Expedition. DeWhitt fled and the tow truck driver was sent to the hospital.

DeWhitt was later arrested and charged with criminal recklessness while armed with a deadly weapon, a felony. Criminal recklessness is defined under Indiana law as "an act that creates a substantial risk of bodily harm to another person."[2] Of course, the Expedition was the deadly weapon.

DeWhitt's defense at trial? It was the tow truck driver's fault. According to DeWhitt, his vehicle was moving at a low rate of speed when the driver came out of the towing office and tried to close the gate. He said that he hit the gate "notwithstanding the fact that he tried to swerve to avoid colliding with it." In essence, DeWhitt argued that if the towing company employee had just stayed in the office and let him drive out, no substantial risk of bodily harm would have occurred and there would be no crime.

In the case of *DeWhitt v. State*, the Indiana Court of Appeals refused to buy into DeWhitt's argument. Noting that the evidence showed that the tires were squealing and the engine was revving, the court concluded that "it was DeWhitt, not [the towing employee], who created the substantial risk of bodily injury ..."[3]

DeWhitt was sentenced to one year of home detention, followed by two years of probation. Too bad for DeWhitt that he was not a key player for a college football powerhouse. The incident might have turned out to be just a big misunderstanding.

---

[1] David Jones, Arrest of Florida Safety Joiner May Be Misunderstanding, USAToday, October 2, 2007
[2] Ind. Code § 35-42-2-2
[3] 829 N.E.2d 1055 (Ind. Ct. App. 2005)

§ 4:8 Lien Sale Theft Case Trumped by Federal Deregulation

The facts of the case may ring familiar to many tow company owners: An owner-operator from Georgia, disgusted with his structurally-defective Kenworth truck, abandoned it in the parking lot of a Nashville truck stop after it failed a DOT inspection. Before leaving, he stripped the vehicle of all personal items and identifying documents. He removed the company name, DOT numbers and license plates from the exterior of the vehicle.

More than a year passed before the truck stop security guard called a Nashville towing firm to haul the truck off the lot. The company responded and impounded the vehicle as requested.

The Tennessee statutes set forth the procedure for disposing of unclaimed impounded vehicles.[1] Generally, certified written notice with specific information must be sent to owners and lienholders within a certain timeframe. If the vehicle remains unclaimed, a newspaper advertisement with specific information included must be published before an unclaimed vehicle can be sold to recoup the towing and storage fees.

Immediately after the impound, the towing firm sent the state-mandated form to the Tennessee DMV, detailing the make, model and VIN of the truck, and asked for the vehicle owner/lienholder information needed to send out the requisite certified notices. The Tennessee DMV returned the form marked "Contact Georgia DMV." The towing firm then sent a similar owner/lienholder request to the Georgia DMV but never received a response. Without any ownership information, the towing firm was unable to send any lien notices.

About three months after the impound, the truck owner decided that he needed the truck as evidence in a breach of warranty lawsuit that he had filed against the dealership that sold him the defective truck. When he went to the truck stop, he was told the truck had been impounded. He contacted the towing company by telephone and was advised that he could retrieve the vehicle upon payment of all outstanding towing and storage fees. Based on information obtained during that phone call, the towing firm immediately sent certified letters to the owner and the lienholder notifying them of the location of the truck and the amount of the charges due. The notice also stated that the truck would be sold at auction if it was not picked up within ten days.

The truck owner's attorney sent several letters to the towing company complaining about the impounding of the truck; however, despite having notice of the pending sale, neither the owner nor the lienholder came to recover the truck. Accordingly, an advertisement was placed in the local newspaper and the truck was sold at public auction. No outside bidders showed up for the sale, so the towing company owner put in a bid and he acquired title to the truck.

The truck owner filed a federal lawsuit against the towing firm alleging conversion — the civil law equivalent of the criminal charge of theft. He claimed that the towing company did not fully comply with the state law regarding abandoned vehicles because the certified notice was inadequate and the newspaper ad was incomplete. The truck owner demanded reimbursement for the full value of his truck (which he claimed to be worth $80,000), plus punitive damages.

In the trial court, I argued on behalf of the towing firm that even if there were minor violations of the abandoned vehicle statute, the lawsuit should be thrown out because the 1994 federal trucking deregulation law forbids the enforcement of any state law relating to the "price, route or *service*" of towing-motor carriers. (See § 5:1). It was my contention that the truck owner's claim for conversion constituted the enforcement of a state law relating to my client's services.

The trial judge agreed. In a decision rendered on January 12, 2007, in *Danny Ware v. Tow Pro Custom Hauling & Towing,* the federal court in Nashville held that the truck owner's claim for conversion was an attempt to enforce a state law relating to the towing company's services; therefore, the lawsuit was prohibited by federal law.[2] The judge ruled that the truck owner's claim for conversion "including any claims regarding alleged unauthorized storage charges or . . . alleged violations of Tennessee statutes regarding notice as to storage fees and sales, are preempted by federal law." He tossed the case out of court.

His ruling was affirmed by the federal court of appeals.[3] The ruling from the appellate court could have legal implications far beyond claims relating to the processing of abandoned vehicles. Since federal deregulation protects towing firms from lawsuits for conversion, it may also shield them from a wide variety of other civil causes of action.

---

[1] Tenn. Code Ann. §§ 55-16-105 and 66-19-103

[2] No. 3:04-0528, 2007 WL 108885, Memorandum Opinion (M.D. Tenn., January 12, 2007)

[3] 289 Fed. Appx. 852 (6th Cir. 2008)

§ 4:9 Damage Release Forms
Worth the paper they are written on?

I see one at the bottom of almost every towing impound release form. Above a signature line, something like: "I have inspected my vehicle and acknowledge that there was no damage caused by the towing company."

Since the vast majority of tows do not result in any damage to the towed vehicle, the signing of the release form is usually inconsequential. But what about those times when things do go wrong? Is it legal to require a customer to sign such a form before the release of the vehicle? Even if it is legal, does it really protect the tow company? What if the vehicle owner simply refuses to sign the release?

In 1985, Larry Jordan was arrested by the Baton Rouge Police Department on suspicion of burglary. The Buick he was driving at the time of his arrest was impounded at Dealer's 24-Hour Wrecker Service and put on "hold" by the investigating officer. When Jordan went to the police department about three months later to obtain a written release of the hold, he was required to sign a form stating that he released the police department from all "claims or demands whatsoever" relating to the impounding of the vehicle.

When he then went to the wrecker service to retrieve his car, he was informed that Dealer's had already sold his car at a lien sale. Jordan sued the police department and Dealer's for the loss of his vehicle. In its defense, the police department tried to rely on the release form that Jordan signed before going to the towing impound yard.

The Louisiana Court of Appeals was unconvinced. In *Larry Jordan v. City of Baton Rouge*, the appellate court noted the general rule that a release or waiver is valid only when there is "free and deliberate" consent by the person giving the release. The court went on to hold that "the circumstances surrounding the execution of the release in this case clearly show that Jordan did not freely consent to the document he signed. He was given no alternative but to sign the form in order to get his car back. As a result, the release is without effect."[1]

The *Jordan* case teaches that compelling a vehicle owner to sign a damage release form without first being given an opportunity to inspect his vehicle will most assuredly invalidate any release signed. Indeed, given the coercive nature of a vehicle damage release, that court ruling casts doubt on the validity of any such release.

At least three states, Illinois, Connecticut, and Florida, specifically forbid towing companies from requiring any type of damage release as a prerequisite to releasing a vehicle impounded for unauthorized parking.[2] The Illinois law was at the center of a federal lawsuit arising out of an impounding incident in Macomb, a small town in west central Illinois.

Phillip Cross operates a towing company in Macomb and had a contract with an apartment management company to tow unauthorized vehicles from the apartment's parking lot. On April 13, 2006, the owner of an impounded vehicle paid the fees for the release of her vehicle; however, Cross also insisted that she sign a "damage form." When the car owner refused to sign, brouhaha ensued. Somebody finally called the Macomb Police Department. The officers responding to the scene told the car owner that she could not be forced to sign the form and called Cross a "crook and a con artist." Soon after that, things turned ugly and the police officers eventually handcuffed Cross and placed him under arrest for theft. On the way to the police station with Cross, one of the officers telephoned an assistant district attorney who prudently advised the officers to release Cross.

Cross sued the police officers and the City of Macomb for false arrest and violation of his civil rights. In a pre-trial ruling, the judge in *Phillip Cross v. David Burnham*, considered whether the officers had a justifiable reason for arresting Cross.[3] Central to the court's analysis was whether requiring the "damage form" was a violation of the state statute prohibiting damage waivers.

Despite Cross's contention that the form was just for noting any observable damage, the judge held that it was, in fact, a release. The form included the following clause: "This is a total and unconditional release from all towing liabilities in the tow of said vehicle." The judge wrote, "Cross does not explain how this is not, objectively, a violation of [the state law]."

Ultimately, the judge decided to leave it to the jury to decide whether the police officers had probable cause to arrest Cross. But, significantly, the judge suggested that the refusal of a vehicle owner to sign a release does not justify continued possession by the towing firm: "[Cross's] possessory lien, if any, was limited to the towing and storage charges."

In other words, if a vehicle owner pays the towing and storage fees, under Illinois law it appears he is entitled to retrieve his vehicle without any further conditions or requirements, including the signing of a damage waiver form.

---

[1] *Jordan v. City of Baton Rouge*, 529 So.2d 412 (La. Ct. App. 1988) writ denied 532 So.2d 152 (La. 1988)

[2] 625 Ill. Comp. Stat. 5/4-203(f)(10); Conn. Gen. Stat. § 14-145b; and Fla. Stat. § 715.07(2)(a)9

[3] No. 07-1091, 2008 WL 345547, Order, (C.D. Ill., Feb. 7, 2008)

§ 4:10 The Bankruptcy Quandary
When the owner of an impounded vehicle files bankruptcy

The sheriff's department directs you to impound the car being driven by a person who has a suspended driver's license. You tow it to your vehicle storage facility and hold it pending a release from the sheriff's department as well as payment of the tow fee and any storage charges.

Pursuant to state law, you mail notices to the registered owner and any lien holders advising that the car will be sold at auction to satisfy your outstanding charges if not picked up by a specified date. Nobody claims the vehicle and the auction date is rapidly approaching.

Then, a few days before the scheduled sale, you get a nasty letter from an attorney representing the vehicle owner. He encloses a copy of a court notice indicating that the vehicle owner has filed a petition in bankruptcy. The lawyer warns that if you do not cancel the sale and give the vehicle back – without charge – all sorts of bad things are going to happen to you. He uses threatening terms like "violation of automatic stay" and "contempt of court."

What do you do now?

Bankruptcy is a powerful tool and provides a variety of protections for debtors. Perhaps most important is the "automatic stay" found in Section 362 of the Bankruptcy Code.[1] Under that provision, creditors are forbidden from pursuing any collection activities against a debtor after a bankruptcy case is filed. Violation of the automatic stay can result in harsh sanctions from the bankruptcy court, including an award of punitive damages to the debtor. Another section of the Bankruptcy Code, Section 542(a), requires persons who are in possession of property of the debtor, and who have been notified of the bankruptcy, to turn that property over to the bankruptcy trustee.[2]

There are, however, some exceptions to both the automatic stay and the turnover provision. Pursuant to Section 362(b), a creditor does not violate the automatic stay if it continues to enforce a security interest, including a possessory lien, which was in effect *before* the bankruptcy case was filed. That is referred to as a "pre-petition" security interest. Thus, if a towing firm impounds a vehicle *before* the debtor-vehicle owner files bankruptcy, and if the laws of the state in which the towing firm is located provide towing companies with a valid possessory lien in situations like that in which the debtor's vehicle was impounded, the towing firm would not be in violation of the automatic stay by refusing to release the vehicle until its charges are paid.

But it should not sell or transfer a vehicle without a further order from the bankruptcy court. The owner of Tiger's Auto Body, in

Waldorf, Maryland, got popped for almost $50,000 in damages and attorney's fees, including $20,000 in punitive damages, for auctioning, titling, then reselling, an unclaimed 2000 Lincoln despite having been notified that the vehicle's owner was in bankruptcy.[3]

If an impounded vehicle is of little or no value, the trustee will likely abandon the vehicle to the towing firm and allow it to proceed with the foreclosure sale. If the trustee does not take the initiative to do so, a towing company might contact the trustee (whose contact information is on the notice of bankruptcy) and request that the vehicle be abandoned by the bankruptcy estate. However, if the vehicle has substantial equity and adds value to the debtor's bankrupt estate, the trustee can file a lawsuit against the towing firm, called an adversary proceeding, to obtain possession of the vehicle. The good news is that Section 363(e) of the Bankruptcy Code allows a possessory lien holder to request an order conditioning a turnover on terms that are necessary "to provide adequate protection of [the lien]."[4] In the case of a towing/storage lien that protection could be payment of the towing and storage charges or providing the towing firm with some other assurance. For example, the bankruptcy court might require that a lien in favor of the towing firm be noted on the certificate of title before the vehicle is released to the trustee.

A few points that should be emphasized: First, if a vehicle is impounded *after* a debtor-vehicle owner files bankruptcy, the exception to the automatic stay for possessory liens does not apply. Failure to release a vehicle impounded "post-petition" could subject the impounding towing company to severe sanctions imposed by the bankruptcy court. In order to recover its fees, the towing company may have to file a claim with the bankruptcy court or seek payment from another source, such as an insurance company or the impounding law enforcement agency. Second, the exception from the turnover rule applies only if there is a valid possessory lien for towing and storage fees under state law. No statutory lien, no exception. Finally, if a towing company is required to turnover a vehicle it should ordinarily be surrendered to the trustee, not the vehicle owner, unless the court orders otherwise.

The bankruptcy laws are complex. If you receive notice that the owner of an impounded vehicle has filed bankruptcy, you are urged to promptly contact an attorney specializing in representing creditors in bankruptcy cases.

---

[1] 11 U.S.C.A. § 362
[2] 11 U.S.C.A. § 542(a)
[3] *In re Bennett*, 317 B.R. 313 (Bkrtcy. D. Md. 2004)
[4] 11 U.S.C.A. § 363(e)

Chapter 5   **Federal Trucking Deregulation Law: Regulation of Safety and Non-Consent Tow Rates**

§ 5:1   Deregulation and the Tow Truck Industry 144

§ 5:2   Supreme Court Deals Setback to Towing Deregulation . 146

§ 5:3   Deregulation's Death Rattle? 148

§ 5:4   The Short and Unhappy Life of Towing Price Deregulation 150

§ 5:5   Price Controls: Naughty or Nice? 152

§ 5:1 Deregulation & the Tow Truck Industry

On January 1, 1995, Title IV of the Federal Aviation Authorization Act of 1994 became effective in all states except Hawaii. Title IV of the law amends the Interstate Commerce Act, providing in part as follows:

[A] State [or] political subdivision of a State ... may not enact or enforce a law, regulation, or other provision having the force and effect of law related to price, route, or service of any motor carrier...with respect to the transaction of the property.[1]

In one fell swoop, Congress mandated deregulation of the economic activities of intrastate motor carrier of property. Although specifically forbidding regulation of the "price, route or service" of a motor carrier of property by a state local government entity, the law preserves the right of states to continue to regulate in matters of "safety," size and weight, transportation of hazardous cargo and minimum insurance requirements.

How will deregulation impact the towing industry? Unfortunately, there are many more questions than answers. However this much is certain:

1. A State government or state agency may no longer require a towing firm to obtain an operating permit or certificate of authority based on public need and necessity. As noted above, states may continue to enforce compliance with "safety" regulations and a certificate of compliance, or fitness, may be required, but those safety requirements cannot be so restrictive as to amount to "backdoor" economic regulation.

2. A local or municipal government can no longer require that a towing firm obtain an operating permit or certificate of authority based on public need and necessity.

3. Tariffs and price-controls for consensual tows are eliminated.

But many questions remain:

What did Congress mean when it said that state and local governments cannot regulate in matters pertaining to "price?" Certainly states and local governments can no longer control prices for towing services provided to commercial accounts or for non-emergency consumer calls, but what about the regulation of rates when emergency towing services are rendered at the behest of a government entity pursuant to a noncompulsory dispatch program such as a rotation list? If the government unilaterally sets those rates by statute, ordinance or rotation list rules — not through competitive contracting — is that an unlawful regulation of "price" forbidden by the federal law or is it simply a case of a willing buyer and a willing service provider? (See § 1:35).

What is included in the term "service?" Can state and local governments continue to regulate hours of operation of storage yards? Require mandatory check and credit card acceptance? Prohibit wreck chasing or call jumping? Require posting of signs on private property before tow-aways?

Litigation will inevitably resolve many of these questions. Whether or not a state or local regulation will be upheld or struck down under the landmark federal law will depend on the exact language and scope of the particular regulation.

---

[1] 49 U.S.C.A. § 14501(c)

§ 5:2 Supreme Court Deals Setback to Towing Deregulation

Immediately after the enactment of the Federal Aviation Administration Authorization Act of 1994 (FAAA Act of 1994), federal courts across the nation invalidated local laws licensing and regulating tow truck businesses. Since 1995, injunctions were issued forbidding municipal governments from continuing to enact or enforce a myriad of ordinances regulating towing operations in non-price matters. Towing license applications and fees, tow truck inspections, driver permits and a variety of other local tow truck regulations were outlawed by federal courts from Miami to San Francisco.[1]

Those court rulings were based on a 1994 federal law that deregulated intrastate trucking, outlawing certificates of public need and necessity, tariffs and route restrictions. However, one very important exemption to that federal law is the so-called "safety exemption," which provides that a state's "safety regulatory authority" is not affected. In other words, although it generally deregulated intrastate trucking, Congress left *state governments* with the authority to regulate the safety of commercial motor vehicles subject to the state's jurisdiction.

With regard to the authority of *municipalities* over commercial motor vehicle safety, most federal courts held that the law left only the states with authority over the safety of intrastate carriers, and that the law forbids the states from *delegating* or transferring that authority to its cities and towns. The majority of courts found that Congress intended for safety and insurance regulations pertaining to commercial motor vehicles, including tow trucks, to be enacted on a uniform, statewide basis. Congress' plan, they reasoned, was to eliminate the "patchwork" of inconsistent and duplicitous local truck regulatory ordinances that has existed over the years.[2] Those court rulings were particularly a boon to the towing industry. Towing companies, long subjected to licensure by every local jurisdiction in which they operated, were relieved of a tremendous administrative and financial burden.

Then the U.S. Supreme Court heard arguments in the case of *City of Columbus v. Ours Garage and Wrecker Service*.[3] Like so many others, that city's tow truck ordinance had been struck down by a federal trial court relying upon the 1994 deregulation law. On appeal, the City of Columbus contended that nothing in that federal law prohibited a state from delegating its trucking safety authority to its cities and counties — like Ohio had done. Ours Garage, on the other hand, argued that such an interpretation would allow cities to circumvent the entire purpose of the federal deregulation law.

On June 20, 2002, the Supreme Court announced its decision. Writing for the majority of a divided Court, Justice Ginsburg said that the 1994 deregulation law "does not bar a State from delegating to municipalities and other local units the State's authority to establish safety regulations governing motor carriers of property, including tow trucks." The high court effectively overruled many of the previous lower court decisions and reopened the door to municipal tow truck regulations.

Although the *Ours Garage* ruling is, without a doubt, a body blow to the towing industry, it does not necessarily forebode a return to pre-1994 regulation of the towing industry by local governments. First, the Court only held that states *may* delegate their safety regulatory authority over commercial motor vehicles to local governmental entities. Not all states have done so. The decision-making with regard to the future of tow truck safety regulation now shifts from the courts to the state legislatures. Even though they have the power to statutorily delegate their regulatory authority over tow truck safety to local governments, state legislatures may well decide that a uniform statewide law is the preferred manner of regulating towing safety.

In states that have not already delegated their authority to regulate towing safety, it remains to be seen whether they will retain the exclusive authority or if they will turn tow truck safety regulation over to local governments. Likewise, in those states that have already delegated towing safety authority to cities and counties, that local authority could be taken away.

Secondly, the Supreme Court was careful to note that, even if it has properly-delegated authority, a local government cannot use its safety regulatory authority as a guise for economic regulation. "Local regulation ... of tow trucks that is not genuinely responsive to safety concerns garners no exemption from [the 1994 law]," wrote Justice Ginsburg. Thus, local tow truck regulations unrelated to safety or the price charged for nonconsensual towing are still preempted by the 1994 federal law. (See § 5:3).

---

[1] *See, e.g., Anna Petre d/b/a Magnum Towing v. City of Toledo*, 246 F.3d 548 (6th Cir. 2001); *Tocher v. City of Santa Ana*, 219 F.3d 1040 (9th Cir. 2000); *Galactic Towing, Inc. v. Miami-Dade County, Florida*, No. 00-cv-3677, Final Judgment and Order of Settlement, (S.D. Fla., June 14, 2001); and *Cedar Bluff 24-Hour Towing, Inc. v. City of Knoxville*, 78 F.Supp.2d 725 (E.D. Tenn. 1999)
[2] *R. Mayer of Atlanta, Inc. v. City of Atlanta*, 158 F.3d 538 (11th Cir. 1998)
[3] 536 U.S. 424 (2002)

§ 5:3 Deregulation's Death Rattle?

In 1994, Congress enacted a dramatic piece of legislation that forbids state and local governments from regulating motor carriers of property in matters relating to "price, route or service." In essence, that sweeping federal law "deregulated" trucking businesses engaged in hauling property in intrastate commerce. It is commonly referred to as the "FAAA Act of 1994". (See § 5:1).

That law was received by most in the towing industry with great enthusiasm. It meant the elimination of economic barriers to market entry such as permits and certificates based on proof of need and public necessity. It wiped away price regulations and tariff requirements imposed on consensual towing and storage. Tow operators were relieved of expensive and burdensome government reporting requirements.

However, Congress did not take away the authority of the state governments to regulate with regard to insurance and the safety of motor vehicles.[1] For years after the enactment of the law, debate raged in the federal courts about whether that authority resided solely with the state governments or whether *both* state and local governments could regulate under the so-called "safety exemption." That was an important question. The answer would determine whether intrastate motor carriers would be subject to one state-wide, uniform safety regulation or, as one court characterized it, "a patchwork" of divergent local safety regulations. The U.S. Supreme Court settled that debate in its 2002 ruling in the case of *City of Columbus v. Ours Garage and Wrecker Service*.[2] In a disappointing decision, the high court held that a state government could delegate its safety regulatory authority to its local governments. (See § 5:2). The law is now clear: With *properly delegated* state authority, cities and counties can also regulate the safety of tow trucks under the "safety exemption."

But what regulations are encompassed within the "safety exemption?" The federal statute says that the federal deregulation "shall not restrict the safety regulatory authority of a State *with respect to motor vehicles.*" On its face, the exception permits only safety regulations relating to motor vehicles, e.g., brakes, lights, tires, etc. However, most courts are painting the "safety exemption" with a much broader brush.

For example, a federal court held that New York City's towing laws requiring the public display of consumer information and certain record keeping and reporting requirements were okay because they are "directly related to safety."[3] How so? In California, the state court of appeals ruled that a statute requiring written authorization before the towing of a trespassing vehicle was a "safety regulation" and therefore lawful.[4] Such a regulation "serves to protect vehicle owners ... from both towing mistakes and outright theft of vehicles from private property," said the California court. Fine, but what do those interests have to do with *motor vehicle safety?*

If a tow operator tows the wrong vehicle, he can be sued in civil court. If he is stealing cars, he should be arrested under the state criminal statutes. Those concerns are not legitimate safety concerns.

In a 2002 case, *Cole v. City of Dallas*, a federal appellate court opined that a city law precluding the issuance of a tow truck driver's permit to anyone with a recent felony drug conviction fell within the safety exception because it was "designed to curtail confrontation between tow operators and non-consenting vehicle owners."[5] Really? And how does it accomplish that? And what does that have to do with motor vehicle safety?

How far does the "safety exemption" go? It seems the courts are stretching the exemption far beyond what was intended by Congress. The scope of the safety exemption is specifically limited to safety "with respect to motor vehicles." How much clearer could Congress have been? As I stated to a panel of judges at the U.S. Court of Appeals in St. Louis during oral argument in the case of *Tow Operators Working to Protect their Right to Operate on the Streets (TOW PROS) of Kansas City v. Kansas City:* "A regulation requiring tow operators, at their own expense, to produce and distribute brochures on home fire prevention is clearly a 'safety regulation,' but is that what Congress meant when it said governments could regulate motor vehicles in matters of safety?"[6]

If, with the blessing of the courts, government entities can avoid preemption by merely slapping a "public safety" label on any towing regulation, then deregulation has come full circle. Arguably, a regulatory scheme which includes motor carrier permits based on public need and convenience and full-blown rate regulation is a "safety regulation" because such a system might curtail a fist fight between two fiercely competitive truckers engaged in a heated discussion at a trade association meeting.

Unfortunately for the towing industry, given these court decisions, the "safety exemption" in the FAAA Act of 1994 is being transformed into a virtual magic wand that state and local governments can simply wave over any motor carrier regulation and thereby avoid federal deregulation. Sadly for the towing industry, absent a change in this judicial trend or clarifying federal legislation, meaningful deregulation may soon be little more than a pleasant memory.

---

[1] 49 U.S.C.A. § 14501(c)(2)(A)
[2] *City of Columbus v. Ours Garage and Wrecker Service*, 536 U.S. 424 (2002)
[3] *Ace Auto Body & Towing, Ltd. v. City of New York*, 171 F.3d 765 (2nd Cir.) *cert. denied* 120 S.Ct. 166 (1999)
[4] *People ex rel. Renne v. Servantes*, 103 Cal.Rptr.2d 870 (Cal. Ct. App. 2001)
[5] 314 F.3d 730 (5th Cir. 2002)
[6] *Tow Operators Working to Protect their Right to Operate on the Streets of Kansas City ("TOW PROS of KC") v. City of Kansas City, Missouri*, 338 F.3d 873 (8th Cir. 2003)

§ 5:4 The Short and Unhappy Life of Tow Truck Price Deregulation

On January 1, 1995, the Federal Aviation Administration Authorization Act of 1994 (FAAA Act of 1994) went into effect which preempted, or deregulated, the intrastate regulation of motor carriers of property by state or local governments.[1] That law states as follows:

> GENERAL RULE. *[A] State [or] political subdivision of a state, ... may not enact or enforce a law, regulation, or other provision having the force and effect of law related to price, route, or service of any motor vehicle carrier ... with respect to the transportation of property.*

In short, Congress simply exercised its federal muscle and told the states and local governments that they could no longer regulate motor carriers of property within their respective jurisdictions by restricting market entry and competition through the issuance of operating permits, by limiting the routes of such carriers, or by setting prices or price ceilings for transportation of property by motor carriers. Congress did, however, leave state governments with the power to regulate the safety of motor carriers of property.

Tow trucks are motor carriers of property. Thus, by enacting that law Congress, whether intentionally or unintentionally, stripped away any legal authority that state and local governments might have had to regulate the "price, route, or service" of towing operations. A literal reading of the law led to the inescapable conclusion that thousands of state and local laws, which regulated towing prices, were wiped off the books virtually overnight.

As you might expect, that federal law spawned a litany of lawsuits. From New Jersey to California, towing companies and towing organizations filed lawsuits asking the courts to declare certain towing rate regulations unlawful. At the same time state and local government associations charged up to Capitol Hill pleading, "You've made a terrible mistake!" State and local officials were particularly concerned about the loss of control over non-consent towing rates. If they did not have authority to regulate non-consent towing prices, government officials argued to Congress, the motoring public would be subjected to horrible price gouging by unscrupulous towing operators.

The rulings in the lawsuits were fairly inconsistent: Some courts held that local tow truck regulations had been outlawed by Congress; others looked beyond the language of the law and held that Congress did not intend to deregulate tow truck operations.

Congress, however, eliminated the uncertainty regarding tow truck price regulation when, as part of the ICC Termination Act of 1995, it amended the law to restore the authority of state and local governments to regulate the price charged for services rendered by tow trucks in any situation in which service is "performed without the prior consent or authorization of the owner or operator of the vehicle."[2]

Three comments about the 1995 amendments to the federal transportation law:

First, the only regulatory authority restored to state and local governments was that relating to the price charged for non-consent towing. State and local laws relating to the "routes" or "service" of tow truck operator remain preempted.

Second, the 1995 amendment is quite vague with regard to the scope of state and local governments' authority over tow truck pricing. The law does not mandate that any regulated towing prices be "compensatory" or that it be "reasonable." Would an unreasonably low non-consent price regulation established by a city council be subject to court challenge as "non-compensatory," or, under the new federal law, do states, cities and towns now have unbridled discretion with regard to setting non-consent tow rates? (See § 2:3).

Finally, if all pre-1995 non-consent towing rate regulations were preempted by the FAAA Act of 1994, must not a state or local government agency wishing to reinstate such regulations necessarily need to repromulgate the regulations as if they never existed in the first place? Arguably, it would be legally improper for a state or local agency to simply reinstate the pre-1995 rates, without any rate making process or opportunity for industry input, as though the rates had never been preempted.

---

[1] 49 U.S.C.A. § 14501(c)
[2] 49 U.S.C.A. § 14501(c)(2)(C)

§ 5:5 Price Controls: Naughty or Nice?
A Yuletide story of towing rate regulation

"Can the government regulate my towing rates?" It is one of the most frequent questions I get from towing company owners. Hark, the herald angel sings.

Unless you have been cooped up in a workshop at the North Pole for several years, you should be aware that the business of transporting goods in intrastate commerce by truck was "deregulated" by the federal government in 1994. In a law commonly referred to as the "FAAA Act of 1994," Congress made it unlawful for state or local governments to regulate intrastate motor carriers in matters relating to their "*price*, route or service."[1] Frosty the Towman is unquestionably a motor carrier of property, so in enacting that law Congress forbade state and local governments from imposing any economic regulations on intrastate tow truck operations.

Many tow truck company owners, having some vague awareness of federal deregulation, have seized upon the word "price" in the federal statute and assumed that state and local governments may no longer regulate or control their towing prices. That assumption is only partially correct.

Soon after the law went into effect, several lawsuits were filed by towing firms asking courts to knock out local towing price controls, claiming they were illegal after federal deregulation. Like Rudolph's nose, those cases shed a bright light on an apparent oversight by Congress. With the enactment of the 1994 law and the ban on "price" regulations, Congress intended to eliminate the need for trucking companies to file rate tariffs with state governments. Perhaps unwittingly, in passing that broadly-worded legislation, Congress took away the authority of state and local governments to control towing rates.

That meant cities and states also lost the power to control the prices charged for nonconsensual towing — those situations in which a vehicle owner does not authorize or consent to the tow, for example, private property impounds. Government officials were hot as chestnuts roasting on an open fire. Those wise men rushed to O' Little Town of Washington, D.C., pleading, "You've made a terrible mistake!" According to them, if Congress did not restore their power to regulate nonconsensual towing prices, the motoring public would be subject to uncontrolled price gouging by unscrupulous Grinches engaged in *nonconsensual* towing.

And it came to pass in those days that Congress added an exception to the deregulation law that allows state and local governments to control the price charged for for-hire motor vehicle transportation services rendered by tow trucks at the request of a law enforcement official or in any situation in which the transportation service is provided without the consent of the vehicle owner — basically, private property impounds. That amendment took effect on New Year's Day 1996.[2]

So, the status of towing rate regulation is as follows: state and local governments are forbidden from regulating the price charged for consensual towing services — for example, direct calls from customers or "COD" calls — but they may control the price charged for *nonconsensual* towing and, as confirmed by a California court of appeals ruling, storage fees relating to that type of towing.[3]

"Bah! Humbug!" you say? Does that mean cities and towns now have unbridled discretion with regard to setting nonconsent tow rates? Can a city council simply pull a list of rates out of the air, or average nonconsent tow rates in the area and then require all nonconsent towing companies to abide by those rates?

Not according to the congressman who proposed the law that cleared the way for nonconsensual rate regulations. He stated that any nonconsensual towing prices regulated by a municipal or state government should be "*compensatory* and *reasonable*."[4] What does that mean? Generally, "compensatory and reasonable" means a rate that covers costs and guarantees the tow operator a reasonable profit margin and return on investment. To use an extreme example, it would be unlawful for a town to arbitrarily cap nonconsensual tow rates at $5 per tow.

But what about $75 or $90 or $115 per tow? Who has the burden to determine whether or not an established rate is, in fact, "reasonable" — the regulating government body or the regulated towing companies? The answer to that question is critical because, done correctly, rate analysis is an expensive process. Financial experts must be hired to review cost data, i.e., fuel, insurance, labor, equipment, evaluate towing operations, and make an assessment of a fair and reasonable nonconsensual towing rate. Unfortunately, I do not bring you good tidings of great joy in that regard. Although there have been scant cases on that issue, a federal court in northern Texas held that the burden of proof is on the towing operators to prove the unreasonableness of a nonconsensual tow rate fixed by a governmental agency.[5]

So, yes, Virginia, there is law that gives cities and states the authority to regulate the price of towing. But that power is limited only to nonconsensual towing and storage fees, and any rates regulated must be compensatory and reasonable.

Merry Christmas to all, and to all a good night!

---

[1] 49 U.S.C.A. § 14501(c)
[2] 49 U.S.C.A. § 14501(c)(2)(C)
[3] *CPF Agency Corp. v. R&S Towing Service*, 34 Cal.Rptr.3d 106 (Cal. Ct. App. 2005)
[4] Cong. Rec. H15602 (daily ed. Dec. 22, 1995)(statement of Rep. Rahall)
[5] *A.J.'s Wrecker Service, Inc. v. City of Dallas*, Civ. A 3:97-cv-1311D, 1998 WL 185521, Memorandum Opinion and Order, (N.D. Tex., April 15, 1998)

154 TOWING and the LAW

Chapter 6   Local Licensing Laws

§ 6:1   Tow Truck Licensing Laws 155

§ 6:2   A Tale of Two Cities... 157

§ 6:3   Big Win in the Big Apple 159

§ 6:1 Tow Truck Licensing Laws

Those working in our industry are, in all likelihood, quite familiar with a special kind of license that pertains specifically to the towing business. Call them what you will — permits, medallions, T-stickers, E tags, TW plates — they are all the same thing: licenses on the right to operate an automotive towing business.

Just as they come under a variety of names, tow truck licenses come in a variety of "flavors" as well. Some states require statewide licenses to the exclusion of any and all local licenses. In other states, there is no statewide licensing scheme, but a multiplicity of local, municipal licenses dominate. Emergency, non-consent towing is the focus of some licensing laws, while other jurisdictions require licenses of all towing firms performing any type of towing within the respective jurisdiction.

The "vanilla" flavor of towing licenses, however, is probably a local law based on certain fundamental public or consumer safety factors. Typically, a local tow truck license law requires businesses performing towing services (as defined by the license law) to:

1. Complete a license application, which usually asks for general information about the business ownership, towing equipment and office location,

2. Provide proof of liability insurance, and

3. Pay a license fee. The standard license fee is a base fee of about $100 plus a per truck fee of $25 to $50.

In general, business licensing laws which have some reasonable relationship to promoting the public's health, safety and welfare are upheld by the courts. Tow truck licensing laws have certainly not been an exception to that rule.

A frequent complaint about local tow truck licensing laws is their scope. Typically, a local tow truck licensing law will apply to "all businesses performing towing within the City of _____." A tow truck company with a principal place of business perhaps 50 or 100 miles away from the licensing city would be required to have a license from that city if it picked up a customer's vehicle from within the city limits. Under a literal interpretation, a tow truck merely passing through the city while in tow would be subject to the licensing law.

Results of litigation on this topic have been mixed. Licensing requirements imposed on towing businesses for simply "passing through" a jurisdiction while in tow have been struck down by many courts. On the other hand, licenses imposed on towing businesses "picking up" within the licensing jurisdiction have been upheld by several courts as a valid exercise of their police powers.

In the 1990s, a tow truck license law in Cincinnati was challenged in federal court by the Interstate Towing Association and several local towing associations. In the case of *Interstate Towing Association vs. City of Cincinnati*,[1] I pointed out to the federal court of appeals that there were approximately 200 cities and towns within a 25-mile radius of Cincinnati. If they were all to adopt an ordinance similar to Cincinnati's — requiring a license for all towing firms that pick up vehicles within the city limits — a local towing firm would have to spend over $100,000 in license fees and at least 200 hours of inspection time just to be able to operate freely in that 25-mile radius. And, I added, its tow trucks would have so many license decals the drivers wouldn't be able to see through the windshield!

The court of appeals, however, determined that towing operations are "local" in nature. According to the court, they are more like local building contractors than long-haul trucking companies. The court held that it was lawful for the City to require towing firms to obtain a local license, regardless of their base of operation.

That 1993 court ruling, and any ruling like it, was called into question the following year by the 1994 federal intrastate trucking deregulation law prohibiting economic regulation of all motor carriers by local municipalities. (See §§ 5:1 and 6:2). Although, under that federal law, municipalities retain their authority to regulate in all matters of motor carrier safety, the question remains as to whether that continuing safety regulatory authority provides municipalities with the legal basis for requiring out-of-town towing firms to obtain a local license. At least one court has said they do not.[2]

---

[1] 6 F.3d 1154 (6th Cir. 1993)
[2] *City of Wellford v. Scruggs*, No. 53409 EA, Order, (Wellford Municipal Court, May 11, 2010)(copy on file with author)

§ 6:2 A Tale of Two Cities
The menace of local business licenses

Max owns a towing company based in the City of Terra Cotta. Max is headed to the small town of Lipsville, located about 35 miles away, to pick up a customer's disabled Honda and tow it back to a repair shop in Terra Cotta. The vehicle is in the parking lot of Valentino's Restaurant.

Max makes tow runs to Lipsville quite infrequently. In fact, Max's last trip there to pick up a vehicle was over a year ago.

When Max arrives in Lipsville, he locates the Honda and begins to load it onto his rollback. He notices a Lipsville Police Department squad car in the convenience store on a nearby corner, but thinks nothing of it. Soon, though, a police captain strolls across the street and asks to see Max's Lipsville business license.

"I don't have a Lipsville license," says Max. "You see, my business is based in Terra Cotta," he explains, pointing to the name and address lettered on the side of his tow truck.

"Son, I don't care if you're from Kalamazoo," says the captain, as he reaches for his ticket book. "If you're gonna tow that vehicle, you're officially doin' business in this town and you can't do business here without a Lipsville business license."

Faced with the threat of a $500 citation, Max agrees to go to the clerk's office at town hall, fill out an application for a Lipsville business license, and pay the $150 business license tax.

The problem demonstrated by this fictitious story, based on many real-life events, is obvious. Automotive towing is an on-demand mobile business operating on irregular and unanticipated routes. Towing firms cannot predict where or how far the next tow call might require them to go. Over time, the typical towing company picks up or drops off vehicles in several different states and dozens, if not hundreds, of local municipalities.

As a practical matter, if my hypothetical town of Lipsville could require that a non-resident towing firm obtain a business license, and pay a business license tax, as a condition of towing vehicles from its streets, then every city, town, and county in the state would be free to impose their business license and fee on non-resident tow trucks. That burden would be stifling.

Imagine the financial and administrative costs that would be incurred by applying for a business license, and paying an annual $150 business license tax, in *every* city and town from which you tow — even those to which you may only travel once or twice in a given year.

Recognizing the predicament of towing firms faced with a myriad of local business licenses and taxes, some state legislatures have enacted remedial statutes. For example, Oregon law completely forbids the imposition of any business license fee or tax on a towing business by a local government entity.[1] Missouri restricts local business licensing to those jurisdictions in which a tow truck company conducts more than 50 percent of its business.[2] California and Utah allow business license taxes to be imposed only by a city or county in which a towing company has a fixed place of business.[3]

Even in states without such a protective statute, a flat business license tax charged to towing companies not regularly engaged in business in the taxing jurisdiction may be unlawful because it unreasonably discriminates. It has the practical effect of imposing a higher "per tow" tax on non-resident tow truckers than on resident tow truckers. In the case set forth above, because it only made that single tow from Lipsville the entire year, Max essentially paid a $150 tax for the privilege of performing that one tow. Compare that to a local Lipsville towing firm making over a thousand tows in Lipsville each year. Its business license tax burden amounts to only a few cents "per tow." The U.S. Constitution prohibits unreasonable tax discrimination against non-resident businesses.[4]

The federal statute deregulating the intrastate motor carrier industry (See § 5:1) would also appear to have a bearing on the issue. However, since the enactment of that law in 1994, one federal court has upheld the application of a general business license law against non-resident tow companies.

In the 2004 case of *Helmrich Transportation Systems v. City of Philadelphia*,[5] a group of out-of-town towing firms filed suit in federal court seeking to stop the City of Philadelphia, from, among other things, requiring them to obtain a privilege license and pay a one-time $250 privilege tax. They claimed the license was a regulation forbidden by the federal law. But the judge ruled that it was so easy to obtain the license (no truck inspection or insurance requirements), the city could not be considered to be "regulating" the towing companies. "[T]he practical impediments to acquiring the necessary licenses are so low," he said, the federal law forbidding "regulation" simply did not apply.

That court decision was unfortunate. Considering the possibility that a towing company might have to obtain dozens of expensive business licenses each year, or perhaps limit the number of towns in which it does business, it would appear that those revenue-generating business license laws are precisely the type of burdensome local laws imposed on motor carriers of property that Congress intended to eradicate in 1994.

---

[1] Or. Rev. Stat. § 822.230(2)
[2] Mo. Rev. Stat. § 301.344
[3] Cal. Veh. Code § 12111 and Utah Code Ann. § 72-9-604
[4] *American Trucking Associations, Inc. v. Scheiner*, 483 U.S. 266, 270, 107 S.Ct. 2829 (1987)
[5] No. Civ. A. 02-2233, 2004 WL 2278534, Memorandum, (E.D. Pa., Oct. 8, 2004)

§ 6:3 Big Win in the Big Apple
Out-of-towners get relief from NYC tow truck licensing law

Imagine receiving a call from a friend or family member who tells you that her car is in a shopping mall parking lot and it won't start. The shopping center is located in a major city in a neighboring state about 70 miles away. She asks you to tow the vehicle back to your shop. You travel to the mall, locate the car, hook it up and start back with the disabled car in tow. Within a few minutes of leaving the parking lot, you are stopped by a city police officer for operating a tow truck without a towing license issued by that city. You are issued a citation and face a $1,000 fine. Your truck is impounded and subjected to a $2,000 release bond.

Outrageous as that may sound, that is exactly what was happening in New York City. Tow trucks operated by companies based outside NYC traveling to the city to drop off or pick up vehicles — or simply driving through the city — were being stopped and seized by NYC law enforcement agencies for no reason other than that they did not display a city tow truck license or medallion. Even poor George Kellerman (of the 1970 *The Out-of-Towners* movie) was not treated so rudely by The Big Apple!

The enforcement of the city's tow truck license law marked a dramatic departure from previous policy. For many years, the city honored a reciprocal agreement by which it allowed tow trucks licensed in other states or cities to make inter-city tows. But in March 2004, with an apparent financial motive, New York City reneged on that long-standing accord and initiated an aggressive campaign against unlicensed out-of-town towing firms. It seized 21 tow trucks in just two days.

In order to avoid the wrath of NYC, outsider towing company owners who refused to obtain a NYC license, pay the $600 per truck license fee, and comply with the burdensome NYC regulations, including an in-city truck inspection, began to radically alter their business practices. A relay, or "hand-off," system was devised. If a tow company from New Jersey or Connecticut needed to retrieve a vehicle from a NYC garage, it would call a NYC-licensed tow company to tow the car from the repair shop to the city limits. The out-of-state tow company would meet the NYC tow truck, transfer the vehicle and continue the tow. The reverse was true for calls terminating in the city — the vehicle would be handed off to a city-licensed tow at the city line. It was a costly process; customers had to pay for two hookups. Tow trucks traveling from outside New York to points on Long Island took costly circuitous routes around the city to eliminate the risk of a stop and seizure.

Fortunately, a federal judge put a stop to all that nonsense. In March 2006, in the case of *Automobile Club of New York Inc. v. Dykstra*,[1] Judge Richard Owen ruled that the city's tow truck licensing law, at least to the extent it applied to out-of-town tow operators only picking up or dropping off vehicles, or just passing through the city, was unconstitutional. He said that the burden placed on interstate commerce by that local license law outweighed its purported safety benefits and, thus, violated the Commerce Clause of the U.S. Constitution.**2**

The city argued that the law was justified by the criminal background check of tow truck drivers which it claimed protected consumers from becoming crime victims. It introduced evidence at trial demonstrating that 70 percent of driver applicants had criminal histories. In its ruling, the court acknowledged that the city has a right under federal law to regulate the safety of tow truck operations, but it questioned the practical impact of the city's criminal background checks. The judge pointed out that the vast majority of driver applications were approved by NYC's Department of Consumer Affairs despite criminal histories that revealed drug and alcohol abuse, possession of stolen property and gun charges. "I am utterly unable to conclude that the fact that the city, however well motivated, checks criminal records [has] had any measurable impact on the safety to any car owner or anyone else in New York City ..., certainly not sufficient to justify prohibiting an out-of-city tower licensed by the state or any other state from entering the city to deliver or pick up a car or merely driving or towing through. There must be a stronger showing than that of impact on safety to justify such marked interference with interstate and intrastate commerce," wrote Judge Owen.

The bottom line, as succinctly stated by the court: "[S]eizure by a City agency of any outsider tow truck in New York City is prohibited where the only ground the agency reasonably has and can assert for the seizure is that the tow truck is not licensed by the City of New York. All tow trucks lawfully operating, with or without a tow, from anywhere outside New York City, whether based within the State or elsewhere, are to be permitted the same access to and use of New York City's roads as those towers licensed by New York City."

Good stuff.

---

[1] 423 F. Supp.2d 279 (S.D. N.Y. 2006) *aff'd* 520 F.3d 210 (2d Cir. 2008); *see also* Michael McGovern, *A Funny Thing Happened on the Way to the Courthouse*, Tow Times, January 2010, at p. 15
[2] U.S. Const., Art. 1, § 8, cl. 3

Private Property (Trespass) Towing **161**

Chapter 7 Administration, Dispatching and Staffing

§ 7:1 Disability Act Regulations Make Hiring Complex 162

§ 7:2 How Much Should You Know Before You Tow? 164

§ 7:3 Criminal Past Not Always Roadblock to Towing Future . 167

§ 7:4 All Dressed Up and No Place to Go 169

§ 7:5 Driver's Arrest-Related Injuries
       Covered by Workers Compensation 172

§ 7:6 Vicarious Criminal Liability 174

§ 7:1 Disability Act Regulations Make Hiring Complex

The Americans with Disabilities Act of 1990 (ADA)[1] prohibits discrimination against employees, or potential employees, based on a physical or mental disability. The Equal Employment Opportunity Commission (EEOC) has issued a set of rules under the ADA that apply to all businesses, including towing businesses, with more than 15 employees.[2]

The ADA rules prohibits asking certain questions at the initial stage of the hiring process because the EEOC insists that that the "pre-offer" stage — before a job offer is extended — is not the proper time for discussion of a potential employees disabilities. Thus, the rules are intended to prevent discrimination against applicants with hidden disabilities.

Under these regulations, an employer cannot ask about the existence, nature or severity of a disability at the "pre-offer" stage. Also, a business may not conduct medical examinations until a conditional offer is made. That provision is difficult to reconcile with the separate DOT regulations applicable to many towing operations dealing with driver fitness, medical qualifications and drug and alcohol testing.

The employer can ask about an applicant's ability to perform specific job-related tasks and may require exams at the "pre-offer" stage that are not medical in nature.

Once a towing firm makes a conditional job offer, then it can require medical examinations and make disability-related inquiries — but only if it does so for all employees within a specific job category, i.e., all drivers, all dispatchers or all mechanics. If the exam is a screening device — if failure means the applicant will not get the job- the criteria used must be essential to the job. Moreover, the employer has the burden of proving that the essential functions of the job cannot be performed with reasonable accommodation.

For example, take the case of a towing firm seeking a new dispatcher. Obviously getting in and out of the radio dispatch room is an essential function of the job, but let's assume that the dispatch room is up a short flight of stairs or has a very narrow entrance. Suppose that one of the job applicants is extremely obese or confined to a wheelchair. The company owner may suspect that the applicant would not be able to get in and out of the dispatch room but it would be improper at the "pre-offer" stage to test the applicant by asking them to try and enter the dispatch area. Only after a conditional job offer is made ("You have the job if you can get in and out of the dispatch room.") can the test be required. Then, even if the applicant cannot access the dispatch room, the burden is on the

Administration, Dispatching and Staffing

employer to demonstrate that it would be unreasonably burdensome to accommodate the disabled employee, for example, by building a ramp, widening the door or remodeling the dispatch room.

The EEOC has published guidelines to help employers correctly interview prospective employees, however those guidelines are confusing and require precise wording by the interviewer. For instance, the interviewer can ask about the impairment, but not if the impairment can also can be classified as a disability. The rules almost demand that a job interviewer be both a doctor and a lawyer!

Obviously, the distinctions between "right" and "wrong" questions are small. Towing firms with more than 15 employees, or those that expect to have more than 15 employees, should be cautious of "failure to hire" lawsuits. Lawsuits can be filed against companies simply because the job interviewer phrased a question incorrectly.

---

[1] 42 U.S.C.A. § 12111, *et seq.*
[2] 29 C.F.R. § 1630

§ 7:2 How Much Should You Know Before You Tow?

What is the legal duty of a towing operator to verify that the person requesting the towing of a vehicle is actually authorized to have the vehicle towed?

That was the question posed in a Tennessee courtroom. The routine facts underlying the case, which will be readily recognizable by most readers of this publication, were undisputed: A towing company, that I will call Outlook Towing, received a telephone call for service. The caller gave his name, a description of the car, the location of the car, the license tag number and a residential address to which he wanted the car delivered. The caller also gave the Outlook Towing dispatcher directions and a "call back" number. A routine call.

The Outlook Towing driver was dispatched to the call, found the vehicle as advised and towed it to the location requested. Upon arrival at the tow destination, a residence, the tow truck driver was met by a man who did not identify himself, but directed the driver where to put the car. The man paid the tow bill in cash. The Outlook Towing driver left the scene; another tow mission successfully accomplished.

But the tale does not end there. As it turned out, the caller did not own the car nor did the caller have any permission from the vehicle owner authorizing him to have the vehicle relocated. Evidently, the caller was a thief who knew there were valuables in the vehicle. Wanting the vehicle moved to a secluded place where he could burglarize it, he called for the tow. After the car was delivered by Outlook Towing, the vehicle was broken into and thousands of dollars in items were taken from inside the vehicle.

The vehicle owner sued Outlook Towing, contending that the company was negligent in failing to verify that the caller had authority to have the vehicle towed. He alleged that the towing company had a legal duty to confirm the caller's authority. Outlook Towing admittedly made no inquiries beyond the initial phone call for towing service. According to the vehicle owner, that failure led to the theft and vandalism of the vehicle and Outlook Towing should be liable for all losses sustained.

The legal concept of "duty" can be elusive. Generally, a common-law "duty" or legal obligation, is imposed on an individual when, because of some relationship or contact between he and another person, he is required to act for the benefit of that other person. For example, when a person operates a motor vehicle on the highways, he has a legal duty to operate his vehicle in a safe manner for the benefit of other motorists. If a duty exists, then a person must

Administration, Dispatching and Staffing   **165**

conform his conduct to what is reasonable conduct in light of all of the circumstances. State laws and regulations may also impose legal duties.

Was Outlook Towing negligent? In other words, did the towing company owe the vehicle owner a duty to verify the authority of the caller? If so, did the tow company act reasonably under all the circumstances?

With regard to the first question, I have been representing towing firms for almost 30 years and I am unaware of any federal or state law requiring a tow operator to somehow verify ownership and/or authorization *prior* to responding to a request for towing service. But is there a duty notwithstanding the absence of a statutory duty? Keep in mind that the vehicle owner's loss was directly attributable to a criminal act: the theft by the anonymous caller. The law does not usually impose any duty to protect others from criminal acts committed by third persons unless there is some special relationship. For example, a psychiatrist may owe a duty to his employees to protect them from a criminal assault by a psychotic patient.[1] However, the routine, isolated tow company-vehicle owner transaction does not seem to be the "special type" of relationship which might give rise to a legal duty to warn or protect others from criminal actions.

But assuming that a duty were to be imposed, what is a towing operator supposed to do? Hundreds of thousands of towing jobs originate with a telephone call from a person unknown to the towing company. Almost all of those calls are legitimate requests for service from a vehicle owner or authorized person. To avoid the isolated incident such as that in the Outlook Towing case, is it reasonable to expect a tow operator to make a detailed inquiry on every call-in for service: name, social security number, place and date of birth, driver's license number, date and place of purchase of vehicle, employment information, spouse and children's names, etc.? Even if the dispatcher got that information, what good would it do? How would it help to verify whether or not it was a legitimate call? Quite simply, it wouldn't.

Should the law impose a duty on towing companies to require all customers to appear in person before the tow, either at the towing company office or the site of the tow, with a photo ID and proof of ownership or written authorization? But would that precaution even prevent a truly fraudulent tow? Does the law require fingerprinting of potential customers and a check of the DMV records before initiating a tow? Otherwise, how can a tow operator ever be certain that the person requesting a tow is duly authorized to do so?

My point, of course, is that, given the nature of the towing business, it would be quite unreasonable to impose a legal duty on towing companies to independently verify the legitimacy of every tow call received. Even if verification could actually be made, the delays and inefficiencies occasioned by such a requirement would be overwhelming. The jury in Tennessee apparently agreed and the case against Outlook Towing was dismissed.

The only situations in which the law should impose a duty to verify ownership and/or authorization to tow would be those in which a clear suspicion is raised. For example, if the caller is obviously evasive or can't provide basic information about the car, if there is something unusual about the delivery location, or if any other circumstance about the call would raise a red flag to a reasonable person, then certainly a duty might be imposed upon the tow operator to make further investigation. Absent such a circumstance, however, it is reasonable for a tow operator to rely upon the information provided over the phone by a call-in customer. Following that industry standard should not ordinarily serve as the basis for a finding of negligence if some criminal intervention is later discovered.

---

[1] *Turner v. Jordan,* 957 S.W.2d 815 (Tenn. 1997)

§ 7:3 Criminal Past Not Always Roadblock to Towing Future

Governments have a legitimate interest in protecting motorists from tow truck drivers who might pose a threat to their safety or welfare, especially when the motorist in need is unfamiliar with any towing companies and the governmental police agency must arrange for the necessary towing service on the motorist's behalf. Towing situations frequently place a car owner one-on-one with an unknown tow truck driver, often riding alone with him in a tow truck. To further its obligation to protect motorists from the risk of personal harm or theft, it is not uncommon for governments to enact laws and police department towing rules which prohibit persons convicted of felony crimes from driving a tow truck in nonconsent towing situations.

However, courts in New York and Tennessee have held that blanket prohibitions against *all* felons serving as tow truck drivers, without regard to the nature of the felony or how the conviction might affect the tow truck driver's ability to provide towing services, violate the felon's constitutional rights. "[I]t would be a most unfortunate and most unjust social policy to prevent anyone who had ever been convicted of a felony from engaging in [the towing] occupation. Such a policy would defeat the recognized and highly laudable principles of rehabilitation and instead it could easily act as a spur to renewed criminal activity," said the New York state court.[1]

A federal judge in east Tennessee indicated that before the state highway patrol could ban felons from serving as tow truck drivers on its rotation towing list it must "show that a legitimate government interest is served by a blanket prohibition on felons due to a demonstrated need ... because of problems experienced with persons with felony convictions ...."[2] In other words, a "no felony conviction" rule cannot serve merely as continuing punishment of the felon but must be based on a genuine safety concern based on previous experiences with convicted felons.

There are two factors that bear on the qualification of a convicted felon to serve as a tow truck driver: (1) the nature of the crime and (2) the date of the offense.

Most would agree that a conviction for a serious felony involving physical violence (for example, murder or sexual assault) or auto theft should preclude an individual with such a conviction from driving a tow truck. But what about felony convictions for tax evasion, drug trafficking or smuggling contraband Cuban cigars? Why should felony convictions for such non-violent crimes serve as the basis for prohibiting an individual from making a living as a tow truck driver? A blanket "no felony conviction" law or regulation fails to take into account that many criminal acts have no relationship whatsoever to the qualification to drive a tow truck and interact with the motoring public.

The second factor to be considered in determining whether a convicted felon should be allowed to perform nonconsent towing work is the date of the conviction. Even in the case of a conviction for a serious felony involving violence, is there not some point in time at which the convicted felon has "paid his debt to society" and should no longer be penalized for the prior conviction? Ten, twenty or even thirty years after the offense, should a person still be banned from driving a tow truck on the sole basis of the old conviction?

The Tennessee federal court ruling infers that all courts should look very closely at any such unlimited regulation to determine whether any legitimate governmental interest is actually being furthered by such a lifetime ban from working as a tow truck driver. In the New York case, the individual had been convicted of carrying a concealed weapon more than 15 years prior to his application for a New York City tow truck driver's permit. From the date of his conviction to the date he applied for the license, he had an unblemished record of employment in the automotive industry and three of his former employers submitted affidavits vouching for him. He was recently married and had adopted a child. The judge said that the denial of a tow truck license to that man would have represented "a grave personal injustice as well as an affront to the social principle of rehabilitation." I agree.

"No felony conviction" laws and regulations are intended to keep the keys to tow trucks out of the hands of those persons who pose a legitimate risk to the motoring public. The challenge to government agencies is to accomplish that objective without unfairly excluding from the towing industry other individuals who, although burdened with a felony conviction, present no real danger behind the wheel of a tow truck.

---

[1] *Brown v. Murphy,* 224 N.Y.S.2d 423 (N.Y. Super. 1962)
[2] *Gregg v. Larson,* 732 F.Supp. 849 (E.D. Tenn. 1989)

§ 7:4 All Dressed Up and No Place To Go
FLSA rules for "On-Call" drivers

Most towing companies are open for business 24 hours, seven days a week. Many tow truck drivers probably feel as though they are working every one of those hours. Of course, they are not. But how much time they really are "working" is critically important under the Fair Labor Standards Act (FLSA).[1] That federal labor law provides that employees are entitled to be paid for all "hours worked."[2] Furthermore, nonexempt employees, whether paid hourly or by commission, are entitled to be paid overtime at a rate of not less than one and one-half times an employee's regular rate of pay after 40 hours of work in a workweek.[3]

An accurate calculation of "hours worked" by a tow truck driver is complicated by the fact that the towing business involves a lot of "waiting time." Whether waiting time is to be included in "hours worked" under the FLSA depends upon the particular circumstances. The focus of the inquiry is the control which the employer has over the employee during the waiting time and whether the employee may effectively use that time for his or her own purposes.

While "On Duty"

A lot of waiting time is compensable. Idleness is inherent in all employments like the towing business that require some stand-by time. A readiness to perform a service may be hired, quite as much as the service itself. For example, a dispatcher who reads a book between phone calls or a tow truck driver who watches TV or plays cards at the shop while awaiting a call is working during their period of inactivity. In those situations the employee is unable to use the waiting time effectively for their own purposes. It belongs to and is controlled by the employer. Waiting is an integral part of the job. The employee is "engaged to wait."

The rule also applies to waiting time away from the office or shop. The idle time a driver spends waiting for a police officer to complete an accident report or for a customer to remove personal property from their vehicle is working time. The waiting time is unpredictable and of short duration.

Off Duty

Periods during which employees are completely relieved from duty and which are long enough to enable them to use the time effectively for their own purposes are not included in "hours worked." Whether the time is long enough to enable them to use the time effectively for their own purposes depends upon all of the facts and circumstances of the case. Suppose a driver is sent from Memphis to St. Louis to pick up a straight box truck only to discover, upon his arrival in St. Louis, that the truck has not been unloaded. If the driver is completely and specifically relieved from all duty while the truck is being unloaded, has no responsibility for the cargo and is free to leave the truck terminal, the hours of idle time in St. Louis are not "hours worked."

Drivers who choose to "hang around" the shop after being completely relieved of duty are also off-duty. But be aware that if a driver routinely accepts tow calls even after he has clocked out, or merely rides along and assists other drivers on calls after his normal work shift is completed, the time spent "hanging around" may be interpreted to be compensable waiting time.

Several years ago, I represented a towing company in a Department of Labor audit that was facing tens of thousands of dollars in overtime payments under that very scenario. It is good policy to require all off-duty drivers to physically leave the company premises.

On-Call Time

Because the towing business is a 24/7 operation, it is not uncommon for tow truck drivers to drive a company tow truck while off-duty and be "on call." Employees who can leave the employer's premises, and are free to engage in their own personal pursuits subject only to the understanding that they will respond to a call by cell phone or pager, are considered to be "waiting to be engaged" rather than "engaged to wait." Such "on-call" time is not working time under the FLSA.[4] When a driver does go out on a job assignment in such a situation, only the time actually spent in making the call need be counted as hours worked. Of course, if calls are so frequent or the "on call" conditions so restrictive that the employees are not really free to use the intervening periods effectively for their own benefit, they may be considered as "engaged to wait" rather that "waiting to be engaged." In that event, the waiting time would also be counted as hours worked.

On-Call Drivers Required To Remain At Home

An example of a restrictive "on-call" situation would be one in which a towing firm forwarded its telephone on nights and weekends to the home phone of an "on-call" driver who must remain at home with a tow truck in order to receive tow calls while the main office is closed.

If they have long periods of uninterrupted leisure during which they can engage in the normal activities of living, any reasonable agreement of the employer and driver for determining the number of hours worked will be accepted. The agreement should take into account not only the actual time spent in answering the calls but also some allowance for the restriction on the driver's freedom to engage in personal activities resulting from the duty of staying home to answer the forwarded telephone.

---

[1] 29 U.S.C.A. § 201, *et seq.*
[2] 29 U.S.C.A. §§ 206 and 207
[3] 29 U.S.C.A. § 207(a)(1)
[4] *See* Opinion No. FLSA 2009-17 (Dep't Labor, January 16, 2009); Opinion No. FLSA 2008-14AN (Dep't Labor, December 18, 2008), and Opinion No. FLSA 2008-8NA (Dep't Labor, May 23, 2008)

§ 7:5 Driver's Arrest-Related Injuries Covered By Workers' Compensation
Confrontation with police is risk of job, says court

Businesses are required by law to pay for the medical treatment and lost wages of employees who suffer job-related injuries. In order to avoid potentially crippling expenses in that regard, all fifty states require companies to purchase workers' compensation insurance or be adequately self-insured.[1] Although provisions of each state's laws differ greatly (some require a minimum number of employees, typically between three and ten, before the mandatory insurance provisions apply), the underlying principle is the same — that employers should assume the costs of injuries that occur on the job, without regard to fault.

However, to be covered under a workers' compensation claim, an employee's injury must arise "in the course and scope of employment." A dispute over whether an injury occurred "in the course and scope of employment" was at the center of a 2008 Oregon court ruling involving a tow truck driver.

David Sisco worked as a driver for Quicker Recovery in Portland. Quicker performed tows for the Gresham Police Department (GPD), which requires a 30-minute response time.

On December 15, 2004, Sisco was dispatched by Quicker to respond to a GPD call for a recovered stolen vehicle abandoned in a store parking lot. Enroute, Sisco exceeded the posted speed limit. Sergeant O'Keefe of the GPD saw Sisco's speeding tow truck, turned on his patrol car's overhead flashing lights, and began pursuing Sisco. When Sisco realized that the police were following him, he flashed his own overhead lights and also pointed out the window in the direction of the parking lot where he was headed — just a few blocks away — all in an attempt to signal to the police officer that he was responding to a GPD call. When Sgt. O'Keefe continued to follow him with lights flashing, Sisco pulled over.

Sisco immediately telephoned his dispatcher to tell him that he would not make it to the GPD tow call within the requisite 30 minutes because he had been stopped by a police officer. The towing company dispatcher told Sisco to cooperate with the officer.

Sgt. O'Keefe approached Sisco and requested his driver's license, but Sisco refused. Based on a personal belief, he told O'Keefe that it was his "sovereign right" to refuse to present his driver's license. O'Keefe explained that Sisco was legally obligated to present his driver's license and that he could be arrested if he did not do so. When Sisco persisted in his refusal, O'Keefe told Sisco that he was under arrest. At that point, Sisco locked his truck door and started to roll up his window.

O'Keefe then ordered Sisco to get out of the tow truck. Sisco refused that request as well. When backup officers arrived, Sisco continued to refuse to leave his truck. The officers then used a stun gun to subdue Sisco and forcibly removed him from the truck. Once Sisco was out of the truck, the officers put him on the ground, briefly pinning him on his stomach by putting a knee on the back of his neck, and handcuffed him. Sisco was cited for speeding, failure to present a license, failure to yield, and resisting arrest.

Shortly thereafter, Sisco was diagnosed with a disc protrusion in his neck that doctors believed was likely caused by the altercation with the GPD officers. Sisco filed a claim under his employer's workers' compensation insurance policy. It was denied on the basis that the injuries did not occur in the scope of his employment. According to the employer, the injuries were the result of Sisco's refusal to comply with the officer's request to produce his driver's license — a personal idiosyncrasy unrelated to his work. Sisco sued.

In March 2008, the Oregon Court of Appeals ruled that Sisco's injuries were, indeed, work-related and should be covered by workers' compensation insurance. In *David Sisco v. Quicker Recovery, Inc.*,[2] the appellate court said, first, that ignoring his dispatcher's request to cooperate with the police officer did not mean that Sisco's conduct was outside the scope of his employment. Even though he was not going about it the way his employer wanted him to, Sisco was still performing the ultimate job, which was responding to a tow call.

However, even though Sisco was "on the job," his claim was still subject to be denied if he was on a personal mission when he got confrontational with the police. On that question, the court found that the nature of the employer's towing business, including routinely racing to meet the 30-minute response obligation to the GPD, meant that Sisco's work necessarily involved some interaction with law enforcement personnel. "[T]he risk of proximate interaction with law enforcement officers after being stopped for speeding, while responding to a tow call, is manifestly a risk related to [Sisco]'s employment," said the court. "[S]uch interactions can escalate, sometimes resulting in physical injury."

In other words, at least for purposes of workers' compensation, getting roughed up by a police officer while responding to a law enforcement tow is just all in a day's work for an Oregon tow truck driver.

---

[1] www.workerscompensation.com
[2] 180 P.3d 46 (Or. Ct. App. 2008)

§ 7:6 Vicarious Criminal Liability
Tow company owners responsible for criminal acts of employees?

In violation of a local towing ordinance, a tow truck driver appears at the scene of an auto accident in his company-owned tow truck without being dispatched by the police department. Can the police officer write a citation to the owner of the towing company?

To facilitate response time to nighttime tow calls, a tow truck driver takes his truck home at night. But overnight parking of commercial vehicles is prohibited in the driver's neighborhood. If a citation is issued for a violation of the local zoning law, who gets it? The driver? Or his towing company employer?

Without his employer's knowledge, a tow truck driver gets high on pills while working his shift. He runs a red light while on a tow and smashes into a car, killing one of the passengers. Can the towing company owner be convicted of vehicular homicide?

Vicarious liability is the imposition of liability on one person for the actionable conduct of another, based solely on a relationship between the two persons. There are numerous court rulings holding corporations or sole proprietors civilly responsible for the negligent acts of an employee acting within the scope of his or her employment. But can an employer be held *criminally* responsible for the *criminal* acts of its employee? Under certain limited circumstances, yes.

Many regulatory statutes and ordinances specifically impose criminal liability upon business owners for the acts of their employees. For instance, alcohol regulations typically impose sanctions on tavern owners for unlawful liquor sales by their bartenders. Some towing ordinances and regulations also provide for vicarious liability on company owners. A police regulation imposing liability for the criminal conduct of an employee will contain language like that found in the New York City tow truck licensing law: "Licensees may be held responsible for any act or omission of any of their employees ...."[1] If the hypothetical ordinance referenced in the first paragraph of this article contained such a clause, the wreck-chasing citation could indeed be issued to the company owner.

But criminal laws or regulations for which employers may be held vicariously liable are limited to minor violations that are punishable only by a fine. Imprisoning an employer for the serious criminal act of one of his employees would violate the Due Process and Excessive Punishment Clauses of the U.S. Constitution.[2] As the Pennsylvania Supreme Court once said, "It would be unthinkable to impose vicarious criminal responsibility in cases involving true crimes."[3]

Administration, Dispatching and Staffing

Also, employers are ordinarily not held responsible for the criminal act of an employee that requires a specific *mens rea*, or state of mind. Most criminal statutes require that the offender have acted with a certain mental state, for example, that he acted "intentionally," "knowingly," "fraudulently" or "recklessly." However, many regulatory statutes do not require that an offender act with any particular mindset. Those are called strict liability laws. The crime of speeding is an example of the latter. It is not a defense to a speeding citation that the violator did not intend to speed or that he "accidentally" exceeded the posted speed limit. The defendant's mental state simply does not matter.

Thus, because the crime of vehicular homicide requires some wrongful mental state by the offender ("recklessness" or "gross negligence"), in the absence of a statute imposing liability, a towing company owner would not be criminally responsible for the unexpected criminal act of the pill-popping driver in the third paragraph above. On the other hand, petty offenses like wreck-chasing and zoning law violations are generally strict liability crimes, punishable only by a fine, for which a governmental body could assess liability on an employer on a vicarious basis.[4]

Also, if the towing firm is organized as a corporation or limited liability company, criminal conduct on the part of the company president or manager will usually be imputed to the corporation or LLC.

It is important to distinguish between *criminal* liability and *civil* liability. Vicarious civil liability can be imposed on an employer for the criminal conduct of one of his employees even in the absence of vicarious criminal responsibility. In the vehicular homicide example, if the employer was aware of the driver's drug problem he might be found civilly liable under the theory of negligent hiring or retention.[5]

Finally, because many towing companies are subject to licensing or permit requirements, a word of caution is in order. Even if the law does not allow criminal sanctions to be imposed on a towing company owner for an employee's criminal actions, an employee's conduct in violation of a towing regulation might still provide the basis for revocation of the company's towing license.[6] Again, that depends on the language of the licensing law. Fortunately, although the court rulings on the matter are not consistent, some judges have held that the Due Process Clause forbids a license revocation based on a non-managerial employee's criminal conduct unless the license-holder knew or should have known of his worker's unlawful actions.[7]

[1] Rules of the City of New York, *Consumer Affairs*, tit. 6, § 2-363(h)
[2] U.S. Const., amend. VIII
[3] *Commonwealth v. Koczwara*, 155 A.2d 825 (Pa. 1959)
[4] *State v. Hy Vee Food Stores, Inc.*, 533 N.W.2d 147 (S.D. 1995)
[5] *See, e.g., Morris v. JTM Materials, Inc.*, 78 S.W.3d 28 (Tex. Ct. App. 2002); *but see Magill v. Bartlett Towing, Inc.*, 35 So.3d 1017 (Fla. Ct. App. 2010) (no vicarious liability where assault committed by tow truck driver while driving tow truck did not occur during dispatched tow call) and *Kaliszewski v. Stevens Towing*, No. 89-L-14-144, 1990 WL 174130 (Ohio Ct. App., November 9, 1990); and *see, generally,* John C. North, Note, *The Responsibility of Employers for the Actions of their Employees: The Negligent Hiring Theory of Liability,* 53 Chi.-Kent L. Rev. 717 (1977)
[6] *Atlanta Taxicab Co. Owners Ass'n, Inc. v. City of Atlanta*, 638 S.E.2d 307 (Ga. 2006)
[7] *Lee v. City of Newport*, 947 F.2d 945 (Table)(6th Cir. 1991)

Chapter 8   Billing and Collection

§ 8:1   A Dividing Issue 178

§ 8:2   I'm Mad As Hell, and I'm Not
        Gonna Take This Anymore!............................... 180

§ 8:3   Who Is Going To Pay?... 182

§ 8:4   A Good Start 184

§ 8:5   Sue 'Em All, Let the Judge Sort 'Em Out 186

§ 8:6   Deadbeat Driver Dodges License Suspension 188

§ 8:7   A No-Win Proposition?...................................... 190

§ 8:8   Salvage Vehicle Abandonment
        by Insurance Companies................................... 192

178 TOWING and the LAW

§ 8:1 A Dividing Issue

Consider the following hypothetical incident:

A late-model conventional Peterbilt tractor pulling a refrigerated trailer loaded with boxes of Dairy Queen Dilly® Bars overturns, causing little damage to the tractor but splitting open the trailer and strewing the cargo all over the highway. The investigating police officer calls the contracted zone tow company or the "next scheduled wrecker," who is obligated to respond and recover the wreck. Although the tractor is easily righted, the recovery job takes more than eight (8) hours because of the time required to pick up the busted trailer and scattered cargo. In fact, about 75 percent of the total time spent on the job is recovering the trailer and cleaning up thousands of melting ice cream bars. The towing company has to hire temporary labor and rent some equipment to clear the mess from the roadway. The tractor, trailer and load are eventually transported to the towing company's storage facility.

Assume that the total bill is $10,000 and there is no dispute about the reasonableness of the charges. Further assume that the trailer is a lease trailer and that the tractor, the trailer and the load are each insured by different insurance companies.

Shortly after the job is complete, the FDA condemns what little cargo was salvaged, rendering it worthless. The insurers for the destroyed trailer and ruined cargo never show their faces, abandoning the trailer and cargo because the total towing and recovery fees exceed the salvage value of either the trailer or the cargo. Soon, though, the insurer for the tractor comes to the tow lot seeking to recover possession of the slightly damaged tractor. How much does the tractor insurer have to pay in order to retrieve the tractor?

Typically, the towing company will demand payment of the entire towing and recovery bill — the full $10,000 — before releasing the tractor. The tractor insurer, however, will insist that the towing company divide the $10,000 bill between the tractor, the trailer and the load and that it be required to pay only the portion allocable to the tractor. The dilemma for the towing company, of course, is that even though the majority of the labor and charges relate to the trailer and cargo, the tractor is the only salvage that has any residual value and thus the only item that can stand to secure payment of the $10,000 bill. If the towing firm lets the tractor go for $2,000 — the percentage of the bill that accounts for labor performed in recovering the tractor — it'll have a helluva time getting paid for the balance of the invoice.

Must the tow operator divide the bill or may he hold the tractor until the entire bill is paid? The answer depends entirely upon the laws of the state in which the accident occurred. Every state, by statute, provides repairers, materialmen, mechanics, warehousemen, etc., with possessory liens — the legal right to keep possession of items repaired or improved until they are paid for services rendered. Ordinarily, those state laws also provide towing firms with a possessory lien for the value of services performed in recovering wrecked vehicles. That means that a towing firm can legally refuse to release a vehicle that it has recovered and is storing until all reasonable charges for towing, recovery and storage are paid. Clearly, a possessory lien is a powerful collection tool.

However, a possessory lien is usually specific to a particular item of property. For example, if a pair of shoes and a pair of boots were taken to a repair shop for new soles and the charges were $30 for the shoes and $45 for the boots, the cobbler would have a lien — the legal right to maintain possession of the shoes and boots — until those amounts were paid. But if the owner later tendered $30 to pick up only the shoes, the cobbler could not withhold possession of the shoes until the entire $75 was paid, because his lien against the shoes is only for the value of the labor he performed on the shoes.

Arguably, a bill for towing, recovering and storing a wrecked tractor-trailer and load is somewhat different than the shoe repair example because the tractor, trailer and load can be viewed as a collective single unit for purposes of the possessory lien laws. On that issue, the specific language of the state's lien law is important. If the statute provides that a towing firm shall have a possessory lien for the value of services performed in recovering a "vehicle," if the lien was challenged, it is likely that a state court would order that the bill be severed, or divided, among the different entities. On the other hand, if the towman's lien is upon "all items" or "all units" recovered from an accident, the bill and the lien should be indivisible, requiring the tractor insurer to pay the entire bill before release of the tractor. Reimbursement can then be sought from the other parties.[1]

The same would apply to a cargo insurer seeking to recover salvageable cargo. Under a good possessory lien law, the cargo insurer should pay the entire bill in order to obtain a release of the cargo, then seek reimbursement from the negligent carrier or its insurer.

Keep in mind that the absence of a lien does not affect the status of the debt for the services rendered. In my example above, even if the tractor insurer was able to recover possession of the tractor by payment of only $2,000, the towing firm is still entitled to be paid the $8,000 balance remaining on the bill. However, without any property of value upon which a possessory lien can attach, collection of the bill against an out-of-state carrier may be considerably more difficult.

---

[1] *See, e.g.*, Va. Code Ann. § 46.2-644.01(F)(owner or lessee of truck or truck tractor responsible for entire vehicle combination)

§ 8:2 I'm Mad as Hell, and I'm Not Gonna Take This Anymore!

Sitting in on a Loss Prevention Conference (LPC) in Atlanta, Ga., I couldn't help but be reminded of that famous line shouted by newscaster Howard Beale in the classic 1976 movie *Network*. During the LPC meeting I listened to many trucking company executives, insurance claims representatives and cargo loss managers complain of what they perceived to be clear cases of overcharging and, in some cases, outright fraud by towing companies. I heard about a $10,000 charge for a 15-minute pull-out, and about a tow operator who gave intentionally misleading directions to a lost truck driver, sending him crashing into a low bridge — the vulture-like tow operator arriving moments later to recover his prey. Admit it: it's a small minority of the industry, but it happens.

I left the LPC conference with the impression that most motor carriers and claims reps have a very reasonable expectation with regard to heavy-duty recovery rates and will usually pay a well-documented invoice without complaint or hesitation. However — be they justified or not — many trucking company representatives and their insurers feel that they are frequently being price gouged for heavy-duty recovery jobs. The "price per pound" billing method seems to have particularly raised their dander. Another hot button is hourly charges for extra "standby" equipment that is hardly, if ever, used during a recovery operation. Like Beale in *Network*, many trucking firms are saying they "aren't gonna take it anymore" and have determined to challenge those invoices which they believe are unreasonable or excessive. That, of course, is their prerogative under the law.

However, tow operators have a distinct advantage whenever a heavy-duty recovery bill is disputed: In most cases, they have the tractor, trailer and load in their impound yard, and the law usually gives them the legal right to maintain possession of that property (a possessory lien) until the bill is paid. And, while a trucking company, shipper or insurance company haggles with the towing company about the invoice, the storage meter is ticking, sometimes to the tune of $100 or more per day.

Faced with that situation, a trucking company desiring to get its truck back on the road, or the shipper seeking its perishable cargo, has two choices. One, it can pay the disputed invoice, and then later sue the towing company for reimbursement of the alleged overcharge. Alternatively, the law in most states provides a mechanism by which the trucker or shipper can file a petition with the appropriate court, post a cash bond or surety in at least the full amount of the disputed invoice, and obtain a court order for possession of its property.

That process is called an action for recovery of personal property or "replevin."[1]

As an example of replevin, suppose that you perform a rollover job. You tow the tractor, trailer and load back to your storage facility. The bill is $10,000. The insurance claims adjuster, for whatever reason, thinks the bill should only be $6,000. If the two of you cannot come to an agreement, the insurance company can file a replevin action in the local court and obtain a court order commanding you to release the equipment and load. But, as a condition of obtaining such an order, the insurance company must pay into the court's registry at least the amount of your bill, in my example, $10,000. The cash bond substitutes for the equipment as your security for payment. Some states require that double the amount of the bill be posted.[2]

A writ of replevin allows the owner of the property to recover its property and cut off the storage meter while the parties work out their differences over the bill. If the parties still cannot come to an agreement, a trial must be held. There, after hearing testimony (usually from other towing operators), the court will decide what is fair and reasonable under all the circumstances. If, in my example, the court decides that $10,000 is the appropriate fee, the $10,000 is taken from the court's kitty and paid to the tow operator. If, on the other hand, the court decides that, say, $7,500 is a fair charge, $7,500 is paid over to the tow company and $2,500 of the bond is refunded to the insurance company.

If the sheriff comes knocking with a writ of replevin, the reputable tow operator needn't be concerned. Remember, in order for a writ of replevin to have been issued somebody deposited cash in the amount of the tow bill with the court clerk. The bond guarantees that funds are available to pay a reasonable fee for services rendered. That is what the tow operator is entitled to under the law, no more, no less. If a fair and reasonable fee was charged, there is nothing to worry about - the full amount of the invoice will be paid. Furthermore, in most states, the law provides for the payment of statutory interest on the amount eventually recovered against the bond.

---

[1] *See Weise v. Rivers Garage & Towing*, No. 97-P-0078, 1998 WL 684176 (Ohio Ct. App., September 30, 1998); *Equilease Corp. v. Neff Towing Service, Inc.*, 418 N.W.2d 754 (Neb. 1988); and *Navistar Financial Corp. v. Allen's Corner Garage and Towing Service, Inc.*, 505 N.E.2d 1321 (Ill. Ct. App. 1987)
[2] *See* Pa. R. Civ. P. 1075.3; 735 Ill. Comp. Stat. § 5/19-112; Mo. Sup. Ct. R. 99.06; and Conn. Gen. Stat. § 52-518

§ 8:3 Who Is Going To Pay?
The derelict vehicle problem

To fulfill its duty to remove wrecked, disabled and derelict vehicles from the roadways within its jurisdiction, a government entity will typically utilize private towing companies, either by means of a rotating call list or a bid contract. Pursuant to the rotation rules and regulations or the terms of the contract, the police department of the governmental entity dispatches a private towing company whenever towing service is needed. The towing company expects to be paid by the vehicle owner or insurer.

Ordinarily, either system works fine with regard to wrecked or disabled vehicles with value. The wrecked or disabled vehicle is towed in, then the owner or claims adjuster comes to the impound lot, pays the towing and storage fees and retrieves the vehicle. The police agency is happy because the obstructing vehicle was removed from the highway. The tow company is happy too, because it gets paid.

The rub comes with junk or derelict vehicles. If a towing firm is called to tow a derelict vehicle, the police agency is still happy (the vehicle is removed), but the tow company is not. It will not get paid for towing and vehicle storage. It will likely have to go through a lengthy and expensive administrative process to obtain a junk title. Then, especially if scrap metal prices are depressed, it will recover a small percentage of its total bill in the sale of the junk to a salvor.

Therein lies the fundamental problem with many towing systems utilizing private towing firms — no provision is made for payment of towing and storage fees when there is no owner or insurer to pay. And for the most part, law enforcement agencies are unsympathetic because under the terms of most towing agreements the towing service agrees to look solely to the owner of the vehicle or their insurer — not the governmental entity — for payment of towing and storage fees.

Over the years, I have spoken with countless state and local officials about the tremendous financial burden incurred in the towing and processing of derelict vehicles. Many officials consider it simply a "cost of doing business" with the government. Well, it shouldn't be — especially in our disposable society in which used-up automobiles are being dumped on the roadsides in ever-increasing numbers.

Using several different legal theories, some tow operators have successfully sued government entities to recover the costs associated with towing and processing junk vehicles. In the 1980s, in a highly-publicized case, the Town of Egg Harbor, New Jersey, agreed to pay a tow operator $750,000 to settle a lawsuit demanding payment for the towing and storage of abandoned vehicles.[1] But as happened in New Jersey, state and local legislatures are quick to enact laws or change the towing rules to limit or cut off the possibility of similar suits. Litigation is not the ultimate answer to the problem.

Several states have enacted statutes imposing sanctions on the registered owners of abandoned or unclaimed vehicles, i.e., fines or revocation of driver's licenses or vehicle registrations.[2] Such laws, although proven effective in some instances, have had minimal impact on the overall problem.

The issue of derelict vehicles really boils down to this: Who is going to pay to remove junk vehicles from the streets of our nation? As it is now, in most jurisdictions the costs are being borne by one of two groups. In a towing system without regulated towing and rates, the tow operators often pass along the cost of processing abandoned vehicles to those who do not pay. In that situation, those who pay for towing and storage are subsidizing the cost of removing abandoned vehicles from the roadways. Where towing and storage fees are regulated or fixed by contract, it is the tow operators who are subsidizing the cost of removing derelict vehicles.

The abandoned vehicle issue requires special consideration. First and foremost, governments should have a *separate* agreement or rule for the towing of derelict vehicles. That avoids the improper, and perhaps illegal, subsidization referenced above.

Second, state laws should provide a method for the expedited disposal of junk and derelict vehicles. If junkers could immediately be sold to a parts yard or scrap metal facility without the necessity of time-consuming, costly paperwork and public auction sales, a private hauler might be attracted to a contract to remove derelict vehicles.

Finally, governments must recognize that the derelict vehicle problem is *everybody's* problem. If a private contract for hauling junk vehicles is not financially feasible, then *everybody* should pay a portion of the cost of removing and processing those eyesores. That is accomplished by allocating a portion of the government's budget to pay for the service. If it requires an increase in taxes or license tag fees to cover the expense, so be it. The removal and processing of derelict vehicles benefits the general public; therefore, the service should be funded by tax dollars. That is true whether the government performs the service with its own trucks, personnel and storage facilities, or it is handled by a private contractor. Tax dollars are often used to pay private companies for certain highway maintenance, such as sign or guardrail installation and street cleaning. Why can't tax dollars be used to pay private towing companies to tow and process junk vehicles?

---

[1] *Little John's Towing v. Egg Harbor Township* (N.J. Super. Ct., Atlantic County, 1985)

[2] *See, e.g.*, Fla. Stat. § 705.103(4)

§ 8:4 A Good Start
Attorney must pay $18,000 of storage

An Indiana court ruling gives new meaning to a well-known lawyer joke.

Stanley Levandoski operates a small towing service in northwest Indiana. On September 30, 1995, he was dispatched to the scene of an intersection accident by the La Porte County Police. A Dodge van had been broadsided by a truck. Levandoski towed the wrecked van to his storage lot.

The owners of the van, Franklin and Darlene Brown, were seriously injured in the accident. They hired Timothy Kelly, a personal injury attorney in Dyer, Ind., to represent them in a lawsuit against the at-fault trucking company. Within a few days, Kelly called Levandoski to inquire about the Browns' wrecked van. Kelly told Levandoski to "hold on to it" because he needed the van as evidence. He asked Levandoski to send him a copy of the bill. Kelly also told Levandoski he would be paid when the case was over.

The Browns' case dragged on for many years. Over that time, Kelly's office called Levandoski on four or five occasions to request updated copies of the storage bill. Each time Levandoski generated bills and forwarded them to the attorney. When the trial finally got underway in October 1999, the storage charges totaled $18,827.

In his summation to the jury, Kelly asked that the Browns be awarded almost $1 million in damages, including Levandoski's storage bill. The jury came back with a disappointing $132,000 verdict. After taking his 40 percent contingency fee and paying the sizeable litigation expenses — all except the vehicle storage bill — Kelly gave what little was left to the Browns. When Levandoski later requested payment of the storage bill, Kelly ignored him. At one point, Levandoski told Kelly he would accept $500 and the title to the vehicle just to settle the matter. Kelly refused. Aggravated and angry, Levandoski hired his own lawyer and sued attorney Kelly for his entire $18,827 bill.

Kelly vigorously fought the storage fee claim. He contended that he never had a binding contract with Levandoski for the storage of the van. He said that he was only acting as an agent for the Browns, therefore they should pay the vehicle storage fees out of the relative pittance they received after shelling out Kelly's contingency fee and litigation costs. Kelly further insisted that if the Browns were not responsible for the bill, then the La Porte County Police should pay it since they initially called Levandoski to tow the Browns' van from the accident scene.

The jury in the storage fee case flatly rejected attorney Kelly's arguments and awarded Levandoski his entire $18,827, plus interest. On April 18, 2005, in the case of *Kelly v. Levandoski*,[1] the Indiana Court of Appeals upheld the judgment against Kelly.

According to the appellate court, resolution of the dispute boiled down to the basics of contract law: offer and acceptance. Kelly's request for Levandoski to hold the van, to send copies of the bill, and to wait for his payment until the litigation was over, could reasonably be construed as an offer to form a contract for storage. Levandoski accepted that offer by sending the bills as requested and holding the van longer than he would have because he believed he would be paid. As Levandoski testified, "All I can say is that I sure as heck would not have stored this vehicle from October 6, 1995 to October 20, 1999, four years, if it were not for the representations and instructions by Mr. Kelly!"

Although Kelly was undisputedly acting as the Browns' attorney and agent, the court held that he could still be personally responsible for the storage deal he made on their behalf. Under Indiana law, attorneys are responsible for their clients' litigation expenses unless they expressly disclaim personal liability. Kelly admitted that he never told Levandoski that the Browns, not he, would be responsible for payment of the storage fees.

The court also addressed Kelly's claim that the police department was responsible for the vehicle storage charges. Kelly asserted that there was no additional benefit, or "consideration," to him from Levandoski because Levandoski was already obligated to provide his services for the police department. The court saw it differently.

Even though the police department initially requested Levandoski's services, within a week Kelly had directly made his own arrangements for the storage of the van. He asked that the vehicle continue to be held because he needed it for the lawsuit. According to the court, that request, followed by Levandoski holding the van for four years, provided the consideration for a legally binding contract between Kelly and Levandoski.

So ... what do you call a personal injury lawyer ordered to pay over $18,000 in vehicle storage fees? A good start.

---

[1] 825 N.E. 2d 850 (Ind. Ct. App. 2005)

§ 8:5 Sue 'Em All, Let the Judge Sort 'Em Out
Collecting heavy-duty recovery bills

When dispatched by a law enforcement agency to a heavy-duty rollover accident, you respond immediately with expensive equipment and skilled workers. Ordinarily, you do not know who owns the wrecked truck, who may have a lien on the vehicle, the nature of the cargo, whether the vehicle or cargo is insured, or—most importantly—how you are going to get paid.

But you go anyway. A difficult truck incident can take many hours and require the use of multiple wreckers and tow trucks, rented equipment (forklifts, dump trucks, etc.) and extra laborers. The total charges, including out-of-pocket expenses, can easily exceed $10,000. You sweat while working the recovery, not just from the manual labor but from fear that you might not get paid.

But you do the work. And you probably will get paid because most states, by statute, provide towing companies with possessory liens. (See § 4:1). Those laws allow towing firms to keep possession of vehicles that they have recovered until they receive payment. Some statutes also provide a lien on the cargo. (See § 4:4). A statutory lien is a powerful collection tool, and a tow operator's primary source of protection: "If you want your vehicle or cargo back, pay me."

However, a possessory lien is only as good as the property being held in lieu of payment. Consider a tractor-trailer hauling a load of glass products that rolls over and burns, scattering the broken cargo. The tow operator may have a bill of $15,000 (including pay-outs) for recovery of the vehicles and cleanup of the cargo. Sitting in his storage yard is the charred hull of the tractor, what little is left of the trailer, and a small mountain of busted glass. Nobody wants any of it. In that instance, the legal right to hold the worthless vehicle and cargo does the tow operator absolutely no good.

Without the leverage of possession of property with some value, getting paid can be much more difficult. Frequently, all the players — the owner of the truck, the owner/lessor of the trailer, the shipper, the consignee, the lienholder, the broker, and their respective insurers — deny liability and point fingers at one another. Next, they want the charges divided three ways: Truck, Trailer and Cargo. Then, Trailer says that Truck is responsible for all costs associated with the Trailer; Truck says it's not paying for the cargo cleanup, and Cargo says it doesn't have insurance to cover cleanup costs. It can be a bigger mess than the wreck itself.

Through compromise and cooperation of all the parties, disputes over heavy-duty recovery bills are usually worked out amicably. If not, there is always the courthouse.

I have handled many lawsuits over heavy-duty recovery charges. There is an old Marine credo: "Kill 'em all, let God sort 'em out." That pretty much sums up my strategy in those cases. All the entities involved are made defendants so the court can allocate responsibility. Since a towing company does not have a written, enforceable service contract, the suit is based on *quantum meruit*. Pursuant to that legal theory, if you provide services that benefit someone else, you are entitled to payment of the reasonable value of your services, even if the other person or company did not specifically request your assistance. The owner of a wrecked truck has an obligation to remove it from the highway. The tow company providing that service is entitled to payment.

The charges relating to cargo cleanup are often a sticking point. In a rollover incident, the cost of salvaging the load frequently constitutes the bulk of the charges, sometimes 75-80 percent of the final bill. If the cargo is completely destroyed in the wreck, e.g., perishable food products, the cargo insurer might pay the casualty loss but ignore the towing firm's cleanup bill. In that event, the owner of the cargo — either the shipper or consignee — should be sued for those charges. If cargo is spilled on the highway, its owner has a legal duty to clean it up, regardless of who spilled it. If a tow company provides that cleanup service for the cargo owner, it is entitled to payment.

Three practical tips regarding litigation for wreck recovery charges: First, you can file suit in the county where the accident occurred and "make them come to you." That is a tremendous strategical advantage in any litigation. Second, you need to know who to sue. The names of the owners or lessees of the vehicles are generally easy to ascertain. The owner of the cargo is determined by the bill of lading. Depending on the terms of that transportation contract, title transfers from the shipper to the consignee at either the loading dock or at the delivery point.

Thus, when working a rollover it is critical that you obtain as much information as possible about the shipment, shipper and destination. If possible, get a copy of the bill of lading. Finally, litigation of this type can be expensive. Legal fees can render any court-ordered payment for naught. (See 8.7). Your state law may allow an award of attorney's fees plus your recovery bill. If not, you should seek an attorney who will handle your case on a contingency fee basis.

§ 8:6 Deadbeat Driver Dodges License Suspension
Kentucky court nixes tow firm's
Financial Responsibility claim

In May 5, 2002, Joshua Grimes wrecked a borrowed 1991 Ford Ranger in Frankfort, Kentucky. The Kentucky State Police (KSP) investigated the accident. The KSP dispatched Holbrook Towing from its local towing rotation list. Holbrook towed the Ranger and stored it at its impound yard in Frankfort.

The Ranger, which was totaled, carried no insurance and went unclaimed by its owner. Eventually, Holbrook Towing filed suit against Grimes and the vehicle owner in small claims court for its towing and storage bill. It received a judgment in the amount of $1,500, however, that judgment went unpaid.

Mike Penn, owner of Holbrook Towing, then turned to the Kentucky Financial Responsibility Law.[1] That law, similar to the financial responsibility laws in other states, generally provides for the suspension of the driver's license of any person who fails to pay a judgment arising out of a motor vehicle accident.

The law works like this: Following a motor vehicle accident, motorists must demonstrate that they have the ability to pay for any loss or injury that they may have caused. The person responsible for the accident must file a statement with the state motor vehicle department showing proof of liability insurance or proof that they have otherwise satisfied any claims relating to the accident. If the vehicle owner has no insurance or does not pay the claim directly, the injured party can sue the responsible vehicle owner and obtain a judgment for their loss or injuries. If that judgment goes unpaid for 60 days, the state motor vehicle department can, upon request of the injured party holding the judgment, suspend the driver's license of the person at fault until the judgment is paid.

As a practical matter, if the judgment amount is not exorbitant, the liable party will often pay off the outstanding judgment in order to restore his or her driving privileges. Insurance companies have long used the financial responsibility laws and the potential of driver's license suspension as a powerful tool to collect their subrogation claims against uninsured vehicle owners.

Penn looked at the Kentucky law and thought, "I've got an unpaid judgment for towing and storage fees that are the direct result of a motor vehicle accident. Why shouldn't I be able to take advantage of the state's power to suspend Grimes' license to help me collect my judgment?"

He submitted the proper form to the Kentucky department of motor vehicles, but his request was rejected. So he filed a lawsuit seeking to determine whether his judgment for towing and storage fees arising from the towing of a wrecked motor vehicle might be used to trigger the sanctions under the financial responsibility statute.

The court case turned on the precise definition of a "judgment." The Kentucky statute, like almost every state's financial responsibility law, applies to:

> any judgment . . . upon a cause of action arising out of the ownership, maintenance or use of any motor vehicle . . . or damages because of injury to or destruction of property . . .

Is a judgment for the fees charged for towing and storing a vehicle involved in an accident a judgment arising out of the "use" of a vehicle for damages that were incurred "because of" the destruction of the vehicle? That was the question facing the Kentucky Court of Appeals in the case of *Holbrook Towing and Recovery v. Commonwealth*.[2]

On February 9, 2007, that appellate court ruled that Holbrook's judgment for towing and storage fees was not a "judgment" for purposes of the financial responsibility statute. The court said that the law was intended to "provide compensation for innocent persons injured through faulty operation of motor vehicles," but that Holbrook was not such a person. The court noted that there was no damage or loss to any property owned by Holbrook. "Holbrook's loss entails compensation for services rendered – purely a matter of contract law arising from Holbrook's responding to a call from the Kentucky State Police," the court ruled.

Holbrook Towing pointed out that it did not have a contract with the vehicle owner. The towing companies on the KSP rotation list are called upon to provide services without the benefit of a contract or agreement with the vehicle owner. According to Holbrook, there was a direct connection between the accident and the services that he rendered. The court could not agree: "The interpretation of the statute urged by Holbrook is simply too far a stretch of logic that is contradicted by the literal language of the statute."

In its opinion, the court of appeals recognized that towing companies perform a valuable public service in removing wrecked vehicles from the roadways of the state and suggested that the Kentucky legislature "could easily amend [the law] to include a cause of action for a towing company to be properly covered by the 'Financial Responsibility Law' to satisfy such a judgment in the future."

---

[1] Ky. Rev. Stat. § 187.290, *et seq.*
[2] No. 2005-CA-002436-MR, 2007 WL 419667 (Ky. Ct. App., Feb. 9, 2009)

§ 8:7 A No-Win Proposition?
Legal fees make pursuing some cases financially unfeasible

Litigation is fraught with uncertainty. Until the verdict or judgment is announced, nobody is sure who will win. However, due to the "American Rule" regarding attorney's fees, there are some cases that, from a financial standpoint, a towing company can never win.

The American Rule provides that each party to litigation is responsible for their own attorney's fees.[1] It contrasts with the "English Rule," common in other nations, under which the losing party pays the winning party's attorney's fees. The American Rule is based on the premise that our society would suffer if a person was unwilling to file a meritorious lawsuit out of fear that, if he lost, he would have to pay the opposing party's legal expenses.

There are exceptions to the Rule. Some statutes shift the responsibility for attorney's fees to the losing party, e.g., the civil rights laws. Parties to contracts can agree in advance for the assessment of fees in the event of litigation. Litigants may be ordered to pay an opponent's attorney's fees if they commit a fraud on the court or act in bad faith. But in the vast majority of U.S. court cases, each person pays their own attorney.

Now consider the American Rule in the context of two fairly common towing cases: Case #1: A towing company performs a difficult rollover recovery and demands payment of $25,000 before releasing its lien on the truck, trailer and cargo. The disgruntled insurance company turns around and sues the towing company, alleging that it was overcharged by $10,000. Case #2: A towing company impounds a late-model automobile. Nobody retrieves the car, so it is processed as an unclaimed vehicle in accordance with the state abandoned vehicle law and advertised for a lien foreclosure auction. No outside bidders appear for the auction, so the towing company acquires title in lieu of its $1,000 towing lien. A week later, the towing company sells the car for $20,000. A month later, a bank holding a $15,000 security interest files a lawsuit claiming that the towing company failed to give proper notice of the auction.

Neither claim is covered by liability insurance, so legal defense fees will not be paid by the towing firm's insurance company. Both could involve months of pre-trial discovery, dozens of depositions, hours of legal research, and days of trial.

Assume that the towing defendant in Case #1 proceeds to trial and the jury rules 100 percent in its favor, finding that $25,000 was a fair and reasonable charge for the recovery job. The tow company is the big winner, right? Not necessarily. Under the American Rule, its legal fees cannot be charged to the losing insurance company; the tow company must pay them. If it pays $15,000 in attorney's fees, its "net" judgment for the $25,000 recovery job is only $10,000. Financially, it would have been better off to have reduced its $25,000 bill by the disputed $10,000 before the lawsuit was filed.

Similarly, in Case #2, the tow operator earned a nice $19,000 profit from the resale of the vehicle. If he vigorously fights the lawsuit and is successful in getting the lienholder's claim dismissed, has he really won if he has to pay $10,000-$15,000 in attorney's fees?

Even if he did nothing wrong, the prudent tow operator might have promptly offered the bank $10,000 of his windfall profit in the chance of resolving the dispute before the attorney's clock started ticking.

Granted, there are often motivations beyond the bottom line for defending such a case. Sometimes tow companies want to set a favorable legal precedent. In other cases, emotions and "principles" come into play. I have had many clients tell me, "I'd rather pay you than that #&@^!% insurance company/bank/vehicle owner!"

But if the only issue is money, other than to kowtow to intimidating insurance companies and lienholders, what can be done to avoid the effect of the American Rule? First, as noted above, a statute or contract providing for the assessment of fees against the losing party trumps the American Rule. Towing associations might push for legislation providing for the payment of attorney's fees by the losing party in litigation over towing charges or lien foreclosure sales. Towing firms should incorporate attorney's fee provisions in their towing invoices and release forms.

Another solution is to stay out of court, thereby avoiding the attendant legal costs. When faced with the prospect of expensive litigation, particularly if the amount in dispute is relatively small, tow company owners should consider dispute resolution alternatives like arbitration or mediation.

A 2001 New Hampshire law establishes a procedure by which a person who wishes to challenge the reasonableness of any fee charged for a truck accident recovery may request a non-judicial review by the commissioner of safety.[2] Good law. A national towing organization once discussed a traveling arbitration panel comprised of recovery experts to resolve heavy-duty recovery bill disputes.

Good idea.

Some will say that I am talking myself out of a job. Perhaps. But like most trial lawyers, I want my clients to be satisfied with the outcome of any litigation. Unfortunately, due to the American Rule, some court cases leave even successful towing defendants unavoidably dissatisfied.

---

[1] *Alyeska Pipeline Serv. Co. v. Wilderness Soc'y*, 421 U.S. 240 (1975)
[2] N.H. Rev. Stat. § 262.35-a

§ 8:8 Salvage Vehicle Abandonment by Insurance Companies
"Insurance dumping" costs towing industry millions of dollars

A 10-year-old vehicle runs off the road, rolls over several times, and ends up in a deep ravine. The recovery takes several hours, requiring two tow trucks and some extra personnel. The destroyed vehicle is hoisted from the gorge and transported to the towing firm's impound yard.

The charge for the recovery is $800. After two weeks of storage, the total bill is over $1,000. But the salvage value of the car is less than $300. The towing company might receive a letter from the vehicle owner's collision insurance company that reads something like this:

> *Attached please find the certificate of title on the above-captioned automobile. We are abandoning this vehicle to you in lieu of payment inasmuch as the charges exceed the value of the salvage.*

The inequitable practice of vehicle salvage abandonment by automobile insurance companies, often referred to as "insurance dumping," is widespread. Auto insurers are quick to retrieve late-model wrecks with substantial salvage value, but the burnouts and older model totals are often ignored and abandoned. The problem is worsened when the claims adjuster will not provide the towing firm with the certificate of title, forcing the towing company to initiate expensive foreclosure proceedings to dispose of the junk vehicle. The Towing and Recovery Association of America once estimated that insurance dumping results in annual losses of close to $50 million to the towing industry as a whole.[1]

Insurance dumping is both unfair and illegal. Towing companies are in the business of providing the services of vehicle recovery, towing and storage. The value of those services is completely unrelated to the value of the vehicle recovered. A towing company incurs the same overhead and labor costs to recover and store a late-model Cadillac as it does to recover and store a 1986 Chevy. When a dentist pulls a tooth, the patient's dental insurance company would never ask the dentist to keep the tooth as payment for his services. Yet auto insurers routinely abandon vehicle salvage in lieu of payment for the reasonable value of towing services rendered.

The standard physical damage auto insurance policy [Harco Commercial Auto Physical Damage Coverage (ISO) Form] states that in the event of a crash a vehicle owner has a duty to "[t]ake all reasonable steps to protect the covered auto from further damage."

That duty includes removal from the accident site and secured storage. Because an auto policy requires the insured car owner to take reasonable steps to protect a wrecked auto from further loss, and because that same policy requires the insurer to pay reasonable expenses incurred by the insured in fulfilling that contractual obligation, the insurer is legally obligated to pay reasonable towing and storage fees. In 2008, in the case of *Spurgeon v. Certain Underwriters of Lloyd's, London*,[2] a federal judge in West Virginia relied upon the "duty to protect" clause of an insurance policy in ordering a property damage insurer to pay over two years of storage fees on a wrecked tractor and trailer.

In liability auto insurance contracts, insurers promise to indemnify their policyholders for all damages and expenses caused by their negligent actions. Those insurance contract provisions have been construed to impose a duty on liability insurance companies to pay reasonable auto towing and storage fees incurred by the victims of their insureds' car crashes. The towing company providing that service is a third-party beneficiary of the "at fault" driver's liability policy.

Whenever possible, a towing firm should obtain a written agreement from the vehicle owner, or the owner's legal representative, providing that the towing company will forebear collection efforts against the vehicle owner and continue to preserve the salvage, in return for an assignment of the vehicle owner's contractual right to reimbursement of towing/storage fees from their insurance company. Such an agreement will provide the towing company with a direct cause of action against an insurance company in the event litigation becomes necessary.

Finally, about half of the states have enacted statutes or insurance department regulations designed to protect towing firms from the insidious practice of insurance dumping.[3] Those laws require insurers to pick up insured salvage vehicles, and pay reasonable towing and storage fees regardless of the salvage value of the vehicle, under penalty of administrative sanctions. Furthermore, if the insurance company's refusal to pay an outstanding tow bill is willful and in bad faith, a tow operator might recover three times the amount of the outstanding bill under state laws forbidding bad faith settlement practices on the part of insurance companies.

There is no reason to get "dumped on" by auto insurance companies. Unless you willingly agree to discount or compromise your bill to settle a claim, you are entitled to full payment of the reasonable value of all services provided on behalf of insured drivers.

[1] *National News*, Towing and Recovery Ass'n of America, May 1984
[2] No. Civ.-A 3:05-cv-100, 2008 WL 53111 (N.D.W.Va., January 2, 2008)
[3] *See, e.g.*, Cal. Veh. Code § 22524.5; Mo. Rev. Stat. § 304.156(13); N.Y. McKinney's Insurance Law, § 3412; Nev. Rev. Stat. § 108.300; Tex. Occ. Code Ann. § 2303.156(b); N.C. Admin. Code, tit. 11 § 4.0418; Bulletin #3-84, *Abandoned Automobile Salvage*, S.C. Dept. of Insurance, September 11, 1984)(copy on file with author); Letter from S. David Childers, Director of Insurance, State of Arizona, to All Property & Casualty Insurers and Adjusters, March 25, 1985 (copy on file with author); and Letter from William H. Inman, Commissioner of Insurance, State of Tennessee, to All Authorized Property and Casualty Insurers, October 3, 1986 (copy on file with author)

Chapter 9   Miscellaneous

§ 9:1 You Can Fool Some of the People Some of the Time....... 196

§ 9:2 Cutthroat Competition.. 198

§ 9:3 Scanning for Dollars... 200

§ 9:4 The Truth about AAA.. 203

§ 9:5 I'll Show You Mine if You'll Show Me Yours.................... 205

§ 9:6 In the Zone 207

§ 9:7 The Taxman Cometh... 209

§ 9:8 The Unfairest of Them All.. 211

§ 9:9 Vehicle Damage Claims.. 214

§ 9:10 New Registration Program for Interstate Towing........... 216

§ 9:11 Guns and Tow Trucks 218

§ 9:12 Finding a Competent Attorney....................................... 221

§ 9:13 Government-Operated Vehicle Storage Facilities 223

§ 9:14 It Makes No Cents: Payment in Pennies........................ 225

§ 9:1 You Can Fool Some of the People Some of the Time

Bob had been in the towing business in his small Tennessee town for over 20 years. He operated both heavy- and light-duty modern towing equipment, had a secured towing yard and enjoyed a good reputation in the community.

Business was good but Bob had a nagging problem: Aubrey's Towing. Aubrey's Towing was a fly-by-night company across town that ran one dilapidated tow truck with no markings, without proper licenses, registration or insurance. Aubrey could not keep his auto club accounts because of poor service and customer complaints but he was always trying to steal Bob's accounts by undercutting Bob's tow rates and badmouthing Bob and his company.

The new phone books came out and Bob immediately flipped to the Yellow Pages® to check out his new ad and those of his competitors. What he saw set his blood to boiling: Aubrey's half-page ad included graphics of small tow trucks, car carriers and a large tow truck. The ad said, "LARGE OR SMALL — WE TOW'EM ALL!" At the bottom of the ad were reproductions of various motor club and trade association logos, clearly inferring Aubrey's affiliation.

Bob had a friend call Aubrey's Towing asking for a large tow truck. Aubrey said the big tow truck "was all tied up" and the caller was referred to an out-of-town towing service. When asked about motor club service, Aubrey said that the contract was still being finalized but that the customer could turn in an Aubrey's Towing receipt to his motor club for reimbursement.

Bob sued Aubrey's Towing under the state Consumer Protection Act which prohibits, among other things, (1) representing that goods or services are of certain quality if they are not, (2) disparaging the goods, services or business of another by false or misleading representations of fact and (3) advertising services with intent not to sell them as advertised.

Bob alleged that the ads for Aubrey's Towing were "grossly misleading" and that it had engaged in deceptive and unfair trade practices in violation of the law. He asked for triple the amount of his actual damages (as provided for in the consumer protection law), a declaratory order and an injunction to prevent future violations of the law.

In *Colyer v. Trew*,[1] the Tennessee state court of appeals held that Bob was not entitled to monetary damages because he was not a "consumer" as the term intended in the consumer protection laws. "We think it is clear that [the consumer protection laws are] for the benefit of the consuming public...and is not designed as a tool to enforce unfair competition between competitive or individuals," said the court.

Even though Bob could not pursue his claim for monetary damages, the court held that he could obtain an injunction to prevent further violations of the law by his competitor. "The purposes of the Act can be achieved only through its enforcement ...It is logical that anyone affected by the violation of the Act, even though he is not a consumer, should be permitted to have the actions of the violator declared unlawful and enjoined," concluded the court.

---

[1] 1982 WL 4419 (Tenn. Ct. App., February 12, 1982)

§ 9:2 Cutthroat Competition

Terry ran a good towing operation. After 15 years in business he had developed an impressive customer list, including state and local police departments, as well as the local university. He had a reputation for quality service at a reasonable price.

Although he enjoyed a thriving business, Terry had a dark secret: a criminal past. He didn't intentionally hide his felony record from his customers — it just never came up and, because the crime was completely unrelated to the towing business, Terry didn't see the need to make an issue out of it.

A few years ago, a new competitor, Nick, did feel the need to make an issue of the criminal conviction. Nick got wind of Terry's criminal history and, seizing on what he saw as a competitive advantage, began to aggressively solicit Terry's customers. He urged them to stop using "the convict's towing service" and use his company instead. In fact, he embarked on a virtual vendetta to make sure that every one of Terry's customers knew about Terry's illicit past. Nick broadcast the underlying details about Terry's conviction far and wide. At a local restaurant, he screamed at one of Terry's customers, hollering that the customer should not be using Terry's Towing. At another time, Nick threatened a university transit employee that he would take his scandalous information to the university chancellor if Terry's towing service was not immediately removed from the university's tow call list.

Terry never denied his criminal past and most of his accounts, happy with the quality of towing service he provided, continued doing business with him despite Nick's ranting. Nevertheless, Terry's revenues began to wane. Certain that Nick's backstabbing antics were having a negative impact on his business, Terry filed suit against Nick.

In his lawsuit, Terry claimed that Nick had "tortiously interfered" with his contracts to provide towing services. He claimed that Nick had intentionally and improperly interfered with the long-standing business relationships that he had with his customers.

In his defense, Nick said, "Aw, heck, that's just good ol' All-American competition. Besides, Terry admits he's a convicted felon, so how can I be held liable for simply telling the truth about my competitor?"

The trial judge threw Terry's case out of court. She agreed with Nick that in order for there to be any harm to Terry, the statements made by Nick would have to be untrue. "We have free speech in this country," the trial judge said. Since Terry was indeed a convicted felon, the case was dismissed by the judge before it got to the jury.

Terry appealed to the state court of appeals. In an opinion issued on March 7, 2001, that court reversed the decision of the trial court and sent the case back for trial. In *Hayes v. Advanced Towing Services, Inc.*,[1] the appellate court stated the general law on the claim of tortious interference:

> One who intentionally and improperly interferes with the performance of a contract . . . between another and a third person by inducing or otherwise causing the third person not to perform the contract, is subject to liability to the other ...

Whether a person's interfering conduct is "improper" depends on a number of factors, said the court, including the nature of his conduct, his motive, the nature of the contract interfered with, and the balance between freedom of competition and the contractual interests of another.

"Generally speaking, one business can solicit business from a competitor's client; however, there are limits," said the court. "The real question is whether the actor's conduct is fair and reasonable under the circumstances." Because some jurors might have found Nick's conduct to be unreasonable, the appellate court determined that the case should have gone to trial. "After all [Nick's] conduct does not fit within the traditional concepts of business inasmuch as it may have caused [some customers'] decisions to be based on factors other than economics or quality of service."

With regard to Nick's defense of truthfulness, the court said, "[A]lthough a truthful statement may be less likely to be considered improper, we are not disposed to create a per se rule that under all circumstances an actor is justified in interfering with either a contractual relationship or a business expectancy so long as the interference is in the nature of a truthful statement." In other words, just because a statement is true, the law does not give a person the right to freely disclose the information under all circumstances without exposure to civil liability. That, said the justices, "would plainly be contrary to the law."

I suppose the moral to this story is if you can't find anything good to say about somebody, best not say anything at all.

---

[1] 40 S.W.3d 800 (Ark. Ct. App. 2001)

§ 9:3 Scanning for Dollars

Is it unlawful for a tow truck driver to monitor police radio channels with an electronic scanner and then, after overhearing a traffic officer dispatched to the scene of an auto accident, proceed to the scene of the accident and solicit towing work from the owners of the vehicles involved in the collision?

The Wire Interception and Interception of Oral Communications Act ("the Wiretap Act")[1] generally provides that it is unlawful for any person to use any electronic, mechanical, or other device to intercept any oral communication. There are, however, many exceptions to the Wiretap Act's prohibitions. One rather obvious exception is a radio communication that is intended for the use of the general public.[2] It is not a crime for me to intercept the radio signal of my favorite country music station on my car radio.

Another exception provides that it is not unlawful for any person to "intercept any radio communication which is transmitted ... by any governmental, law enforcement, ... or public safety communications system, including police and fire, and readily accessible to the general public ..."[3] Thus, it is perfectly legal to listen-in on police and fire radio channels with an electronic scanner. But the inquiry does not end there.

Another federal law, the Communications Act of 1934,[4] provides that "[n]o person having received any intercepted radio communication or having become acquainted with its contents ... shall ... use such communication (or any information therein contained) for his own benefit...."[5] Any person willfully violating the Communications Act for "commercial advantage or private financial gain" is subject to a fine of $50,000 and/or two years imprisonment.[6] A "commercial advantage" violator is also exposed to a civil lawsuit with potential liability of up to $100,000 for each violation.[7] Although most of the current prosecutions under the Communications Act involve theft of satellite cable television programming, the scope of that law is not limited to cable television piracy.

The Federal Communications Commission (FCC), the federal agency charged with enforcing the Communications Act, has rendered an opinion that while the *mere interception* of a law enforcement radio broadcast by means of an electronic scanner is not unlawful, the *use* of that broadcast for personal benefit or gain is a violation of that law. In a "Fact Sheet" issued in 1997,[8] the FCC stated as follows:

An example of using an intercepted call for beneficial use in violation of [the Communications Act] would be someone listening to accident reports on a police channel and then sending his or her tow truck to the reported accident in order to obtain business.

Despite that FCC proclamation, to my knowledge no tow truck operator has ever been convicted or sued for violating the Communications Act as a consequence of monitoring a police scanner and then proceeding to the scene of the accident to solicit towing work. There may be some practical reasons for the absence of "wreck chasing" cases.

First, it would seem to be difficult to prove such a case. Without a confession by the defendant tow truck driver, or the testimony of an employee or co-worker that the defendant responded to an accident scene based on information he obtained from a scanner, a prosecution would be based on shaky circumstantial evidence. Another practical consideration is the apparent lack of motivation on the part of the federal law enforcement agencies to prosecute police radio-scanning tow truck drivers. The U.S. Attorney's Office has wide discretion with regard to which violations of federal law it chooses to prosecute. Most federal prosecutors have better things to do than indict tow truck drivers eavesdropping on police communications.

Secondly, although, as noted above, the law provides for an award of civil damages arising out of an unlawful interception, the Wiretap Act states that a civil suit must be filed by the person "whose … communication is intercepted."[9] In the case of a tow operator's unlawful use of a police scanner, that would be the police agency whose frequency is monitored.

But unlike a cable TV broadcaster whose programs are pirated and rebroadcast, a police department suffers no financial loss from a tow operator's unlawful conduct. Although injunctive relief is available in a civil suit, what are the odds that a police chief will pursue a difficult-to-prove civil lawsuit against a tow operator just to stop him or her from using a police scanner for profit?

Note, however, the difference between monitoring a police channel and listening-in on a *competitor's* radio frequency. If a tow operator is intercepting his competitor's base-to-truck radio dispatch and then "jumping" the calls by beating his competitor's driver to the location of the call, the competitor — the person whose communication is intercepted — would have a legitimate civil action for both an injunction and money damages.[10]

[1] 18 U.S.C.A. § 2511, *et seq.*
[2] 18 U.S.C.A. § 2511(g)(ii)(I)
[3] 18 U.S.C.A. § 2511(g)(ii)(II)
[4] 47 U.S.C.A. § 151, *et seq.*
[5] 47 U.S.C.A. § 605(a)
[6] 47 U.S.C.A. § 605(e)(2)
[7] 47 U.S.C.A. § 605(e)(3)(C)(ii)
[8] Interception and Divulgence of Radio Communications, *Fact Sheet* (Federal Communications Commission, January 1997)(copy on file with author)
[9] 18 U.S.C.A. § 2520
[10] *See, e.g., Cafarelli v. Yancy*, 226 F.3d 492 (6th Cir. 2000)(alleged interception of taxicab radio calls by competitor)

§ 9:4 The Truth About AAA

"Isn't it price-fixin' or something?" He was a AAA contractor and had telephoned me to complain about the low rates he is paid for towing and service calls he performs for the world's largest motor club.

In an attempt to show how AAA pricing does not constitute a violation of the antitrust laws, I told him about the time I was presenting a legal seminar at the annual convention of a statewide towing association in a Midwestern state. My presentation was early in the morning. Later in the day, four of the towing association members, who were also AAA-contracted tow operators, approached me.

"We've scheduled a meeting this afternoon with the AAA road service manager at AAA's regional office down the street. We want an increase in our service call and tow rates," they said. "Could you go with us?"

I told them that I'd be happy to attend the meeting but, because I was completely unfamiliar with the particulars of their AAA contracts or their costs of operation, I could not speak on their behalf. They said they would like for me to go with them anyway, so I tagged along.

We arrived at the AAA office and were escorted to the back of the building where the road service manager had a tiny office. He greeted us warmly, pulled five more chairs into his office and offered us coffee. The extra seating took up all the floor space. Without being introduced, I squeezed around the desk and quietly sat off to the side while the four tow operators sat directly in front, their knees touching the front of the manager's desk. The Man in charge of the AAA contractors propped his feet up on his desk, leaned back in his chair with his fingers laced behind his head, smiled broadly and asked, "Now, what can I do for you boys today?"

The tow operators, hats in their hands, told the service manager how their costs of operation had increased over the recent years. They compared their current insurance and fuel costs with those of two or three years prior. They adequately explained the need for the newer, safer but more expensive towing equipment, and they told him how they were spending money to properly train their drivers in towing safety.

The Man, still reared back in his chair, listened intently with his brow furrowed, nodding from time to time in apparent concern for their financial woes. The towmen then complained that despite the rapid increases in their costs of operation, the AAA contract rates had not increased. I recall that the rate was surprisingly low.

They finished their spiel by asking for a rate increase. The room went quiet for what seemed like 10 minutes but was probably only 15 or 20 seconds.

"You boys finished?" asked The Man. They all nodded silently.

The front legs of The Man's chair slammed down onto the concrete floor with a loud bang, startling everybody, including me. He leaned forward across his desk, the big smile draining from his face.

"Let me tell you boys something. This ain't no f——ing marriage. If you don't like what I'm paying you — quit!" he said bluntly. With his left hand he reached down and pulled a yellow legal pad out of one of the drawers of his desk and tossed it towards the now wide-eyed tow operators. The names and phone numbers of a dozen or so towing companies were handwritten in a list on the top of the pad.

"See that list? Those are all towing companies that want your contracts and are willing to tow for me at the same rates that I'm paying you now." The Man stared at the towmen for a few seconds, then he leaned back in his chair, smiling broadly again. "So, is there anything else I can do for you boys today?"

In the parking lot outside that AAA office, those tow operators were understandably angry. "What an SOB!" they fumed. "The nerve of that guy!" They turned to me. "What do you think of that?!" I agreed that the manager was a jerk, but I told them, "I suppose he's right."

AAA is not engaged in price-fixing. So-called "vertical price fixing" occurs when a supplier attempts to regulate a resale price, for example, a winch manufacturer coercing all its distributors to sell its products to the end-users at the same retail price.[1] But a AAA service contract does not present a vertical price fixing situation because the tow operator is not charging fees to a third-party consumer at a rate fixed by AAA. The auto club, acting on behalf of its members, IS the customer.

A towing service contract with AAA is a basic "arms-length" independent contractor agreement. No tow operator is *obligated* to perform towing services for AAA and its members. Every towing contractor serving the motor club does so voluntarily. And, as I explained to the AAA contractor on the phone, AAA tow rates are not determined by an illegal price setting scheme; they are set according to the length of the list on the yellow legal pad in the road service manager's desk drawer.

---

[1] *Pierce v. Ramsey Winch Co.*, 753 F.2d 416 (5th Cir. 1985)

§ 9:5 I'll Show You Mine If You'll Show Me Yours

It is illegal for two or more competing towing operators with businesses located in the same city to agree how much they will charge for various towing and recovery services. That would constitute a blatant violation of the federal antitrust laws. Tow operators in Arizona and Maine were once charged with criminal violations of the antitrust laws after they made deals among themselves regarding how they would bid on pending governmental towing contracts.[1]

But does a tow operator in Bushnell, Florida, violate those same antitrust laws if he posts his rates on a towing industry Internet bulletin board? Does the mere posting of those rates expose him to antitrust liability if his competitors read his post and then adjust their rates to conform with those he posted?

First, it is important to understand that the sole objective of Congress in enacting the federal antitrust laws was to assure a competitive economy. That purpose, the Supreme Court has explained, "rests on the premise that the unrestrained interaction of competitive forces will yield the best allocation of our economic resources, the lowest prices, the highest quality, and the greatest material progress ...."[2] Fair competition is the bedrock of America's economic system.

The Sherman Antitrust Act is one of two federal antitrust statutes.[3] It very broadly forbids "[e]very ... conspiracy in restraint of trade or commerce ..." The fixing of prices amongst competitors, called horizontal price-fixing, is considered one of the most egregious restraints of trade. Violators are subject to both criminal and civil sanctions, including treble damages.

However, in order for an antitrust violation to occur under the Sherman Act, there must be a "conspiracy." An exchange of price information among competitors, with no intent to regulate pricing, is not per se illegal. Indeed, every time you pick up a vehicle from your competitor's storage facility you get a receipt that discloses his towing and storage rates. And some jurisdictions require tow operators to prominently post their rates in their places of business. Simply looking at a receipt or perusing a rate sign posted in the office of a competitor does not implicate a tow operator in a price-fixing scheme. The essential characteristic of prohibited price-fixing is a "conspiracy" — any type of *understanding* or *consensus* among competitors, direct or indirect, to fix prices.

Back to our website rate-poster from Bushnell. Is he entering into a conspiracy to fix prices when he posts his rates? Is that Internet bulletin board post any different than the posting of his rates in the lobby of his place of business required by local law? Yes.

Unlike providing a customer with a receipt or displaying towing charges for the benefit of consumers, the posting of rates by a tow operator on a towing website serves no purpose other than to share those rates with fellow tow operators. The absence of any other legitimate purpose makes such an exchange of rate information highly suspect. Granted, the tow operators viewing the rates on the bulletin board may not all be in direct competition with the poster, but there remains a genuine risk of a "silent" conspiracy among competitors to fix prices. The tendency of bulletin board participants to follow the rates posted by others in their geographic area goes without saying.

The Federal Trade Commission, the agency charged with enforcing the antitrust laws, was once asked to review the practice of a trade association that was publishing its members' service rates. In its advisory opinion, the FTC said: "Even though couched in the form of a suggestion, the natural and probable result [is] to persuade substantial numbers of the [association] members to charge the rate suggested, thus leaving an almost inescapable inference of an agreement among competitors to charge a common rate."[4]

It is the danger of that "inescapable inference" of a conspiracy to fix prices that has prompted industry Internet bulletin boards to forbid the posting of specific rates on their websites. In response to a tow operator who was angrily complaining to me about one such "no prices" policy, I asked, "If not to conform your pricing to those who have posted their prices, why else do you want to see tow rates posted on the bulletin board?" He had no answer.

Of course, the fact that towing competitors may be charging approximately the same rates for similar services does not, of itself, indicate illegal price-fixing. It could well be, and often is, the result of independently-reached pricing decisions based on similar cost factors. But if similar rate schedules among competitors were to follow an exchange of pricing information via the Internet, the FTC might take notice.

---

[1] *State v. Randy's Inc.*, No. 88-467, Consent Decree, (Me. Super. Ct., Androscoggin Co., November 30, 1988)(copy of file with author) and *State v. Northern Arizona Towing Assn., et al.*, No. CV-93-18730, Consent Decree (Ariz. Super. Ct., Maricopa County, Nov. 1995)(copy on file with author)

[2] *Northern Pacific R. Co. v. United States*, 356 U.S. 1 (1958)

[3] 15 U.S.C. § 1

[4] Advisory Opinion Digest No, 257, (1967-70 Transfer Binder) Trade Reg. Rep ¶ 18, 393 (F.T.C. 1968); 33 Fed. Reg. 11701 (August 17, 1968 (copy on file with author)

§ 9:6 In the Zone

Zoning ordinances are intended to control and regulate urban growth. In order to prevent, for example, the construction of a cement plant in a quiet residential neighborhood, which most people would find aesthetically and economically unsuitable, local governments and their planning commissions have created systems of geographical districts or "zones."

The type of activity that can be conducted within a given zone is set forth in the zoning laws and regulations. The standard zoning code sets forth from 20 to 30 different categories of zones and the uses permitted therein. Some uses, for example, single-family residential housing and light retail activities, are permitted freely in almost any zone, while "sociably objectionable" uses, such as junkyards and waste disposal facilities, are restricted to very limited, usually isolated, areas and subject to a multitude of regulations.

Typically, land use regulations are quite specific in describing the various "uses" or types of activities allowable in the designated zones. But no list of uses can be all-inclusive. It is the use, or intended use, of property in a manner that is not specifically defined that often results in controversy and, frequently, litigation.

An "automotive towing business" is a use that is not defined in most zoning codes. In other words, towing businesses are not "pigeon-holed" as a permitted use in a particular zone. That being the case, in what zone can a towing business lawfully operate? The question comes up all the time. And the answer can be critical, especially if a local zoning board is seeking an injunction to stop a towing company from operating at its present location.

A common problem facing towing businesses, at least from a zoning perspective, is that part of the business operation involves the temporary storage of vehicles belonging to others, most of which are wrecked or damaged. Because of that, zoning and planning authorities tend to classify towing operations as "junkyards" and want to forbid the use anywhere except within a zone designated for junkyards.

Towing company owners argue that their businesses are no different than commercial parking garages, which also temporarily store vehicles belonging to others, so a towing company should be allowed to operate anywhere a commercial parking garage might operate. The fact that some vehicles are wrecked or damaged is insignificant, they contend, because the zones in which motor vehicle parking is allowed do not specifically prohibit the parking of *wrecked* or *disabled* vehicles.

It is well-established that zoning ordinances and land use regulations are within a government's inherent authority to legislate in matters of the public welfare and safety. However, the courts have always been careful to point out that such laws are contrary to the common-law right to use one's land as one chooses. Clearly, zoning and land use regulations place an unnatural or unusual restriction on the free use of one's property. Accordingly, the courts have established a rule of "strict construction" when deciding cases involving zoning ordinances. The rule of strict construction means that any ambiguity in a zoning code is to be weighed against restriction, and any use that is not *expressly prohibited* in a given zone must be allowed.[1]

In other words, zoning ordinances cannot be construed to exclude, by implication, uses that are not clearly prohibited. Furthermore, if a use is not specifically excluded, there is no need for the property owner to seek a zoning variance or other administrative order to continue with a desired use. A variance is necessary only when an intended use is inconsistent with the zone in question.

In the situation described above, in which the parking of wrecked automobiles is not specifically prohibited in a zone permitting the parking of automobiles, it would appear that the use of the property as an automotive towing company should be allowed.

Bear in mind that the rule of strict construction applies in all zoning matters. Towing companies are frequently confronted with regulations affecting the use of their property and business operations: Can a tow truck be parked in a residential driveway overnight? Can the company name be painted in large letters on the side of an office or garage? Can a radio tower or razor wire fence be erected? Can pole lighting or cameras be installed in the storage yard? The same rule applies in those cases — if the desired use is not *expressly prohibited* in the zone in which the use is intended, it should be allowed.

All zoning law disputes require a careful and thorough analysis of the applicable local zoning code. If you are having a problem with your zoning regulations, you should consult with competent legal counsel.

---

[1] *Wheatley v. Joint City-Council Planning Com'n of Nelson County*, No. 2006-CA-489, 2008 WL 4601212 (Ky. Ct. App., Oct. 17, 2008) and *The City of Kingston, Tennessee v. Gary D. Watts*, No. 14,443, Order, (Tenn. Chancery Court, 9th Jud. Dist., Roane County, October 25, 2004)(towing storage lot not "junk yard")(copy on file with author)

§ 9:7 The Taxman Cometh

If you operate heavy-duty tow trucks you may have received an IRS Form 2290, the tax return for the Heavy Highway Vehicle Use Tax (HHVUT). That excise tax, added to the federal tax code in 1956, is a special levy placed on large vehicles to help defray the costs of highway construction and maintenance.[1]

According to Congress, heavy trucks cause a disproportionate amount of wear and tear on our highways, so they should be assessed an extra tax for roadway upkeep. The HHVUT is paid annually and the tax period runs from July 1 through June 30. The Form 2290 returns are due by August 31.

The HHVUT applies to any vehicle with a "taxable gross weight" of 55,000 lbs. or more. The minimum tax is $100 per year and the maximum tax is $550 per year, which is payable on any vehicle with a taxable gross weight of over 75,000 lbs.

Pursuant to the IRS regulations, "taxable gross weight" is defined as the sum of three components: the weight of the highway motor vehicle, plus the weight of the semi-trailers or trailers *customarily used* in connection with such highway motor vehicle, *plus* the weight of the maximum load customarily carried on the highway motor vehicle and on the semi-trailer or trailers.[2] If a highway vehicle is "equipped to tow" a semi-trailer or trailer, then such a semi-trailer or trailer shall be treated as *"customarily used"* in connection with the highway vehicle and the weight thereof included when calculating taxable gross weight.

Certainly any truck-tractors with lowboys or trailers used by a towing firm are subject to the tax based on the weight of the truck, trailer and maximum possible load. (If the vehicle is registered in a state that requires declaration of gross weight in a specific amount, the HHVUT weight can be no less than the weight declared.)

What about conventional heavy-duty tow trucks with tow bars or underlifts? How is "taxable gross weight" of a conventional tow truck calculated for purposes of determining the applicability of the HHVUT? A tow company owner might reasonably assume that since it does not tow trailers and cargo, "taxable gross weight" is the Gross Vehicle Weight Rating (GVWR) of the tow truck only and that any heavy-duty tow truck with a GVWR less than 55,000 lbs. is exempt from the HHVUT.

But in some audits the IRS has contended that the "taxable gross weight" of a conventional-type heavy-duty tow truck for purposes of the HHVUT is the gross weight of the tow truck plus the maximum gross weight of any loaded vehicle, or vehicle combination, that *might* be towed behind it. Since the total *combined* weight of a heavy-duty tow truck and a loaded tractor-trailer can easily exceed 55,000 lbs. or even 75,000 lbs., under that IRS interpretation virtually all conventional heavy-duty tow trucks are subject to the HHVUT — probably at the maximum rate of $550 per truck.

I think the IRS is wrong. First, as noted above, the first two components of the definition of "taxable gross weight" are the weight of the power unit and the weight of the semi-trailers or trailers customarily used in connection with the power unit. Most conventional heavy-duty tow trucks are *not* equipped to easily attach to and tow semi-trailers and trailers. Even if outfitted with a pintle hook or fifth-wheel converter, heavy-duty tow trucks do not *customarily* tow trailers and semi-trailers. Tow trucks *customarily* haul disabled trucks and tractors which, in turn, may or may not be towing semi-trailers or trailers.

Furthermore, requiring tow truck companies to pay the excise tax based on the total weight of their tow trucks plus the weight of any vehicle(s) and load that might be towed constitutes double taxation. Invariably, the owner of any heavy vehicle being towed by a heavy-duty tow truck has already paid the HHVUT based on the taxable gross weight of the vehicle(s) being towed.

Since the HHVUT is a charge levied against heavy vehicles for the exceptional burden they put on highways, it seems logical that the only weight which should be considered for purposes of determining the "taxable gross weight" of a heavy-duty tow truck is the unloaded weight of the tow truck itself. That is the only extra untaxed weight on the road. Unlike the load carried by other heavy vehicles, the "load" carried by a conventional heavy-duty tow truck is another heavy vehicle that has already paid the HHVUT.

In my opinion, Congress did not intend for the taxable weight of a conventional-style heavy-duty tow truck to include the weight of disabled HHVUT-paying heavy trucks and tractor-trailers rigs that are being towed. Unfortunately, the IRS has not asked me to write an interpretive bulletin on the subject. Accordingly, if you have any doubts or concerns about your Form 2290 filing status you should consult your tax advisor or attorney.

---

[1] 26 U.S.C.A § 4481
[2] Treas. Reg. § 41.4482(b)-1

§ 9:8 The Unfairest of Them All

The October 2004 edition of ***Tow Times*** was the annual "Buyer's Guide" issue highlighting the latest in towing equipment, accessories and services. As I do every month, I perused the magazine, catching up on industry news and events, reading the interesting columns and articles, and, in that excellent issue, checking out all the new towing stuff.

There were, however, two related items in that magazine, seventy pages apart, that disturbed me. The first was a Century ad that featured a bright red and yellow heavy-duty rotating wrecker. The words "METRO FIRE RESCUE" appeared in large white letters on the wrecker boom. The second item was an article recapping a heavy-duty recovery performed on an interstate ramp near O'Hare Airport by Illinois DOT Minuteman tow trucks.

What do these two items have in common and why did I find them troubling? Both portray tow trucks owned and operated *by governmental entities*. The Century rotator depicted in the ad is obviously owned by a local fire department. The Minuteman tow truck program is run by IDOT on the major thoroughfares in Chicagoland and has been the subject of substantial controversy over the years. Both serve as stark reminders that some governments are providing towing or vehicle recovery services in direct competition with the private towing industry. A government towing operation can be funded by tax dollars and provided at no cost to the consumer of the service, i.e., the vehicle owner or their insurance company, or provided for a fee under a tax-exempt basis. Either way, it holds a most unfair business advantage over private enterprise.

Many think it is wrong for government to engage in a service business in competition with, or to the exclusion of, taxpaying private businesses. It seems especially wrong when the business is one which has traditionally been conducted by the private sector and is also one over which the government exercises monopolistic authority, like accident scene clearance.

Not surprisingly, the issue of governments competing with private enterprise has been the subject of many court challenges by aggrieved business owners. For example, in 1997 the owners of private campgrounds sought to enjoin the City of Branson, Mo., from operating its own campground. When a sinkhole swallowed up an entire block of Winter Park, Fla., in the early 1980s, a private photographer sued to stop the city from competing with him in the sale of photographs of that notorious geological event. Other published cases concern city-owned parking garages, athletic fields and arenas, hotels, a water slide and a skating rink.

Generally, the courts have ruled that governments may engage in a business commonly carried on by a private enterprise if the business is "for a public purpose" and not merely to make a profit. If the business advances the public welfare, say the courts, the government may even levy taxes to support the business and compete with private interests engaged in a like activity. The City of Branson's campground was upheld as being for legitimate "recreational" purposes.[1] The Florida photographer lost his case because the court found an "educational and scientific" purpose behind the city's sale of sinkhole photographs.[2]

Does clearing roadways of wrecked vehicles serve a public purpose? Of course. But does that justify the exclusive use of government-run tow trucks when qualified private sector tow trucks are available? Eliminating motor vehicles with safety defects from the highways serves a public purpose, but private businesses still perform auto repairs. Bear in mind that, unlike the Branson campgrounds and the Florida photographer who were still able to compete with their new governmental competitors, government-run tow trucks typically operate to the total exclusion of private towing companies for the particular service provided, i.e., highway clearance or scofflaw vehicle towing. (In such a situation, is there "competition" at all?)

Speed of response time and fast accident scene clearance is often advanced as the "public purpose" justifying government tow trucks. However, the "IDOT Quick Clearance" article effectively debunks that myth. The writer reports, "With a state police escort, IDOT arrived on the scene [with a heavy-duty wrecker]." *With a state police escort*, any of the many competent private towing companies in the area could have been on the scene just as quickly.

Nor is IDOT's light-duty freeway towing patrol justified on the basis of public purpose. The California Department of Transportation and CHP provide the same highway service quite effectively utilizing *private towing contractors.*

In 1988 the Iowa legislature enacted a "non-competition by government act," which, generally, forbids government entities in that state from providing "services to the public which are also offered by private enterprise ...."[3] Good idea, but the law has a loophole large enough to drive the Century rotator through. The law provides that the providing of competing services by government is proscribed "unless specifically authorized by statute, rule, ordinance or regulation." Thus, a government body can "self-authorize" itself to compete with private enterprise.

Whenever a government undertakes to operate a public hospital, a waterworks system, an electric plant, a parking system or a garbage collection system, it is in reality engaged in competition with private business "for a public purpose." Government needs to ensure that essential services will always be available to its citizenry. But when the government's power is used primarily for a private purpose, it runs afoul of the cornerstone of our democracy — the free enterprise system. Privately-owned towing companies should not be forced to face unfair competition from any government unit under the guise of a public purpose.

---

[1] *Siegel v. City of Branson*, 952 S.W.2d 294 (Mo. Ct. App. 1997)
[2] *City of Winter Park v. Montesi*, 448 So.2d 1242 (Fla. Ct. App. 1984)
[3] Iowa Code § 23A.2

§ 9:9 Vehicle Damage Claims
Avoid inflated assessments of vehicle damage claims

In 1990, Murel Laughlin purchased a wrecked 1989 Ford F-350 four-wheel-drive tow truck for $12,000. He restored the truck and put it in service towing vehicles through the hills and dales of upper east Tennessee.

Seven years later, in 1997, a car coming from the opposite direction crossed into the on-coming lane of traffic and collided with the Ford tow truck being driven by Laughlin. The tow truck chassis was "demolished," according to Laughlin, who was only slightly injured in the accident.

Laughlin sued the driver of the at-fault vehicle for the damages sustained to his tow truck. After many continuances, the case went to trial in 2004.

On the witness stand, Laughlin was asked to describe his tow truck. "Well, you've got the truck, and then you have the wrecker, but the wrecker part goes on the back with a boom and a wheel-lift. You can lift cars up by the wheels, or you can lift them underneath," he explained to the jury.

When asked to place a value on his tow truck at the time of the collision in 1997, Laughlin testified that the unit was worth "twenty-four thousand or something." However, on cross-examination it was revealed that the truck had 129,000 miles on it at the time of the wreck, that the liner was missing from the door of the truck, and that the truck body had been sanded and was unpainted. When asked if the tires were bald, Laughlin replied, "I say the tires were, you know, getting — some of them were ready to replace."

Witnesses called to bolster Laughlin's opinion about the value of his truck were not much help. A retired tow truck dealer, and friend of Laughlin, testified that in his opinion the unit was worth $22,000. However, upon further questioning he said that his valuation was based on a 1989 Ford F-350 tow truck in good condition and he admitted that he did not know the condition of Laughlin's truck. He also testified that the removable wrecker crane, which was only slightly damaged in the crash, was worth $10,000. "Just the [wrecker] unit is worth more than the truck," he said.

Another local towing operator testified that not long before the trial he had sold a similar tow truck in good condition for $6,000.

The jury rejected Laughlin's demand for $24,000 and awarded him only $3,500 for his tow truck. Laughlin appealed, but the Tennessee Court of Appeals upheld the jury's verdict. In the case of *Laughlin v. Fillers*,[1] the appellate court said, "[T]here is material evidence to support the jury's award of damages for the wrecker, and we find no abuse of the Trial Court's discretion in approving the award."

Although the Laughlin ruling involved damage to a tow truck, it contains an important lesson for towing company owners who frequently find themselves on the other side of the courtroom — defending a claim for damage to a towed vehicle. When a party claims damages to a vehicle, the declared value or cost of repair must be supported by credible documentation or testimony.

Proof of the value of a vehicle, or cost of repairs, can be established in a variety of ways. Generally, the owner of a vehicle may render an opinion of the value of his or her vehicle before the damage occurred and the (diminished) value after the damaging incident. The difference of the two, of course, is the measure of the loss.

As a practical matter, however, a vehicle owner's testimony is necessarily tainted by bias. A vehicle owner-plaintiff wants to obtain as large a judgment as possible and tends to inflate the damages to their vehicle. As the Laughlin case demonstrates, an owner's testimony should be taken "with a grain of salt."

In order to avoid that inherent partiality, a plaintiff seeking reimbursement for property damages needs to present expert testimony. If the vehicle is a total loss, that usually comes from an auto dealer who can testify regarding the sale price of similar vehicles. Many courts will allow a plaintiff to rely on published used car value guides like NADA or the "Blue Book." In cases involving body, engine or transmission damage, the testimony should come from an auto body repairman or mechanic who can testify about the estimated cost of repair. If the vehicle has already been fixed, the repair bill is the best evidence. Of course, a towing company defendant can call his own expert witness to refute the opinions of the vehicle owner's experts.

Unfortunately, towing accidents do happen. But when faced with an unreasonable claim for vehicle damage or loss, the prudent tow operator will obtain an independent appraisal or estimate and force the vehicle owner to prove the true value of his claim by competent evidence.

---

[1] No. E2005-00107-COA-R3-CV, 2005 WL 2300383 (Tenn. Ct. App., Sept. 22, 2005)

§ 9:10 New Registration Program for Interstate Towing
Uniform Carrier Registration

If you have a U.S. Department of Transportation (DOT) number on the side of your tow trucks and you haul vehicles or property in interstate commerce, you have received a letter or notice from your state commercial motor vehicle office about the Uniform Carrier Registration (UCR). You may wonder: *"What the heck is this?" "I've already got a US-DOT number, so do I need to file the UCR application?" "What happened to the Single State Registration System (SSRS)?"*

Relax. It's not that big of a deal. Basically, the UCR replaces the SSRS, but with a few new twists.

Some background: State governments have the legal right, granted by Congress, to regulate the safety of trucks operating within their respective jurisdictions, even trucks traveling from other jurisdictions. Included in that regulatory authority is the right to require an interstate motor carrier to register its federal operating authority, thereby proving that it carries the federally mandated levels of liability insurance. By doing so, and paying a registration fee, a carrier obtains operating "authority" from each state in which they operate. Years ago, interstate carriers filed registrations in each state in which they operated. Decals or stickers from each state were kept on a "bingo card" maintained in the truck cab as proof of registration.

In 1991, in order to reduce the administrative burden that the "bingo card" system imposed on interstate motor carriers, Congress directed the implementation of the Single State Registration System (SSRS). Under the SSRS, an interstate carrier registered in only one state, its base state. The carrier would designate the other states in which it was going to operate and pay the appropriate fees, which the base state would then distribute.

In the federal highway funding legislation passed in 2005 — commonly referred to as SAFETEA-LU[1] — Congress eliminated the SSRS, which had been criticized as fiscally unfair. In its place, a comprehensive new plan was implemented. The law has two aspects: the Uniform Carrier Registration System, a national database of motor carriers, and the Uniform Carrier Registration Agreement, which replaces the SSRS.[2]

Under the new law, an interstate towing company still registers with a base state, but does not have to pick and choose the states in which it will operate. A carrier's federal operating authority is automatically registered with the participating states. And everyone now has to register, not just for-hire motor carriers. That includes private and regulated carriers, freight brokers, freight forwarders and leasing companies. That provides for a broader fee base.

Unlike the SSRS, which was on a per-truck basis, the cost for UCR is per-carrier and will be the same for all states. The fee is tiered, based on the total number of vehicles in a company's fleet. There are four levels between 1 and 100 vehicles: $39 for up to 2 trucks, $116 for 3-5 trucks, $231 for 6-20 units, and $806 per year for 21-100 units. The number of vehicles to be reported is the number reported in the carrier's most recent Form MCS-150 filed with the FMCSA.

Law enforcement will know whether or not you paid. They use computer records to verify UCR registration. Noncompliance could result in confiscation of the tow truck.

If your interstate towing company is not based in one of the states that currently participate in the UCR you will need to register in a neighboring state. Of course, towing companies that operate solely within a state (intrastate carriers) do not need to comply with the UCR.

Interstate towing firms should not confuse the UCR registration with their US-DOT registration. The US-DOT number on the sides of your trucks only indicates that you have *federal* authority to operate interstate. The new UCR program provides interstate towing companies with the necessary *state* authority.

Interstate towing operators should contact their state motor carrier enforcement offices with any questions.

---

[1] Pub.L. 109-59, 119 Stat. 1144
[2] 49 U.S.C.A. § 13908

§ 9:11 Guns and Tow Trucks
Right to carry concealed weapon has limitations

On June 26, 2008, in a decision of major significance for gun advocates, the United States Supreme Court confirmed the constitutional right of individuals to possess handguns in their homes for self-defense. The Second Amendment of the U.S. Constitution states that "the right of the people to keep and bear Arms shall not be infringed."[1] In the case of *District of Columbia v. Heller*,[2] the high court ruled that a local law in the nation's capital that completely forbade the possession of handguns violated that constitutional provision.

However, the court was careful to note that, like most constitutional rights, the right to keep and bear arms is not unlimited. State and federal laws forbid certain categories of people from possessing firearms. There are also many state and local laws regulating the carrying of concealed weapons outside the home. Those laws were not affected by the Supreme Court ruling.

Unfortunately, towing can be a very dangerous occupation, especially if the tow is a repossession or private property impound. There are documented instances of tow truck drivers being killed or seriously injured by enraged vehicle owners. Consequently, many tow truck drivers carry handguns on their person or in their tow trucks for protection. But, as noted above, there are some restrictions on the constitutional right to bear arms.

First and foremost, under federal law and most state laws, it is illegal for a person who has been convicted of *any* felony to *ever* be in possession of any type of firearm or ammunition.[3] It is also unlawful for a person convicted of misdemeanor domestic violence, someone under a domestic restraining order, or a drug addict (as defined by statute), to be in possession of a gun.[4] The penalties for violating the federal statute are severe.

Some police agencies try to use the "felon in possession" law as a justification for excluding convicted felons from participating on the towing rotation list. Their rationale is that a tow truck driver might haul a vehicle containing a firearm, or transport a customer in the cab of his tow truck who is carrying a firearm, and be deemed to be in constructive possession of the weapon and, thus, subject to prosecution.

However, I am unaware of any prosecution of a tow truck driver under those circumstances. That is probably because the statutes require that a felon be in *knowing* possession of a weapon and that he exercise some dominion or control over it. Certainly, if a driver with a felony conviction was completely unaware of the presence of a gun in a towed vehicle or in a customer's pocket, he could not be found guilty of the "felon in possession" law.

Even if a tow truck driver is not subject to an outright prohibition on possessing a weapon, such as the state and federal "felon in possession" statutes or the domestic violence disqualifications, as noted by the Supreme Court in *Heller*, there are still lawful restrictions on the right to carry a weapon outside the home. According to the National Rifle Association (NRA), there are over 20,000 state and local "gun control" laws in the United States.

Many of those laws pertain to the carrying of *concealed* weapons. By definition, the act of carrying a concealed weapon includes keeping a handgun hidden in your pocket or in a location such that it is readily accessible for use. An example of the latter would be a handgun in an unlocked glove box or under a truck seat.

Every state has a criminal statute making it illegal, to some extent, to carry a concealed, loaded weapon in public. Many have outright prohibitions. Others allow carrying a concealed gun only under limited circumstances. For example, Mississippi bans concealed weapons unless the weapon is in a motor vehicle.[5] You may carry a concealed weapon in Vermont unless you have "the intent or purpose" to injure another person.[6] Tennessee prohibits carrying a gun "with the intent to go armed."[7] A Wisconsin statute forbids carrying a concealed weapon, but an amendment to that state's constitution guarantees citizens the right to have a concealed gun for "defense."[8]

Even though, as a general rule, concealed, loaded weapons are outlawed, forty-seven states allow a person to apply for and obtain a permit to carry concealed weapons, a "carry permit." Most states have "shall issue" laws, meaning that if an applicant for a gun carry permit meets certain minimum standards, the permit will automatically be issued. Typically, the permitting agency will require a minimum age (usually 21 years), proof of citizenship and residency, fingerprinting, firearms training, and the absence of any disqualifying convictions or characteristics. About eight states have more restrictive, discretionary standards making carry permits more difficult to obtain. Many states have reciprocity agreements so that a carry permit issued in one state is recognized in another state.

If you desire to carry a concealed weapon for your protection, and are not disqualified from possessing a firearm, you should contact the attorney general's office in your state to determine if a permit is available or needed and, if so, how to obtain one. The NRA also has a helpful website with a compilation of the state gun laws for all 50 states and the District of Columbia.[9]

[1] U.S. Const., amend. II
[2] 554 U.S. 570 (2008)
[3] 18 U.S.C.A. § 922(g)(1)
[4] 18 U.S.C.A. §§ 922(g)(3),(8) and (9)
[5] Miss. Code Ann. § 97-37-1(2)
[6] Vt. Stat. Ann., tit. 13, § 4003
[7] Tenn. Code Ann. § 39-17-1307
[8] Wisc. Stat. Ann. § 941.23 and Wisc. Const., Art. 1, § 25
[9] www.nraila.org

§ 9:12 Finding A Competent Attorney

How many times have you received a call for a quote to retrieve a car that's "just barely stuck in the mud"? You quote the fee and the caller says, "That much?! Thanks, anyway. I guess we'll just try to get it out ourselves." About two hours later you get a call back. Unable to free the vehicle, the caller is resigned to using your service. You arrive on the scene and find boards, ropes and chains scattered all around. The car is now mired up to its door handles in mud, the result of the car owner's amateur efforts at vehicle recovery. Your fee for recovery is now twice as much as the amount quoted on the first phone call.

I recall many such episodes when I was driving a tow truck. Well — guess what? — I often see similar situations as an attorney. Some business owners will contact an attorney at the early stages of a legal problem; however, concerned about the cost of legal representation, they will turn down professional help and try to handle the matter themselves, often with disastrous results.

Unfortunately, the towing business is fraught with legal problems. In addition to the "routine" concerns such as liability for vehicle damage and storage loss claims, vehicle registration and licensing laws, size and weight restrictions, contracts with motor clubs and governmental agencies, tax and employment law issues — to name but a few — the modern towing professional is also struggling with legal and legislative monsters like environmental regulations, laws preventing discrimination on the basis of disability and myriad motor carrier safety regulations. If the towing firm engages in government towing, it faces an additional Pandora's Box of contract provisions and rules and regulations.

Just as proper vehicle recovery requires specialized knowledge of certain procedures and methods, proper presentations or arguments before governmental agencies, legislative bodies or courts require specialized skill and knowledge of established procedures. When faced with a legal or legislative issue concerning his or her towing business, the company owner would be well advised to obtain competent legal counsel at the earliest opportunity.

So how do you find an attorney familiar with the issues common to the towing industry? An attorney who knows the difference between a snatch block and a chop block or the difference between a rotation list and a laundry list.

- Ask your state or local towing association. Many associations hire attorneys to assist them in legal and legislative matters, and those attorneys develop a familiarity with the towing industry. Be aware that association attorneys may have potential conflicts of interest that prevent them from representing you in a particular matter, especially if the legal problem involves another member of the association who the attorney also represents.

• Other towing operators in your area are also good reference sources. Many towing firms across the country that have educated their own lawyers about the towing business and are willing to share him or her with other towing firms — again, if it does not pose a conflict to the lawyer or the client towing firm.

• Some state bar associations certify lawyers in certain specialties. There is no certification for towing but certification in other areas, for example civil litigation or tax law, might be helpful if you seek legal assistance in a particular area of law.

• If you need assistance in matters relating to the ICC, OSHA regulations, DOT safety regulations or state trucking regulations, the Transportation Lawyers Association may be able to refer you to an attorney in your area who will have experience with general trucking laws and regulations. The TLA's phone number is 913-895-4615.

• The Martindale Hubbell Directory of Lawyers and Law Firms, available in most public libraries, contains the names and addresses of just about every lawyer in the United States. The directory is arranged geographically and rates lawyers based on opinions of their peers on legal ability, experience, ethics, reliability and other qualifications. Some firms also list representative clients.

Remember, when you are faced with a legal problem and think you are "just barely stuck in the mud," hiring competent counsel early may ultimately save you considerable time and money.

§ 9:13 Government-Operated Vehicle Storage Facilities
A growing threat to the private towing industry

"Study says impound lot could yield $2.4M for city," read the headline in the *North County Times* on May 27, 2009. The article following foretold of a plan by the City of Escondido, California, to renovate a surplus city property (paving, fencing and lighting) and hire several new employees to manage it as a vehicle impound yard. Instead of transporting impound vehicles to their private storage lots as they have done in the past, the four city towing contractors would be directed to take those impounds to that new city-owned storage lot. The towing companies would still be paid the towing fee, but the storage fees, or revenues from the sale of unclaimed vehicles, would be collected by the city. Obviously, if the plan is implemented, the $2.4 million annual gain for the City of Escondido would come at the expense of the private towing vendors.

It is an alarming trend. Municipalities across the nation, strapped for operating revenues, are greedily eyeing vehicle storage fees earned by private towing firms. From Atlantic City, New Jersey, to Long Beach, California, city governments have opened their own storage lots to the financial detriment of private towing companies. The concept of a municipality-run vehicle storage lot raises political, ideological, legal, and economic questions. Economically, the loss of vehicle storage revenues would devastate many private towing firms. Often, the high-margin storage fees charged on law enforcement impounds subsidize the low-margin, or even below cost, law enforcement tow rates. Towing companies that rely upon storage fee revenues to stay in the black would be forced to close.

Ideologically, some believe that it is fundamentally wrong for any government to engage in competition with tax-paying private businesses. After all, private enterprise is the cornerstone of the U.S. economy. Indeed, the state legislators in Iowa and North Carolina have enacted "non-competition by government" laws that generally forbid government entities from providing services to the public which are offered by private enterprise.[1] Such legislative bans are certainly an effective means of fending off city-owned storage lots. Not surprisingly, in states that do not give private industry favored treatment, the issue of government competition has been the subject of a myriad of court challenges by aggrieved businesses. For instance, private business owners have sued to stop city-owned hotels, hospitals, athletic arenas, convention centers, parking garages, water parks, campgrounds, and skating rinks.

Generally, courts have ruled that governments may engage in a business commonly carried on by a private enterprise if the business is "for a public purpose" and not merely to make a profit. If the business advances the public welfare, say the courts, the government may even levy taxes to support the business and compete with private interests engaged in a similar business. (See § 9:8).

In 2005, the City of Toledo, Ohio, was determined to develop and operate its own vehicle storage lot. Its primary motivation? The expected $450,000 in annual storage fee revenues. The city authorized a $2.8 million bond to purchase 34 acres of land and make the necessary improvements. Once completed, the city planned to redirect its rotation towing companies to haul impounds to its own lot. The private storage yards would quickly be emptied of city-ordered impounds.

On March 15, 2005, the rotation towing companies sued the city in federal court, claiming that the city's action constituted improper market regulation. In *Abco Services, Inc. v. City of Toledo* they complained that, as a sovereign government entity, the city enjoyed "unique powers and leverage ... unlike other private market participants." Because their specially-equipped storage lots would be rendered practically useless for their designed purpose, the towing firms also argued that the city had, in effect, illegally confiscated their property in violation of the federal constitution. Only a month after filing, for reasons unknown to this author, the towing firms abandoned their lawsuit and the city storage lot opened for business in September 2005.[2]

Another local towing firm protested the legality of the same city storage lot in *Magnum Towing and Recovery v. City of Toledo*. However, in an order dated May 9, 2006, a federal judge said, "Magnum's recourse is not [in the courts] but through the political process." [3]

Local governments contend that, in addition to generating revenues, city-operated storage lots serve legitimate public purposes, e.g., the convenience and efficiency of a single storage location, and control over criminal evidence. However, those interests can easily be served by designating a single private storage lot or, as in Chicago, hiring private industry to manage a city-owned facility. At least the private sector would still be engaged in the vehicle storage business.

It bears noting that, unlike city-run hotels, parking garages, or campgrounds, where private industry is able to compete with a governmental business rival, government-run storage lots exclude private competitors. The private towing industry has no independent source for the lucrative nonconsensual law enforcement impounds. Those tow-ins are controlled by the same government entity that is feeding its own storage lot.

---

[1] Iowa Code § 23A.2 and N.C. Gen. Stat. § 66-58
[2] No. 3:05-cv-07101-JGC, Order of Dismissal, (N.D. Ohio, April 21, 2005)
[3] 430 F. Supp. 2d 689 (N.D. Ohio 2006)

§ 9:14 It Makes No Cents: Payment in Pennies

If you engage in nonconsensual towing for any length of time, it is likely to happen: One day you will impound a vehicle for a DUI or for parking in violation of a housing complex apartment parking regulations. At some point, the vehicle owner, still angry because he got caught breaking the rules or maybe still hungover, will call to inquire about the amount of the bill. The next day, the smart aleck will show up at your office with over 10,000 loose pennies in plastic jugs that he says is payment for the outstanding charges. If you refuse to accept them, he will cry that the pennies are "legal tender" and that you must accept them or give him his car without charge.

Do you have to accept the pennies as payment for your towing and storage services?

To be sure, pennies are legal tender in the United States. The Coinage Act of 1965, entitled "Legal Tender," states: "United States coins and currency (including Federal reserve notes and circulating notes of Federal Reserve banks and national banks) are legal tender for all debts, public charges, taxes, and dues."[1]

That statute means that all United States money is a valid and legal offer of payment for contractual *debts* when tendered to a creditor. There is, however, no federal statute mandating that a private business must accept currency or coins as payment for goods or services. Unless there is a state law which says otherwise, a businessman could insist that he be paid for his services with jelly beans or casino chips. If a business owner chooses to accept cash (as almost all do), he is free to adopt his own policy on *how* he will accept currency or coins. For example, many passenger bus lines prohibit payment of fares in pennies or dollar bills. Gas stations often refuse to accept bills in denominations over twenty dollars.

I am unaware of any reported court cases involving pennies tendered for towing fees, but in *State of Ohio v. Brian Carroll*,[2] the unhappy defendant in a criminal case in Chillicothe Municipal Court attempted to pay his $123 in court costs with a box full of loose pennies. The clerk of the court, pursuant to her policy, would not accept the pennies unless they were rolled in tubes. The defendant refused to do so. He was later found in contempt of court. On appeal, the defendant pointed to the federal "Legal Tender" law, contending that pennies in any amount must be unconditionally accepted. The Court of Appeals of Ohio disagreed, stating "It defies logic and common sense that this Congress intended such a wooden and broad application of the statute beyond any control of the payee regardless of circumstances."

Thus, if a towing company chooses to accept pennies as payment for its services, it has a right to control the manner in which it will take them. It may outright reject pennies in excess of a certain amount, it may require that large numbers of pennies be rolled, or it might require that bulk pennies be counted out one-by-one in the dispatcher's presence. The key is notice to the customer. If you are engaged in nonconsent towing and have had vehicle owners try to pay with pennies, or want to avoid potential problems, you might consider posting a sign in your office or customer lobby setting forth the conditions under which you will accept the one-cent coins.

Finally, I have heard it said that a business is not required by law to accept more than 100 pennies ($1) towards the payment of any bill. That is incorrect. No law specifies that pennies cease to be considered legal tender when proffered in quantities over a specific amount. The Coinage Act of 1965 makes it clear that pennies are legal tender *up to any amount.* However, as explained above, towing companies are still free to accept or reject pennies as they see fit.

---

[1] 31 U.S.C.A. § 5103
[2] No. 96CA2236, 1997 WL 118064 (Ohio Ct. App., Mar. 13, 1997)